THE EARTHEN LONG BARROW
IN BRITAIN

ALSO BY PAUL ASHBEE

The Bronze Age Round Barrow in Britain

John Thurnam Esq., M.D., F.S.A.

The Rev. William Greenwell, M.A., D.C.L., F.R.S., F.S.A.

THE EARTHEN
LONG BARROW
IN BRITAIN

AN INTRODUCTION TO THE STUDY OF THE FUNERARY PRACTICE AND
CULTURE OF THE NEOLITHIC PEOPLE OF THE THIRD MILLENNIUM B.C.

PAUL ASHBEE

TORONTO
UNIVERSITY OF TORONTO PRESS

© Paul Ashbee 1970

First published in North America 1970
by University of Toronto Press
ISBN 0–8020–1572–7
by arrangement with
J. M. Dent & Sons Ltd, London

Made in Great Britain
at the
Aldine Press · Letchworth · Herts

To Richmal, Edward and Kate
who have lived with long barrows
for so long

CONTENTS

vii

(N.B. Customary and List names are used in Appendices
5, 6, 7, 8 and 9. For references to appropriate
literature see Appendices 3 and 4.)

BIBLIOGRAPHY, 182

INDEX, 200

ILLUSTRATIONS

TEXT FIGURES

xiii

PREFACE AND
ACKNOWLEDGMENTS

The earthen long barrows were first studied as a type separate from, though related to, the stone-built long barrows, by John Thurnam in 1868. To preface his classic publications, treating barrows long and round, he wrote: 'I extracted from the "Ancient Wiltshire", in a tabular form, all the descriptions of the tumuli the opening of which is recorded in that work. It is the results thus obtained, in connection with those yielded by my own researches, and with such other observations as serve to illustrate the subject, which are exhibited in, and form the basis of, the present papers' [Thurnam, 1868, 162].

Like Thurnam a century ago, I have been able to extract a certain amount of information from early sources and set it in its proper place by comparison with those details won from the earthen long barrow excavations of recent years, which include 'my own researches', the Fussell's Lodge and Horslip examples. For the inter-war work, on mounds peripheral to the main concentrations, provided ambiguous details, difficult to integrate. Thus it is only recently that a regular pattern of structures within earthen long barrows has emerged or that a specific relationship with stone-built long barrows has been perceptible.

My first view of an excavated earthen long barrow was of the deserted cuttings into Julliberrie's Grave. Subsequently I have seen a large number of these massive works under various conditions. A number of sites that have not as yet been published in full are mentioned in this book which can be best considered as a measure of earthen long barrow studies as seen up to 1967.

The basis of this inquiry was a degree dissertation at the University of Leicester. There Mr Stanley Thomas supervised my labours with sympathetic guidance and sound advice, and with him I enjoyed many long hours of congenial critical conversation. To him I wish to express my thanks and gratitude.

Works of synthesis invariably owe much to many as is evidenced by the bibliography which embraces a broad span of time and European space. Thus to those whose

xv

books and reports I have read, whose excavations I have seen, and with whom I have conversed and corresponded, my indebtedness is considerable.

Individuals and Institutions have most generously allowed me to make use of their photographs and line drawings, as well as giving me permission to publish. It is with gratitude and pleasure that I acknowledge their kindness: Professor R. J. C. Atkinson; Mrs C. Banks; Dr R. L. S. Bruce-Mitford and the British Museum; Messieurs H. Carré, J. Dousson, P. Poulain; Mr F. Carver; Mr H. J. Case and the Ashmolean Museum, Oxford; Professor W. Chmielewski; Mr A. E. P. Collins and Mr D. Waterman; Mrs M. V. Conlon and the University of London Institute of Archaeology; Dr G. J. Copley; Dr J. G. Evans; Dr R. Feustel; Professor P. V. Gløb and the Danish National Museum; Mr L. V. Grinsell; Miss A. S. Henshall; Mr J. H. Hopkins, Mr A. Pike and the Society of Antiquaries of London; Professor K. Jaźdźewski; Mr R. F. Jessup; Dr I. H. Longworth and the British Museum; the Ministry of Public Building and Works; Miss N. Newbigin; Mr C. W. Phillips and the Ordnance Survey; Professor Stuart Piggott; Dr J. K. S. St Joseph and the University of Cambridge Committee for Aerial Photography; Dr I. F. Smith; Dr B. Soudsky; Frau A. Sprockhoff; Dr B. Stürup; Mr W. H. Styche and the Roundway Hospital Management Committee; Sir Mortimer Wheeler; Mr John Wymer.

I am especially grateful to Mr C. W. Phillips who gave me access to, and every assistance with, the topographical records of the Ordnance Survey, and Professor R. J. C. Atkinson who discussed with me the Wayland's Smithy excavations and the new problems there raised. At all times library usage has been expedited by the unflagging energy and unfailing patience of Mr J. H. Hopkins.

Always while excavating, viewing long barrows, writing and drawing, my work has been encouraged and criticized to its considerable advantage by the realistic and stimulating observations of my wife. At the same time she has been ever there with pencil, tape and trowel. A most distinguished archaeologist and feminist once wrote: 'There is no doubt that love has saved archaeology a considerable sum in wage bills'; *non est disputandum!*

University of East Anglia   PAUL ASHBEE

Chapter 1

INTRODUCTORY

THE PREMISES OF PREHISTORY
CATEGORIZATION
HISTORICAL CONSIDERATIONS

Earthen long barrows, sometimes termed unchambered long barrows, and variously described as wedge-shaped, pear-shaped or rectangular, are normally mounds, sometimes of extravagant length, thrown up from flanking ditches. Human burials were deposited, apparently at one time beneath the often broader, easterly, ends. The bones were housed in structures of turf and timber, found in a collapsed and confused condition. Such structures had sometimes been burnt and the bones that they housed had suffered accordingly. In general, the dimensions of the mounds were out of all proportion to the deposits that they covered. The remains of long cairns, seemingly covering cists, have been included with the foregoing. Long barrows or cairns covering stone chambers to which, it is believed, there could have been periodic access are excluded.

Excavation since the time of the Regency has provided the body of knowledge regarding these monuments. Such excavation can be regarded as either superficial but 'extensive', or else intimately 'intensive'. Evidence from the small second category, supplemented by the first, demonstrates that the denuded arcuate-profiled mounds covered the remains of erstwhile timber enclosures and mortuary houses. The term 'earthen long barrow' is therefore, strictly speaking, a misnomer because other materials are or were involved, but its retention is urged to separate the class from barrows with *stone* chambers. The term 'unchambered' long barrow should be discarded because of the abundant evidence within the mounds of erstwhile structures housing burials. It was considered unfortunate a quarter of a century ago [Childe, 1940, 63].

THE PREMISES OF PREHISTORY

Before an archaeological narrative is embarked upon, the relationship between the student of the present and his subject in the past must be realized and kept under constant review. Like the historic past [Collingwood, 1946, 326], the prehistoric past can be approached only via the prehistorian's mind. The things that we record, classify and analyse were not made and built as archaeological documents. They acquire their specific character only because we apply to them our techniques for access to knowledge of the past. Prehistory is an inferential intellectual concept based upon selected evidence recovered by archaeological methods.

Substantially the material evidence which provides prehistory can be approached in two ways. *Direct* and personal excavation of monuments and relics in the field, supplemented by a no less direct and personal study of relics in museums, and also of unexcavated field monuments, must be supported by *indirect* knowledge of these obtained by the critical appreciation of the descriptions, reports and narratives prepared by others [Ashbee, 1960, 16]. The direct relationship of the prehistorian with his material becomes, when recorded, indirect for all others. Thus while all may agree in general principle regarding an undertaking, the individual outcome must be the product of the qualities peculiar to the person involved. These may range from past experience, through comparative knowledge to obsession [Piggott, S., 1959, 14; Wainwright, 1962, 27]. For these matters are far from objective: the mere mechanics of excavation and subsequent synthesis impose unavoidable subjectivity, while one's preconceptions and knowledge can all too frequently condition one's observation and rationalization [Piggott, S., 1962a, 71]. Awareness of these factors must guide any approach to direct and indirect archaeological evidence.

Indirect archaeological evidence, that is, an excavation or other report, is the history of an operation undertaken in past time. Thus its use calls for the exercise of historical criticism. For such a report is the product of an individual related intimately to his age, and so must be considered in the light of the archaeological aims of that time.

Some diminution of the dangers inherent in individual approach to an excavation problem is possible when two or more persons act in concert. The ensuing catalytic exchanges normally result in an end-product considerably in advance of that possible by one person alone. Indeed, a measure of corporate effort may become the future pattern for complex archaeological undertakings.

With intelligible prehistory as the aim, the value and limitations of any archaeological record must be assessed, and a decision made as to what information can legitimately be distilled from it. Hawkes [1954] considers this as comprising three categories: technological, economic and social. It is in this order that the archaeological evidence varies in its potential reliability. While technological and economic information can be gleaned almost directly, the inferences of social and political details and activities, and of the ideologies that lubricated them, are more subjective and difficult. At the same time, having mind for the competence of evidence, the field of human thought and aspiration [Wainwright, 1962, 32, 111], is so remote from the material culture available to archaeology that its inference is almost impossible. Childe in fact could write [1959, 4] that in his belief any attempt to recapture such subjective motives or emotions was foredoomed.

M. A. Smith [1955, 6] has reminded us that there may be no logical relationship between human activity in some of its aspects and the remaining evidence. Since then Wainwright [1962, 32] has stated that there is no guarantee that observed material distinctions are a true reflection of social distinctions. To this must be added a reminder that what, viewed from **our** vantage point in time, may seem simple and logical processes, were not so for an **early** society, bounded by its contemporary environment and conceptual equipment. Again, monuments important to us, because they have been the subject of well conducted excavations, were not necessarily important to their builders. Indeed, we may see and deliberately seek patterns that may have had no immediate significance to those who produced them.

Generally speaking, the feasibility of writing prehistory shades from the reasonably probable to the almost impossible. Notwithstanding, Childe [1959, 2] put before us what must be our faith in our discipline. His final and resolute declaration was that 'the economic, sociological and ultimately historical interpretation of archaeological data has, I believe, now become a main task that can contribute enormously to human history and should enhance the status of archaeology'.

CATEGORIZATION

Before notions regarding a specific prehistoric problem can be entertained, the materials which are its basis must be ordered into categories. Such categorization involves the identification and grouping together of likes and the counter-process of the disassociation of unlikes. This means that the basic observations cease to be unrelated phenomena because patterns of similarities have been established.

Classification [Childe, 1956, 14] in archaeology normally involves functional, chronological and chorological arrangements. An example of the first could include a number of different types. As the ordering of materials involves human effort, individual or corporate, some subjectivity is unavoidable. Thus, for example, a given class of monument may be grouped according to function and *need not*, unless deemed specifically necessary, be considered upon a chronological or, for that matter, a chorological basis. Therefore the consideration of particular problems pertaining to one class of monument, which might involve identification of specific variants of types, would be but basic categorization without further implication.

The chronological arrangements of variants of types would involve what has been termed 'typological' treatment. Such a concept might be thought a corollary of *any* treatment of types, but in archaeology it has acquired peculiar meaning, based on the assumption that certain constituent forms within an assemblage change, stage by stage, and that their direction can be determined by inspection [Childe, 1956, 69]. This concept, which must differ from categorization based upon presumed function, involves evolutionary systematization according to form, design and ornament.

For about a century now typological concepts have been applied with some success to coins and bronze implements [Evans, J., 1864, 27; 1881, 472]. That this has met with success for such implements is due, perhaps, to the rapid progress of Bronze Age technology and the fact that each bronze is an entity in itself. The danger, as with Abercromby [1912], is of unilinear evolution in a vacuum [Piggott, S., 1963, 54].

With monuments, it is often virtually impossible, except in the most favourable circumstances, to impute more than general relationships [e.g. Piggott, S., 1954, 235]. Indeed, so difficult is the classification of monuments, for views as to the significance of specific detail differ widely, that some basic categorizations [Daniel, 1950, 9] have excited elaborate criticism [Grimes, 1951]. However, the reduction of seemingly discrete phenomena, to produce an order which is a pattern of similarities, necessarily involves categorization, and this is normally possible only upon a morphological basis. Moreover, concepts devised for this purpose by any individual writer can be taken in a quite unintended manner unless a statement of his individual understanding and intended usage [e.g. Malmer, 1962, xxx–xxxv] gives precision to his synthetic work.

The construction of an archaeological narrative should not be based solely upon the classification of a single isolated trait without reference to its fellows, while there must be clear appreciation of the potential limits of relic or monument as evidence. This can only be related to the individual in his age and involves keeping the whole mechanism of conceptual thought under constant critical review.

HISTORICAL CONSIDERATIONS

Patrick, patron saint of Ireland, may have been the first to have had his inquiry into a long barrow's contents recorded [Crawford, 1936, 479; Carney, 1961, 144]. Indeed, Patrick's encounter with an occupant of a long barrow is the earliest and most important example of a 'resuscitation', an accomplishment which is one of the rarer miracles attributed to Irish saints [Carney, 1961, 142]. The story is as follows:

And Patrick came to Dichuil to a great grave, of astounding breadth and prodigious length which his familia had found. And with great amazement they marvelled that it extended 120 feet, and they said: 'We do not believe this affair, that there was a man of this length.' And Patrick answered and said: 'If you wish you shall see him.' And they said: 'We do.' And he struck with his crozier a stone near its head and signed the grave with the sign of the cross, and said: 'Open, O Lord, the grave.' And the holy man opened the earth and the giant arose whole, and said: 'Blessed be you, O holy man, for you have raised me even for one hour from many pains.' Speaking so he wept most bitterly, and said: 'I will walk with you.' They said: 'We cannot allow you to walk with us, for men cannot look upon your face for fear of you. But believe in the God of Heaven and accept the baptism of the Lord, and you shall not return to the place in which you were. And tell us of whom you are.' [And the man said:] 'I am the son of the son of Cas, son of Glass, and was swineherd to King Lugar, king of Hirota. The warrior-band of the son of Mac Con slew me in the reign of Coirpe Nioth Fer, a hundred years ago to-day.' And he was baptized, and confessed God, and he fell silent and was placed once more in his grave.

Long barrows were of significance to the Saxons for they noted the more prominent long mounds in their charters. Crawford [1953, 172] has commented on the Saxon use of an equivalent to the modern term 'long barrow'. A 'langan hlaew' in the bounds of the parish of Tackley, in Oxfordshire, is called Long Banck on a map of Whitehill Farm of 1605 [Crawford, 1930, 358] and was considered as a long barrow by Leeds [1921, 255]. When Crawford saw it in 1930 it had been ploughed very low but was still a perfectly recognizable mound, slightly more stony than the rest of the field. Fieldwork [Dunning, 1946] has rediscovered a long barrow and a round barrow at South Wonston, in Hampshire, recorded in Birch's *Saxon Charters*, 604, A.D. 904 as a 'barrow between two long barrows'.

During the seventeenth and eighteenth centuries, John Aubrey [Powell, 1948; 1949, and William Stukeley [Piggott, S., 1950] visited and recorded long barrows. In his unpublished *Monumenta Britannica*, Aubrey distinguishes long from round barrows] calling them, especially when set about with stones, 'sepulchres'. Stukeley [1743, 45] commented upon the 'pyriform' shape of earthen long barrows near Avebury.

As early as 1702 Lord Winchelsea and Heneage Finch dug to discover the occupant of Julliberrie's Grave (pl. 1) at Chilham in Kent [Jessup, 1937, 126]. However, it was not until the beginning of the nineteenth century that Sir Richard Colt Hoare and William Cunnington [Sandell, 1961] began their spate of opening barrows, both long and round. Into long barrows they dug trenches, termed 'sections' [Colt Hoare, 1810, 55] while ancient soils were recognized and even analysed [Colt Hoare, 1810, 92 and fn.]. The layered character of mounds was indicated in terms of 'marls' and 'moulds' while pits, graves and the circumstances of burials also received descriptive treatment. From his 'extensive' work Colt Hoare was able to describe and define long barrows as a class of monument [Colt Hoare, 1810, 20].

Later in the century the methods and procedures of Colt Hoare and Cunnington were emulated (Appendix 1) in the south by Thurnam [1868; 1870] and in the north by William and Thomas Bateman [1848; 1861], Lord Londesborough [1848], William Greenwell [Hodgson, 1918], and John Robert Mortimer [Mortimer, 1905]. Thurnam (frontispiece) dug into some twenty-two earthen long barrows altogether, about Stonehenge, at the western end of Salisbury Plain, and in North Wiltshire. He assigned them to the 'stone period' and differentiated them from stone-chambered long barrows [Thurnam, 1868, 168].

Associates of the Batemans dug into three long barrows in Yorkshire while Lord Londesborough found the oft-quoted 'Duggleby Type' flint artifacts [Smith, R. A., 1926, 104, fig. 100] in another. Greenwell [1877, 479–80] (frontispiece) showed that the Yorkshire long barrows did not have stone chambers and that their burials had been burned. He considered that neither map nor plan was necessary, and yet Pitt-Rivers [1898, Address, 28] was his pupil. Mortimer investigated only two long barrows and prepared plans and sections to illustrate his accounts.

The modern stage in the history of earthen long barrow excavation began with the total excavation of the Wor Barrow (pl. 11) during 1893–4 by Pitt-Rivers [1898, 62]. Modern intensive excavations (Appendix 3) fall into three groups. First of all there are two enterprises undertaken before 1914, followed by seven more in the decade before the Second World War, since which time the examination of a further series has been concluded. Most were partial excavations, but at least six have been totally or nearly completely excavated.

In 1907, B. H. and Maud Cunnington [Cunnington, B. H., 1909] disclosed, under the Heddington 3 mound which was 'thrown over', details comparable with those revealed by recent work. Unfortunately, no plan was published with the account. Seven years later the Tow Barrow on Wexcombe Down attracted the attention of O. G. S. Crawford and A. E. Hooton [Crawford, 1955, 107]. The outbreak of war curtailed their activities but, nonetheless, structural features were observed and Early Neolithic pottery found.

Earthen long barrow excavations of the inter-war years comprise two groups: those in the south, for the most part in Wessex, and those in the north-east, in Lincolnshire and East Anglia.

The first of the southern series was on Thickthorn Down [Drew & Piggott, 1936]. It was completely removed in quadrants, its ditch emptied, and the whole then restored. Two years later, a long barrow on gravel by the Stour at Holdenhurst was threatened with destruction [Crawford, 1930, 358]. A deep overburden inspired the use of a mechanical excavator [Piggott, S., 1937a]. At Badshot [Keiller & Piggott, 1939] the body of the barrow had been destroyed but the greater part of the ditches remained for examination. When an earlier Neolithic causewayed camp emerged from beneath the Maiden Castle ramparts, excavated between 1934 and 1937, there were, striding across it and in stratigraphical relationship to it, the parallel ditches and mound remnant of a bank barrow of inordinate length [Crawford, 1938, 228; Wheeler, 1943, 20, 86]. The re-excavation of Julliberrie's Grave in Kent was apparently suggested by the landowner after the publication of a novel in which the mound featured [Jessup, 1937, 122].

The study of maps by O. G. S. Crawford led C. W. Phillips to trace at least nine earthen long barrows on the Lincolnshire Wolds [Phillips, 1933b]. Subsequent fieldwork identified three more [Phillips, 1934] and during 1933 and 1934 the almost total excavation of the more prominent of the Giants' Hills was carried out [Phillips, 1936]. Shortly afterwards Phillips [1935] re-examined a mound on Therfield Heath, Royston, while A. H. A. Hogg [1940] examined an enigmatic mound on the Norfolk glacial gravels. At about this time, too, Sir Lindsay Scott explored the short long barrow at Whiteleaf [Childe & Smith, 1954]. The study of pottery from this mound led to a revision of current ideas regarding the character of Later Neolithic wares.

The trends of research in a European context [Piggott, S., 1955] were guiding factors in the excavation of the Fussell's Lodge long barrow in 1957 [Ashbee, 1958; 1966], while a possible relationship with the nearby causewayed camp led to an examination of the low-ploughed Windmill Hill Horslip long barrow in 1959 [Ashbee & Smith, 1960]. The long barrow at Nutbane [Morgan, 1959] disclosed a range of complex structural remains.

A development intimately associated with earthen long barrows is the isolation

6

[Atkinson, 1951, 58] of long mortuary enclosures. A Wiltshire example has recently been excavated [Vatcher, 1961a].

During 1962 and 1963, excavation of Wayland's Smithy, a stone-chambered long barrow in Berkshire, disclosed an earlier earthen phase. Its burials had been housed in a mortuary house pitched against a ridge borne by axial posts. In view of this principle such mortuary houses are described below as of the 'pitched' type. Recognition of these remains rationalized much that was hitherto confused and obscure in accounts of earthen long barrow excavations, for example the tumbled mass covering the bones at Fussell's Lodge and the remains of a burnt structure beneath the recently re-excavated long barrow on Willerby Wold, Yorkshire [Manby, 1963]. Excavation has also been made into the Yorkshire mound dug into by Londesborough a century ago [Vatcher, 1961b], but full details are not available, while examination of what was thought to be one of two adjacent long barrows at East Heslerton [Vatcher, 1965] disclosed a single mound of great length.

Earthen long barrow record and excavation emerge as initially a southern English vocation. There is still a disparity between south and north which is only slowly being redressed. The work of Colt Hoare, Cunnington, Thurnam and Greenwell in particular has provided a wealth of documentation concentrated on Salisbury Plain and Yorkshire which can be termed 'extensive'. It is possible to use this material together with what can be discerned from the records of the more recent and comprehensive undertakings which were 'intensive', although even these are not lacking in subjectivity.

Chapter 2

DISTRIBUTION

FORM AND TYPE
SIZE AND ORIENTATION
THE WEATHERING FACTOR

Following Stuart Piggott [1954, fig. 1, maps I and II, fig. 15, maps III and IV], earthen long barrows can be considered as of either a *southern* or *northern* region. The southern region (fig. 1), bounded on the north by a line from the Severn Estuary to the Wash, approximates to Fox's Lowland Zone of Britain [1952, 29]. The northern region (fig. 2) is primarily the northward extension of his Lowland Zone [1952, 32, map B] together with the remainder of Britain north of this line. Thus, strictly speaking, earthen long barrows might be considered as a Lowland Zone phenomenon. It must be noted that in making this differentiation, and in defining the basic groups of barrows, there is no intention of accepting what have been termed 'Fox's Laws' [Daniel, 1963, 9] or any subsequent debasement of them [Peate, 1961, 251].

Eight groups can be identified in the southern region (Appendix 10): (1) The Dorset Ridgeway and Coast; (2) Cranborne Chase; (3) the Hampshire Uplands; (4) Salisbury Plain East; (5) Salisbury Plain West; (6) the North Wiltshire and Berkshire Downs; (7) Sussex and Kent; (8) the Chilterns and East Anglia. There are two main groups in the northern region (Appendix 10): (1) the Lincolnshire Wolds; (2) Yorkshire. With the Yorkshire long barrows must be included outliers in Westmorland, and also recognizable cairns in Cumberland, Northumberland and Yorkshire. Long cairns in Scotland have also been noted: Henshall's Balnagowan group.

The geological solid that, with notable exceptions in both regions, bears all the earthen long barrows, is the chalk. The long cairns are mostly on acid moors and boulder clays. A major concentration, lying for the most part between Bridport and Dorchester on the downland block between the sea and the River Frome but with outliers over the river on the Purbeck Hills and by the Stour, is the Dorset Ridgeway and Coast group (fig. 3), some incorporating stone structures. Long barrows in linear cemeteries on the north-west–south-east ridges formed by the series of streams flowing into the Rivers Stour and Avon comprise the Cranborne Chase group (fig. 4). Almost all its monuments lie on these relatively low ridges (pl. III), between 200 ft and 400 ft above sea level; the higher ground to the north-west was ignored except for one or two outliers. The Hampshire Uplands group (fig. 5) consists of mounds scattered on the again relatively low blocks of downland between the Bourne on the west and the somewhat higher land to the east. There is a single outlier in Surrey at the west end of the Hog's Back, and others on the high ridge at the western end of the Isle of Wight. The map of Neolithic Wessex [Crawford, 1932] illustrates how separate and distinctive these groups are, while Grinsell's maps [Grinsell, 1959, map 1] emphasize, above all, their chalkland character.

The Salisbury Plain groups (fig. 6), East (Stonehenge) and West, lie upon what has been defined as the Lower Chalk Plain [Gifford, 1957, 6], which is intimately associated with the Salisbury Avon and its tributaries. The eastern group comprises the concentration of eight mounds within a relatively small area, just south-west of Stonehenge [Piggott, S., 1951, fig. 61], the single mound at the eastern end of the Cursus [Stone, J. F. S., 1948, 9, fig. 1], a group of four just east of the Robin Hood's Ball causewayed camp with one outlier on the eastern side of the Avon, eight more astride the block of downland between the Avon and the Bourne, and six others, one of which is stone-structured, just east of the source of the Bourne. These last and the Giant's Grave (Milton Lilbourne 7) (pl. v) are upon the summits of the High Chalk [Gifford, 1957, 4]. The Fussell's Lodge long barrow and another suspected site close by are some seven miles south-east of the Stonehenge cluster and, as far as can be seen, stand in isolation. The Salisbury Plain West group consists of long barrows which cluster about the headwaters of the River Wylie and its tributaries. One is on the flood plain (Sherrington 1), others on the higher plain [Gifford, 1957, 5], while the north-western outliers cling to the high summits. Again, the map of Neolithic Wessex [Crawford, 1932] illustrates the distinctive character of the groups and their components, while Grinsell's maps [Grinsell, 1957, map 2] demonstrate their relationship with the distinctive anatomy of the south Wiltshire chalklands.

It should be noted how intimately certain long barrows are associated with other monuments in Dorset and Wiltshire. A bank barrow lies athwart the Maiden Castle causewayed camp (fig. 7) [Wheeler, 1943, pl. 1], long barrows are set in and beside the great Dorset Cursus [Atkinson, 1955, fig. 1] and there is a mound at the eastern end of the Stonehenge Cursus [Stone, 1948, fig. 1].

Those long barrows, both earthen and stone-structured, which comprise the North Wiltshire (Avebury) and Berkshire Downs group (fig. 8) are in three concentrations. The first is the ten barrows about the headwaters of the River Kennet (and the Avebury great circle); the Windmill Hill causewayed camp conforms to the barrow distribution but is not the focus about which the mounds are set. The second is the eight barrows associated with the southern escarpment of the chalk above the Vale of Pewsey. Two, Adam's Grave (Alton 14) and the Kitchen Barrow (Bishop's Cannings 44), are sited in commanding positions upon the chalk high summits. The two long barrows on the

1. Southern Region: earthen long barrows

Berkshire Downs some ten miles from Avebury, Wayland's Smithy and the composite mound at Lambourn, lie back from the northern escarpment of the chalk.

The long barrows on the chalk downs of Sussex (fig. 9) are in two concentrations [Piggott, S., 1935, 121, fig. 5], forty miles apart. Those in the east are bracketed between the causewayed camps of Whitehawk and Coombe Hill, and those in the west are near the Trundle. Flint mines are associated with and lie between them. This group also includes the Julliberrie's Grave long barrow on chalk by the River Stour in East Kent, more than fifty miles distant from its fellow.

As has been shown by Dyer [1961, fig. 2], most of the long barrows of the Chilterns (fig. 10) line their western escarpment and tend to cluster upon the headwater of the River Lea. The Therfield Heath long barrow lies almost twenty miles distant, and beyond are the West Rudham and Ditchingham mounds on the acid East Anglian heathland (fig. 11).

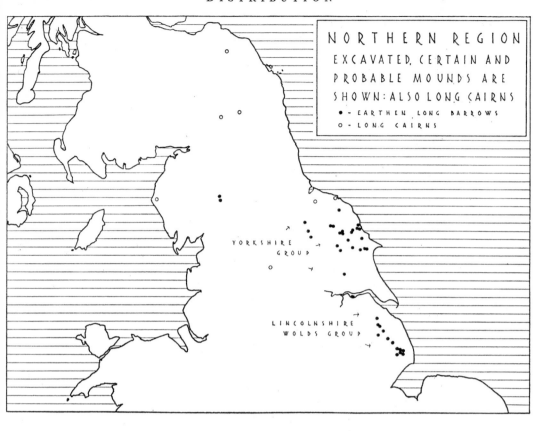

2. Northern Region: earthen long barrows

In the northern region the known long barrows of Lincolnshire (fig. 12), which rigidly adhere to the chalk, cluster in two areas: the valley of the Swinhope Beck in the north and the relatively isolated terminal Wold massif in the south. They stand along the edges of the upper slopes of valleys and close to water [Phillips, 1933a, 7; 1933b, pl. 1; 1936, fig. 1]. The Yorkshire long barrows [Elgee, 1930, 42, fig. 9; Phillips, 1933b, pl. 11; Manby, 1963, 174, fig. 1] also lie in two areas. Those on the chalk Wolds (fig. 13) line their western limit, and form a great half-circle on the western side; north of the Vale of Pickering (fig. 14) there are three distinct small concentrations with one outlier to the north. Those on the northern limestone hills and those on the Wolds which lie to the east and towards the coast seem to focus upon the eastern end of the Vale.

The Crosby Garret long barrow lies on a slope above Sunbiggin Tarn [Grinsell, 1953, 242]. Another possible long barrow is at Crosby Ravensworth some five miles

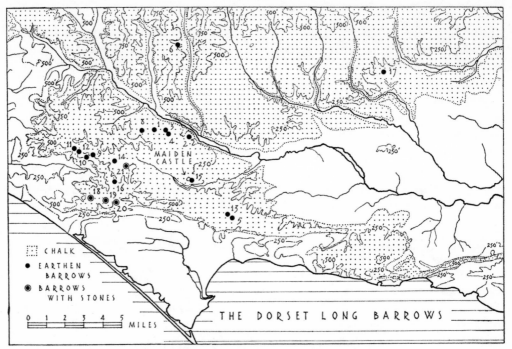

3. Dorset Ridgeway and Coast earthen long barrows

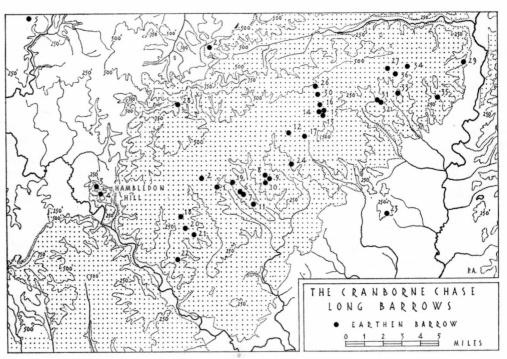

4. Cranborne Chase earthen long barrows

12

to the north-west. Also to be considered are the scattered long cairns on the high moorlands, standing in relative isolation. Little is known of them, but with the shrinkage of the peat blanket in some of these regions there is the possibility that an intelligible pattern may emerge.

Atkinson [1962, 12–13] has noted four apparent earthen long barrows in Scotland which, although on hills, lie on the coastal strip of relatively low land. Henshall's Balnagowan group [Henshall, 1963, 40–44] of long cairns and barrows has been shown to have a noticeably coastal distribution, while conspicuous positions and hill tops seem to be preferred.

Enigmatic mounds are known, such as Shiplea Hill on the edge of the water meadows at Ratcliffe-on-Soar north of Leicester [Thurman, 1868, 170, fn. b; Phillips, 1933a, 7]. There are also records of destroyed sites, like the Adam's Head, Giant's Grave [Phillips, 1933b, 197; Clark, 1947, 17], or long vanished ones, e.g. Mill Hill, Dunstable [Phillips, 1933b, 174]. Their inclusion in or exclusion from an assessment would not unduly alter present distribution patterns. It seems reasonable to suppose that any markedly large long mounds in any number, except perhaps in the most remote regions, would have been noted by Stukeley and others. One factor that might to some extent affect distribution, however, is the progressive exploration of river gravel terraces by air photography [RCHM, 1960]. However, nothing closely resembling the flanking ditches of a long barrow has so far been found.

The earthen long barrows must not be considered against the geographical background of present-day Britain. Coastline, climate and vegetation have changed. Daniel has considered these changes with regard to the chambered tombs [Daniel, 1950, 23], and Stuart Piggott [1954, 1] summarized them when he depicted the natural background for Neolithic settlement in the British Isles. Bare downs and heaths [Dimbleby, 1962] are largely man-made, a fact frequently forgotten in the study of the past. In their natural condition these isles, and indeed much of Europe, would be clad in the deciduous forest of the Temperate Zone [Clark, 1952, 10, fig. 2]. Only such factors as poverty of soil, climatic extremes [Movius, 1942, 89–95], fresh and salt water, and, in the Highland Zone, altitude, inhibited its growth [Clark, 1945; Godwin, 1956, 27–9; Ashbee, 1960, 37]. Neolithic forest trunks have come to light in the silts of East Anglian rivers and radio-carbon dates have been assigned to them—one from near Ely (Q-589, 2535 ± 120 B.C.) was 67 ft in length and without trace of branches. Such trunks are the product of forest conditions [Edlin, 1958, 44].

FORM AND TYPE

Earthen long barrows are elongated mounds with quarry ditches flanking them on either side or, much less frequently, turning about one end or, even more rarely, both ends. Some may be less than 100 ft in length, others almost 500 ft, and a small specialized class are longer still.

The mounds (pl. IV) resolve, on scrutiny, into two varieties. There are those which are

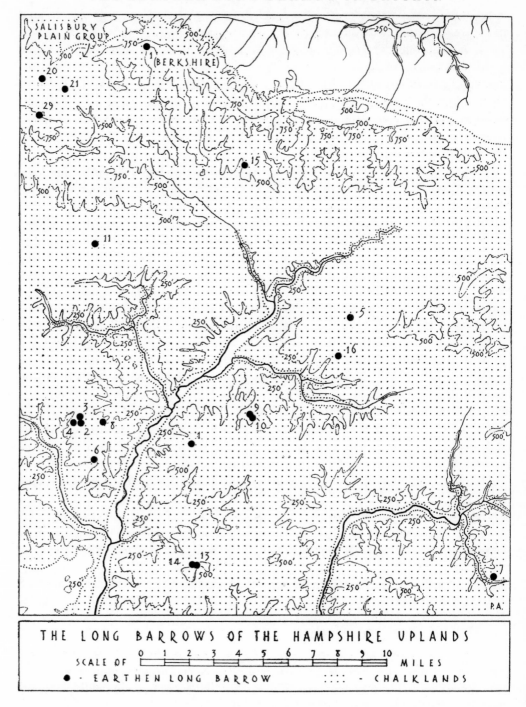

5. The earthen long barrows of the Hampshire Uplands

approximately trapezoidal and those which are roughly rectangular. This dual character of the earthen long barrows, first clearly stated by Colt Hoare [1810, 20], was quoted by Thurnam [1868, 173] and more recently by Grinsell [1958, 24].

All lists published so far (Appendix 2) which record dimensions of earthen long barrows, give only one breadth measurement generally, although this is not always indicated, at the widest point. At the same time orientation (discussed below) is given as *larger end first*. Normally no other note has been made except incidental references to 'wedge-shaped' or 'oblong' [Grinsell, 1957, 137]. The general impression given by the published records is that the trapezoid (or 'wedge-shape' or 'pear-shape', according to the monument's condition) is ubiquitous, but it is not possible to form a precise picture since all dimensions have not been given. The satisfactory identification of earthen long barrows of a rectangular, sometimes called 'parallel-sided', form from published lists has the same inherent difficulties. Grinsell [1958, 24] notes that there is some tendency for the longer examples to be parallel-sided and of uniform height throughout their length.

Bank barrows (pl. vi), parallel-sided and thus rectangular, represent the extremes of length in earthen long barrows. Defined as a class by Crawford [1938], Wheeler [1943, 24] set down their characteristics after his excavation of the example striding across the causewayed camp at Maiden Castle. Recent work [Prehistoric Society, 1962, 4] has disclosed more of their character. The bank barrow Long Bredy 1 is apparently in two parts and its longer part is not straight but changes direction two-thirds of the way along its length. Like the Dorset Cursus [Atkinson, 1955], the Maiden Castle bank barrow [Wheeler, 1943, pl. III] is also on two alignments, the two parts having a 1 : 2 ratio in their lengths. Probing by R. J. C. Atkinson [Grinsell, 1959, 81] has shown that the two Pentridge long barrows, IIa and IIb, are flanked by a continuous ditch and are thus probably a bank barrow.

Two further variants of the basically rectangular earthen long barrow are those in which the ditch, although causewayed, sweeps around one or both ends. The first, which can be termed the U-ditch class, are of medium size and seem to be restricted to Dorset. Holdenhurst, Cerne Abbas 1 and Gussage St Michael I, II, IV, are the classic examples. The second is illustrated by Wor Barrow and the Giants' Hills at Skendleby. Here excavation of the ditch disclosed a single causeway, but complete clearance of the ditch was more than the available financial resources allowed [Phillips, 1936, 65]. Further excavation here, or for that matter at Therfield Heath and West Rudham, might have disclosed arrangements similar to that of the Wor Barrow. The pronouncedly inturned ends of some ditches, as at Netheravon 6 and Gussage St Michael VI, might denote affinity with this class.

Small long barrows, as on Oakley Down, in Cranborne Chase [Colt Hoare, 1810, 242; Crawford, 1928, 174, pl. xxxi], and larger oval barrows were designated a class by Colt Hoare [1810, 22, 242], his *xii. Long Barrow no. 2*. Thurnam [1870, 296] investigated the class and was sceptical regarding their oval mounds, and of late [Grinsell, 1957] they have become identified with enditched multiple round barrows

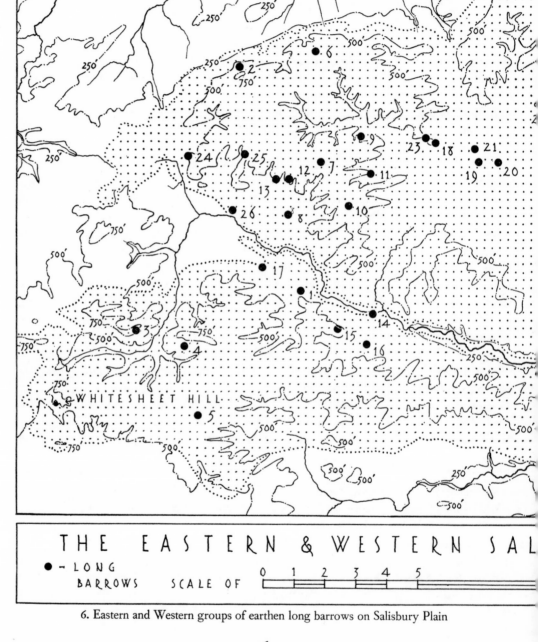

6. Eastern and Western groups of earthen long barrows on Salisbury Plain

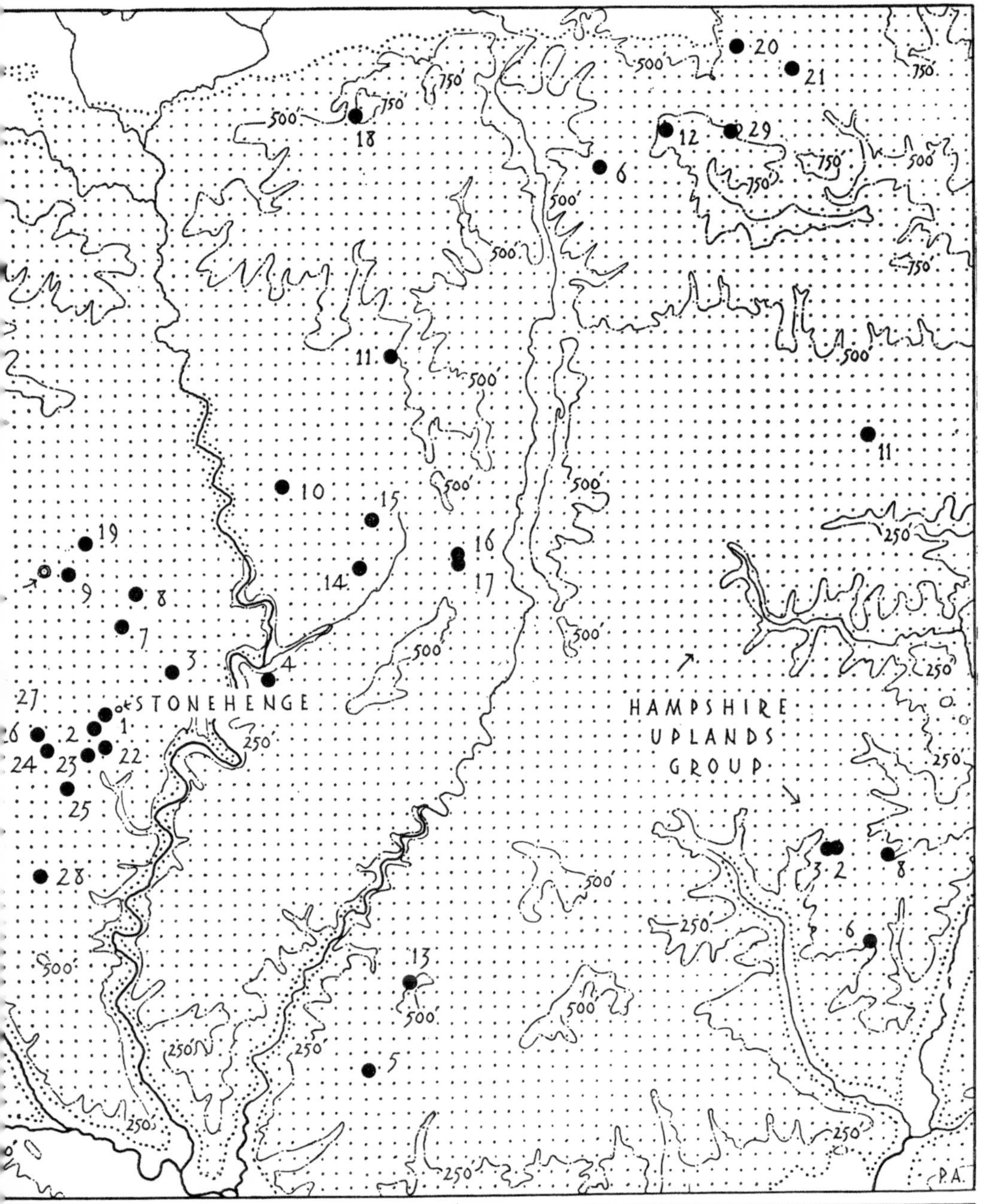

RY PLAIN LONG BARROW GROUPS

15 20 MILES   - CHALK LANDS

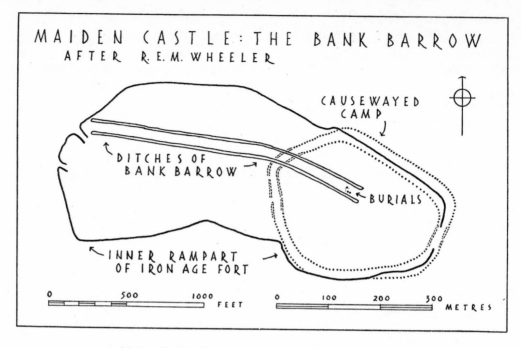

7. Maiden Castle: the bank barrow over the causewayed camp

(Appendix 11). Field scrutiny, if undamaged examples survive, with selective excavation, might restore this class to our archaeological literature.

Long mortuary enclosures (pl. VII) [Atkinson, 1951, 58] should be considered along with earthen long barrows. They recall in plan rectangular earthen long barrows in general and the Wor Barrow in particular. They appear to have been but slight sub-rectangular causewayed-ditched enclosures with an internal bank [Vatcher, 1961a, pl. IX].

The long cairns in the north apparently lack any stone structure other than cists, and thus, as far as can be seen, broadly resemble trapezoid earthen long barrows (pl. VIII). The external characteristics of four mounds, more earthen than stone, have been described by Atkinson; they taper slightly, but are almost parallel-sided, and have high eastern or northern ends and, sometimes, traces of horns.

A series of 'oblong' mounds, here to be considered and dismissed, resemble earthen long barrows; they range from pillow-mounds [Crawford, 1928, 18-24, 162-4, pl. XXVII; Bosanquet, 1928; Piggott, S., 1930, 199] to traces of medieval salt-workings [Thompson, 1957, pl. I].

Of the two basic forms of earthen long barrow, including the northern cairns, the trapezoid form is apparently the more widespread while the rectangular is restricted to the south. Related small and oval long barrows, as well as enditched multiples of round barrows, also seem to be a southern phenomenon, as do the long mortuary enclosures. It might be possible to regard these details of form and type in the light of Childe's early observation regarding chambered tombs [Childe, 1933, 121]: '... the oldest types will be those most accurately reproduced in the greatest number of distinct regions; types localised in specific areas will be later inasmuch as they represent regional variants on the original type or types.'

SIZE AND ORIENTATION

Length is the determinant of the size of earthen long barrows; width can only be used with reserve for, as has been shown above, more than one measurement is needed for the adequate record of most monuments. Little direct evidence of original height is forthcoming on account of denudation processes. Trapezoid mounds are markedly higher at one end while rectangular mounds have a uniform height throughout their length. These basic differences reflect, distantly, the original appearance of the structures.

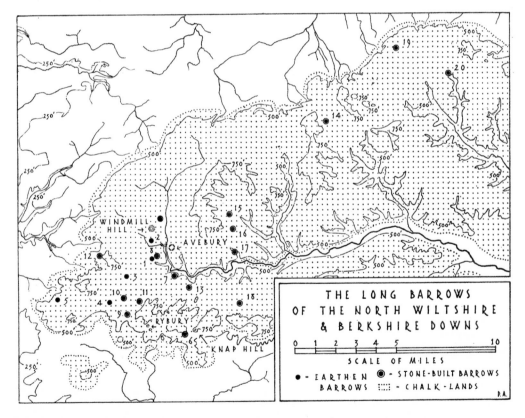

8. The long barrows of the North Wiltshire and Berkshire Downs

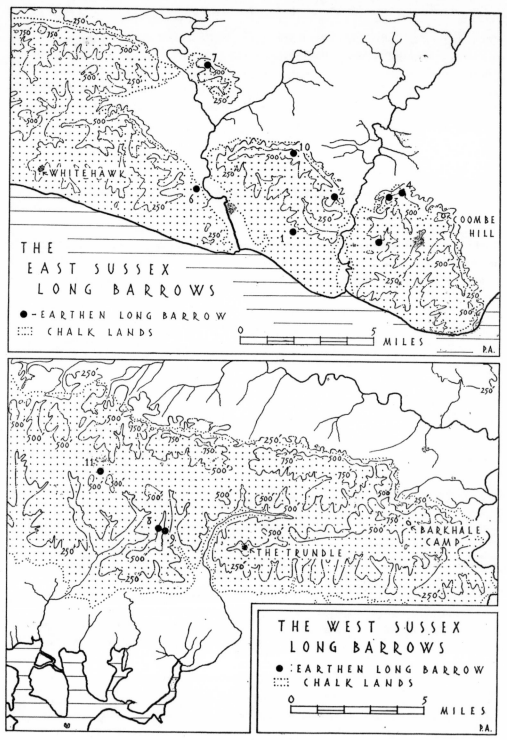

THE
EAST SUSSEX
LONG BARROWS

●—EARTHEN LONG BARROW
▒▒▒ CHALK LANDS

0   5
|___|___|___|___|___| MILES

P.A.

THE WEST SUSSEX
LONG BARROWS

●: EARTHEN LONG BARROW
▒▒▒ CHALK LANDS

0   5
|___|___|___|___|___| MILES

P.A.

9. The earthen long barrows of Sussex

20

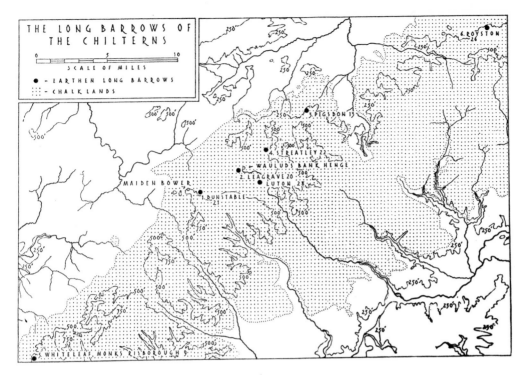

10. The earthen long barrows of the Chilterns

Most (115 of a total of 203) earthen long barrows (figs. 15, 16, 17, 18) are between 100 ft and 200 ft long. Thirty-six are less than 100 ft but over 65 ft, while twenty-seven lie at the other end of the scale, i.e. between 200 ft and 250 ft. Long earthen barrows are relatively few in number: only seven are between 250 ft and 300 ft, twelve between 300 ft and 350 ft and two between 350 ft and 400 ft. The narrow but regular bank barrows, of 500 ft and more, are only four in number.

In the north there are mounds of comparable size to those in the south but they are mostly on a slightly smaller scale and the greater mounds are proportionately fewer. Recently, however [Vatcher, 1965], a Yorkshire mound has been shown to be 410 ft in length.

A seemingly significant pattern emerges on a basis of local groups. While in each group most long barrows conform to the mass, there are smaller examples. However, almost every group has one or more extended or great mounds, which on a size basis stand apart from their neighbours.

Modest mounds are notably relatively common in the vicinity of Stonehenge. The claim that the Sussex long barrows are of smaller than average size [Curwen, 1954, 92] would appear to result more from the absence of lengthy mounds than uniformly modest proportions.

The more-or-less east–west orientation of earthen long barrows has received

21

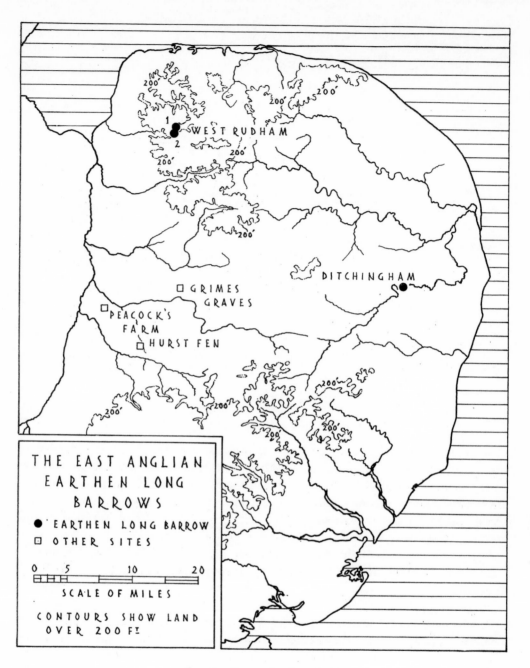

11. East Anglian earthen long barrows

comment from the first [Stukeley, 1743, 46; Colt Hoare, 1810, 21; Williams-Freeman, 1915, 10; Cunnington, M. E., 1938, 73; Piggott, S., 1954, 53]. More than four-fifths are orientated east–west or within 45° of this direction (fig. 19). This pattern is followed

22

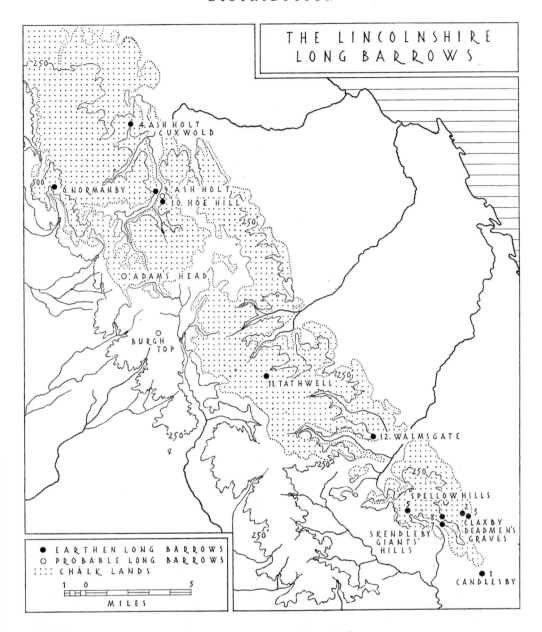

THE LINCOLNSHIRE
LONG BARROWS

4. ASH HOLT
CUXWOLD

6. NORMANBY   9. ASH HOLT
                   10. HOE HILL

O ADAM'S HEAD

O
BURGH
TOP

11. TATHWELL

12. WALMSGATE

SPELLOW HILLS

CLAXBY
DEADMEN'S
GRAVES

SKENDLEBY
GIANTS'
HILLS

CANDLESBY

● EARTHEN LONG BARROWS
○ PROBABLE LONG BARROWS
:::: CHALK LANDS
        1   0   5
MILES

12. The long barrows of Lincolnshire

with minor variations in each region (figs. 20, 21, 22), although everywhere there are
a few mounds with north–south orientation. Only in Cranborne Chase is there a
significant variation from this pattern: this seems to have been brought about by their

23

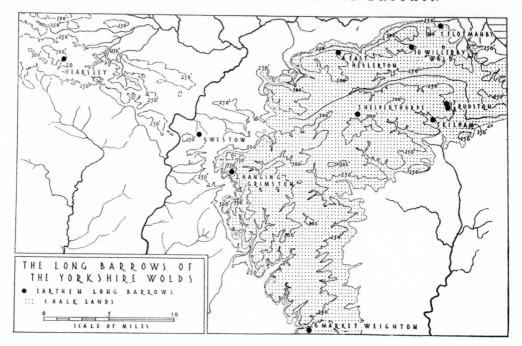

13. The long barrows of the Yorkshire Wolds

siting on predominantly north-north-west to south-south-east ridges [Prehistoric Society, 1962, 5]. In contrast to the rest of the group, the long barrow incorporated in one side of the Dorset Cursus [Atkinson, 1955, 8] is roughly at right angles to the normal trend. This, like the long barrow at the eastern end of the Stonehenge Cursus [Stone, J. F. S., 1948, fig. 1], provides evidence suggesting that, when circumstances demanded, drastic departures could be made from a uniformity dictated, to some extent, by nature.

THE WEATHERING FACTOR

The earthen long barrows, like all man's monuments, have been subject, down the years, to the complex biological, chemical and physical factors which constitute the processes of weathering and denudation, change and decay (fig. 23). The mounds and their stratigraphy as we see them today are the end-product of these factors; the prehistorian is faced with the works of man modified by the forces of nature, and to understand the first he must appreciate the changes wrought by the second.

Stukeley [1743, 17, 38, 44] and Colt Hoare [1810, 92] incidentally observed the effects of nature upon monuments while Pitt-Rivers [1898, 24, Address], at the

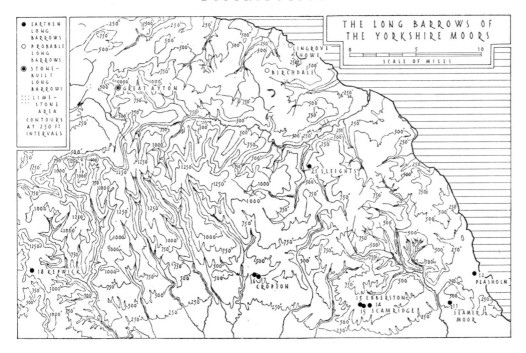

14. The long barrows of the Yorkshire Moors

conclusion of his examination of the Wor Barrow, left the great ditches (fig. 24) unfilled so that he might study silting in action. Such pioneer observations as these, together with developments during the last decade, led to the inception of the Experimental Earthwork on Overton Down (pl. IX), in Wiltshire [Jewell (ed.), 1963], and its fellow on Decoy Heath, near Wareham in Dorset. The first is on chalk, the second on acid-soil heathland with a sandy geological soil. The account of the initial undertaking contains an historical introduction [Ashbee, 1963] which reviews the appreciation of, and references to, natural factors in archaeological literature to the present.

Pitt-Rivers [1876, 371] was the first to differentiate the natural infill of pits and ditches, which he termed *silting* (pl. XI), from fillings put in by the hand of man. He observed that alterations might have been made in the stratigraphy of the Wor Barrow ditch by badgers [Pitt-Rivers, 1898, 100]. Burrowing rabbits, now almost entirely absent from the scene, are probably one of the most continually underestimated factors in field archaeology. Few downland earthworks were free from them two decades ago [Hubbard & Hubbard, 1905, pl. VI; Curwen, 1929, pls. VIII, XXII; Grinsell, 1936, pl. XI; Clark, 1940, pl. 92], and their warrens, sometimes extensive and long used [Thompson & Worden, 1956, 85–91, fig. 10, pl. IIIb], when abandoned and silted, surely account for the lenticular stratification [Grinsell, 1941, 105] recorded from chalkland barrows.

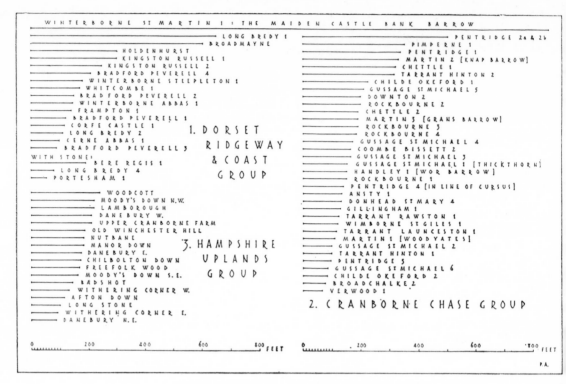

15. Lengths of long barrows: the Dorset, Cranborne Chase, and Hampshire groups

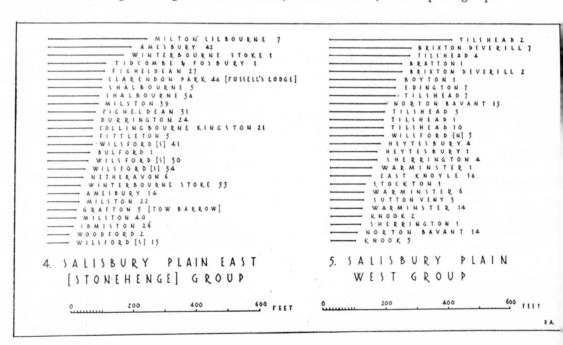

16. Lengths of long barrows: the Salisbury Plain groups

EARTHEN
——————— BISHOP'S CANNINGS 92
——————— AVEBURY 17
——————— BISHOP'S CANNINGS 76
——————— AVEBURY 47 [HORSLIP BARROW]
——————— HEDDINGTON 3
WITH STONE
——————— EAST KENNET 1
——————— AVEBURY 22 [WEST KENNET]
——————— PRESHUTE 3a
——————— LAMBOURN
——————— ALTON 14
——————— ASHBURY, WAYLAND'S SMITHY
——————— CALNE-CHERHILL
——————— LIDDINGTON-WANBOROUGH
——————— BISHOP'S CANNINGS 65
——————— BISHOP'S CANNINGS 91
——————— BISHOP'S CANNINGS 44
——————— AVEBURY 68
——————— WEST OVERTON 12
——————— PRESHUTE 1

6. NORTH WILTSHIRE [AVEBURY] & BERKSHIRE DOWNS GROUP

——————— FOLKINGTON-WILMINGTONS
——————— UP MARDEN
——————— ALFRISTON 55
——————— ARLINGTON 2
——————— CHILHAM, TULLIBERRIE'S GRAVE
——————— LITLINGTON 2
——————— PIDDINGHOE 22
——————— SOUTH MALLING 40
——————— WEST FIRLE 13
——————— STOUGHTON 12
——————— STOUGHTON 14

7. SUSSEX & KENT GROUP

——————— STREATLEY 22
——————— WEST RUDHAM 1
——————— DITCHINGHAM
——————— WEST RUDHAM 2
——————— ROYSTON 26
——————— DUNSTABLE 21
——————— LEAGROVE 20
——————— PEGSDON 13
——————— MONKS RISBOROUGH 9 [WHITELEAF]

8. CHILTERNS & EAST ANGLIAN GROUP

0   200   400   600   FEET

P.A.

17. Lengths of long barrows: the North Wiltshire, Sussex and Kent with the Chilterns and East Anglian groups

——————— WALMSGATE
——————— SKENDLEBY 1, GIANTS' HILLS
——————— NORMANBY
——————— LANGTON, SPELLOW HILLS
——————— SKENDLEBY 2
——————— SWINHOPE, HOE HILL
——————— CLAXBY, DEADMAN'S GRAVE 2
——————— CLAXBY, DEADMAN'S GRAVE 1
——————— SWINHOPE, ASH HILL
——————— TATHWELL
——————— CANDLEBYS
——————— CUXWOLD, ASH HOLT

1. LINCOLNSHIRE WOLDS GROUP

LONG CAIRNS
——————— BELLSHIEL LAW
——————— GREAT AYTON MOOR
——————— BRADLEY MOOR
——————— KIELDER, DEVIL'S LAPFUL
——————— SAMSON'S BRATFUL

EARTHEN MOUNDS: SCOTLAND
——————— CAVERTON HILLHEAD
——————— MACDUFF
——————— GOURDON
——————— SLAINS

THE WOLDS
——————— HESLERTON
——————— RUDSTON 2
——————— FLOTMANBY
——————— RUDSTON 1
——————— KILHAM
——————— WILLERBY
——————— MARKET WEIGHTON
——————— HELPERTHORPE
——————— HANGING GRIMSTON
——————— WESTOW
SCARBOROUGH
——————— EAST AYTON, SEAMER MOOR
——————— PEASHOLM
SCAMRIDGE
——————— EBBERSTON
——————— SCAMRIDGE 1
——————— SCAMRIDGE 2
CROPTON
——————— CROPTON 1
HAMBLEDON
——————— GILLING
——————— OVER SILTON
——————— KILBURN, WASS MOOR
ESKDALE
——————— GROSMONT
WESTMORLAND
——————— CROSBY GARRETT
——————— ENNERDALE
——————— CROSBY RAVENSWORTH

2. YORKSHIRE GROUP

0   200   400   600   FEET

P.A.

18. Lengths of long barrows: the Lincolnshire, Yorkshire, and Scottish long barrows

27

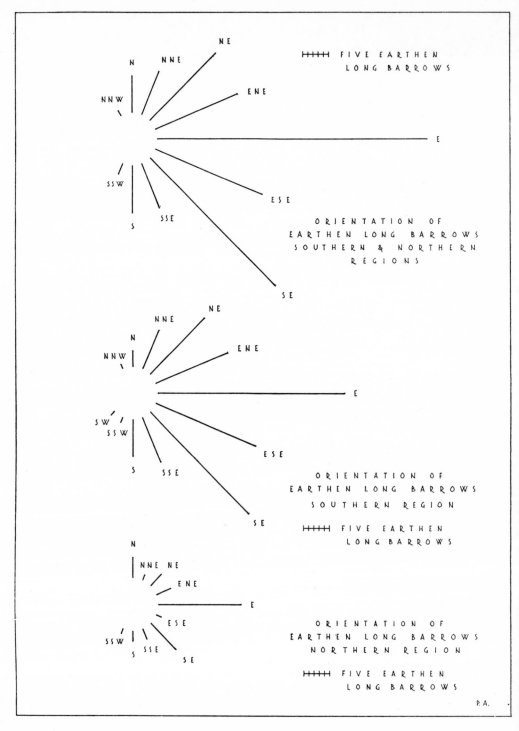

19. Orientation of the earthen long barrows together with orientations of those of the Southern and Northern Regions

28

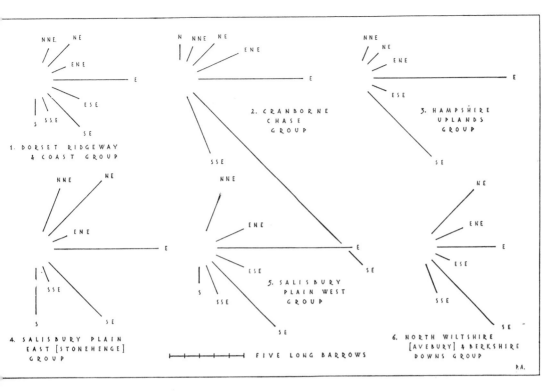

20. Orientations: the Dorset, Cranborne Chase, Hampshire, Salisbury Plain, and North Wiltshire groups of long barrows

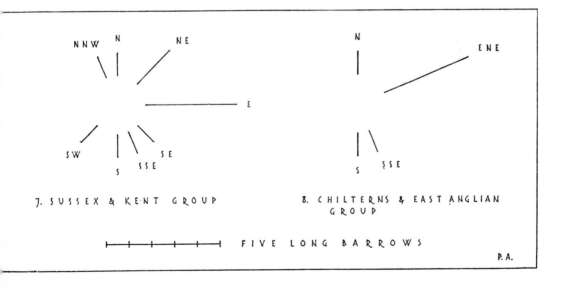

21. Orientations: the Sussex and Kent, Chilterns and East Anglian groups of long barrows

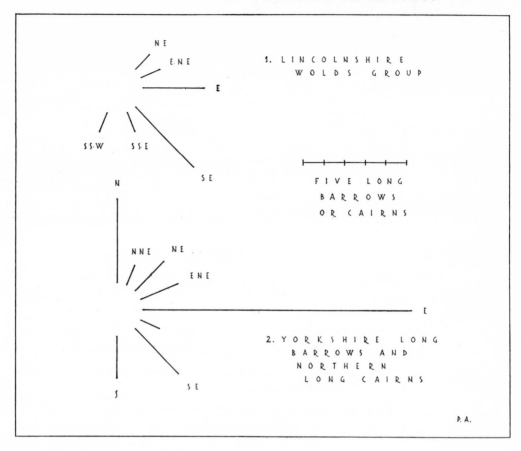

22. Orientations: the Lincolnshire, Yorkshire and Northern groups of long barrows

Roughly circular holes in the gravel at the bottom of the ditch of the Holdenhurst long barrow [Piggott, S., 1937a, 4] and the ill-definable holes noted by Atkinson [1953, 36] when he re-examined a section of the Maiden Castle bank barrow seem to be a product of tree roots, comparable with what has been observed in geological contexts [Arkell, 1947, 240, pl. vi, Lower]. Earthworms carry stones and other small objects to the base of a soil profile [Dimbleby, 1954, 12] and might account for the black earth noted under long barrows by Colt Hoare [1810, 92]. Archaeological aspects of earthworms have been discussed by Cornwall [1953, 131], Atkinson [1957] and Jewell [1958]. The sections of the West Rudham long barrow [Hogg, 1940, pl. iii] show that what appeared to be turf was a water percolation phenomenon [Glasbergen, 1954, 29]. Calcium carbonate, apparently water deposited, has been noted on struck flints in long barrow ditches [Drew & Piggott, 1936, 89; Jessup, 1937, 131]. A river meander, rather than a

Section through old military trench, Thundersbarrow Hill,
showing result of 13 years silting

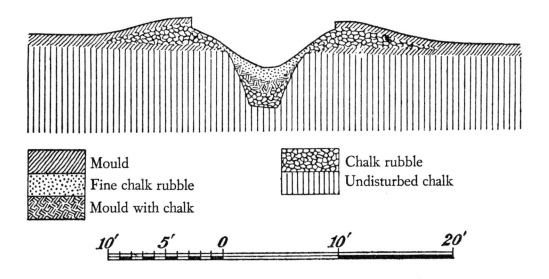

Mould

Fine chalk rubble

Mould with chalk

Chalk rubble

Undisturbed chalk

10'   5'   0   10'   20'

Diagrams illustrating the stages observed in the
process of silting

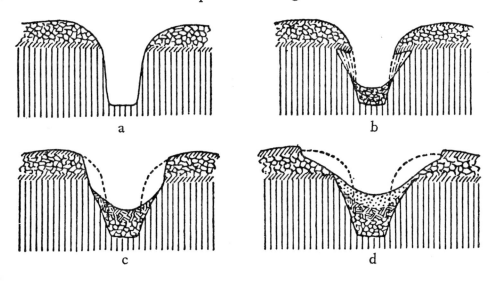

a

b

c

d

23. Silting in action in a chalk ditch

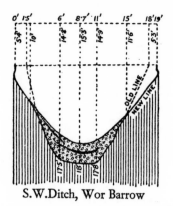

S.W. Ditch, Wor Barrow

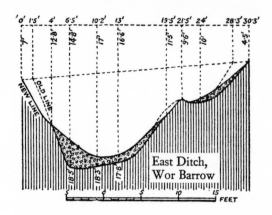

East Ditch, Wor Barrow

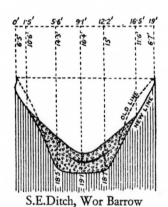

S.E. Ditch, Wor Barrow

24. Silting in the unfilled excavated ditches of the Wor Barrow

chalk pit, may have truncated Julliberrie's Grave [Jessup, 1937, fig. 1]. The progressive lowering of the soil mantle in relation to soils sealed beneath barrows and other earthworks is also relevant [Atkinson, 1957, 228] and is termed differential weathering [Ashbee, 1960, 59, fig. 19].

Such observations as the foregoing allow the evidence gleaned by excavation to be considered in another dimension. Man and his works are a part of nature, not separate from it. The tendency to treat prehistory as a distinct province has led to a mass of 'pits' and 'post-holes' in archaeological literature, which are the misleading progeny of uncritical excavation and evaluation.

Chapter 3

STRUCTURE

MOUNDS · DITCHES
LONG MORTUARY ENCLOSURES
MORTUARY HOUSES

Earthen long barrow structure was largely conditioned by local geology; the materials to hand, earth or stones, were used. There are, therefore, two basic forms: *earthen mounds* and *stone cairns*, but often structure was 'composite', both earth and stones being used. Again, modern intensive excavation has shown that many mounds covered complex timber structures of which now only earthen traces remain.

Detailed knowledge of earthen long barrow structure is based upon the relatively recent 'intensive' examination of a small series in southern England and a smaller series in northern England (Appendix 3). Both series are supplemented by earlier 'extensive' investigations (Appendix 4). Only four of the northern long cairns have been dug into, but some evidence of a common structural pattern has been forthcoming. It is convenient to consider structure under three headings: the *Mounds*, which sometimes cloak the remains of timber or stone features that originally retained them; the *Ditches*, normally still visible, which served as sources of building materials; and the timber, turf and stone *Mortuary Houses*, in which lay the burials.

MOUNDS

It is possible to discern two groups of mound structures. The first consists of timber or stone enclosures which contained spoil dug from the ditches. The second appears to have been built entirely of heaped soil or stacked sods, but sometimes had terminal timber structures. Some of both have massive façades of standing timbers at their easterly, proximal ends (for mound structural components see Appendix 5). For brevity, the term 'proximal' has been used for the end at which the burials were, usually the higher and wider, and 'distal' for the other.

Two bases for division of the enclosures can be seen. First, there are the entranced enclosures to which access could apparently have been gained at some stage, but which

33

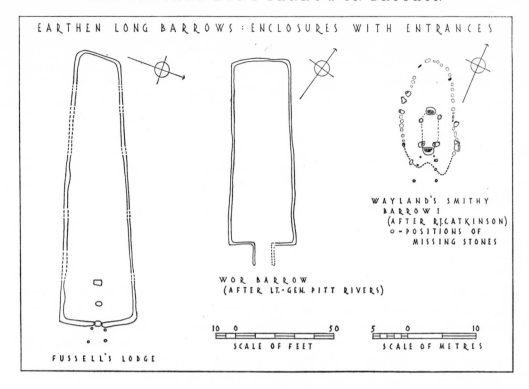

25. Earthen long barrow enclosures with entrances

had no separate façade, and secondly the façaded enclosures. The form of the ground plan provides the other contrast, that between angular and ovoid. Angular enclosures are pronouncedly trapezoid, slightly tapering or rectangular.

The entranced enclosures (fig. 25) have only three examples: the Fussell's Lodge long barrow, the Wor Barrow, and Wayland's Smithy I, the composite monument which preceded the stone-chambered long barrow. The ground plan of Fussell's Lodge was a pronounced trapezoid, that of the Wor Barrow a pronounced rectangle, while Wayland's Smithy I was an ovoid. All had 'porch' entrances.

Beneath the wedge-shaped mound of the Fussell's Lodge long barrow (pl. X; fig. 26) was a bedding trench for vertical timbers. It was trapezoid in plan, some 135 ft long, 20 ft wide at the oblique distal end and 40 ft wide at the broad, slightly convex, proximal end. The record of timbers (pl. XII) in this trench was fragmentary, owing to extreme distortion following upon extensive faulting. There had been an entrance through the middle of the proximal end of this enclosure. This had later been slighted by a post

34

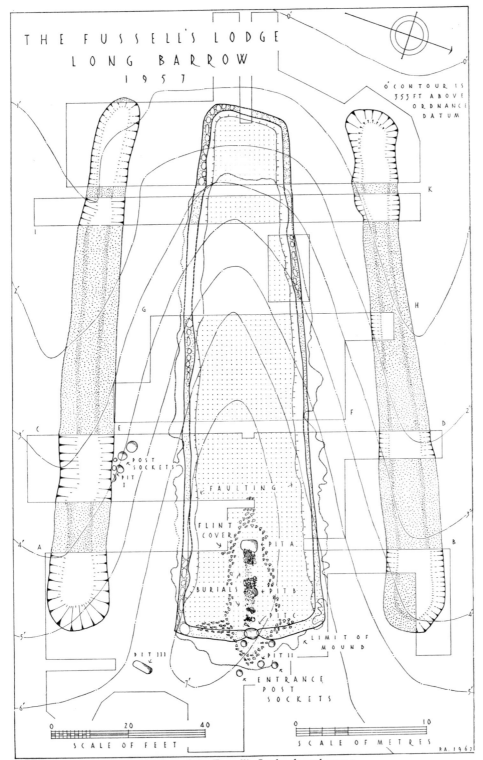

THE FUSSELL'S LODGE
LONG BARROW
1 9 5 7

0' CONTOUR IS
353 FT ABOVE
ORDNANCE
DATUM

K

I

POST
SOCKETS
PIT
I

FAULTING

FLINT
COVER
PIT A

BURIALS
PIT B

PIT C

LIMIT OF
MOUND

PIT III
PIT II

ENTRANCE
POST
SOCKETS

G

H

F

E

C

D

A

B

0   20   40
SCALE OF FEET

0   10
SCALE OF METRES

P.A. 1962

26. Plan of the Fussell's Lodge long barrow

35

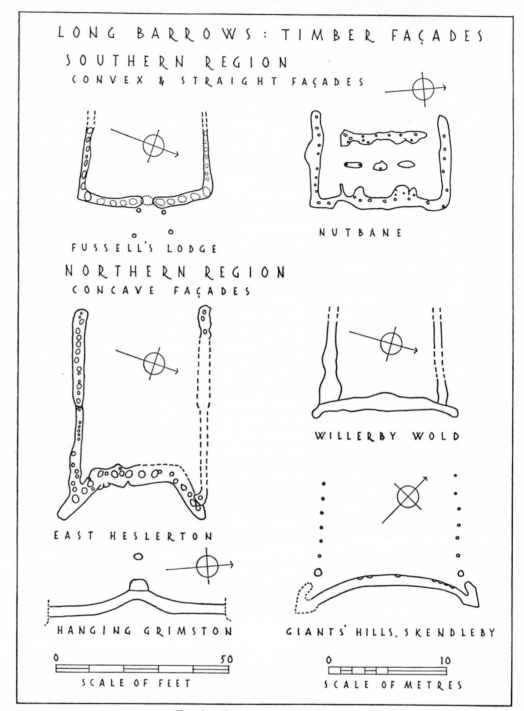

LONG BARROWS: TIMBER FAÇADES

SOUTHERN REGION

CONVEX & STRAIGHT FAÇADES

FUSSELL'S LODGE

NUTBANE

NORTHERN REGION

CONCAVE FAÇADES

EAST HESLERTON

WILLERBY WOLD

HANGING GRIMSTON

GIANTS' HILLS, SKENDLEBY

0   50
SCALE OF FEET

0   10
SCALE OF METRES

27. Façades: Southern and Northern regions

of the axial mortuary house. A setting of four posts at the enclosure entrance, itself trapezoid in plan, may have been the basis of a porch. When the monument was first raised, the enclosure had retained the soil and chalk rubble dug from the flanking ditches.

The Wor Barrow rectangular enclosure was some 90 ft by 35 ft and had a restricted 'passage' at its eastern end. As at Fussell's Lodge, the enclosure had been bounded by trunks, some of them substantial [Piggott, S., 1954, pl. II, b], set in a bedding trench and packed with flint nodules (pl. XIII). As the enclosure lay well within the sub-rectangular mound, it was thought that it might have been a chamber [Pitt-Rivers, 1898, 65], but it has been pointed out [Piggott, S., 1954, 54] that the posts were too small to take the thrust of the roof necessitated by this hypothesis. Whether the palisade was visible after infill is also debatable. One photograph [Piggott, S., 1954, pl. II, b] which might suggest that the enclosure was completely covered in shows in section the mound apparently continuing on either side of vestiges of a substantial post. Had the enclosure retained all the spoil from the ditch, timbers rising some 20 ft above the ancient soil would have been needed. The great height of the mound in relation to its general size before excavating ($13\frac{1}{2}$ ft above the ground level and thus some 12 ft above the ancient soil beneath it) might indicate that it had initially been retained to a considerable height. Such trunks as were detected here would have had a great combined strength, but the well-preserved ancient soil might point to a relatively swift collapse enveloping parts of the palisade. Alternatively, the soil outside the palisade could well be derived from the setting-out trench [Pitt-Rivers, 1898, pl. 249; Vatcher, 1961a, 167, fig. 5, fn.] which possibly co-existed with the free-standing phase of the enclosure.

The Wayland's Smithy I ovoid enclosure was originally delimited by sarsen stones, many of which had been removed leaving only holes. The mortuary house lay on the axis, and the great proximal post was outside. A trapezoid setting of posts, similar to those at Fussell's Lodge, may have formed a porch. Small sarsen stones, presumably from cultivation clearance, had been used as a base to fill this enclosure and were also on either side of the mortuary house, and chalk rubble from the ditches had been heaped on these.

Only three façaded (fig. 27) enclosures have so far been recorded in the northern region: Giants' Hills, Skendleby, with a ground plan best described as slightly tapering, the Willerby Wold G.ccxxII mound, which covered a pronouncedly trapezoid enclosure and the East Heslerton enclosure, only a part of which has been examined. A distinguishing feature of these northern façades is their crescentic character.

The Giants' Hills barrow (fig. 28) was for long the only example of which a complete record of an enclosure was available in the region, or for that matter, in the country, apart from Wor Barrow. A much-spread rectangular mound, some 210 ft long and 75 ft broad, covered a slightly tapering enclosure 200 ft by 45 ft at the proximal end, diminishing to less than 35 ft at the distal. This enclosure was closed across its proximal end by a façade of apparently massive split trunks, bark outwards, housed in a generous palisade trench of convex form with a short return at its northern end. The corresponding return at the southern end, on the downhill side, had apparently been eradicated

37

by the weathering of the ditch. In contrast to the palisade principle of the façade, the posts which delimited the sides and distal end of the enclosure had stood in sockets. These had been set at about 5 ft intervals, in order of diminishing diameter ranging from 2 ft to 9 in. at the proximal end. To retain the mound, horizontal members would have been needed with such an interval. Along part of each side the evidence for standing posts was missing or slight, possibly owing to the close proximity of ditch to enclosure, together with weathering. Apart from the mortuary installations, there was evidence for a light hurdle-work fence with offsets, demarcating bays, on the southern side, in the distal half of the mound.

Greenwell [1877, 487: G.CCXXII (references thus are to the number of each barrow in that work)] dug into the Willerby Wold long barrow, and work carried out between 1958 and 1960 [Manby, 1963] illuminated and amplified his account. Beneath the mound (fig. 28) at the eastern end was the bedding trench of a convex façade, with a trapezoid enclosure attached to it. This was described as 'ditched', but traces of posts were found at one point. It may have been faulted in places, which would account for the varied profile, while tabular chalk from the flanking mound screes had replaced the timbers. The excavation account suggests that the standing posts were connected, even below ground level.

Excavation of the eastern half of the prodigiously lengthy East Heslerton long barrow (fig. 28) [Vatcher, 1965] disclosed a discontinuous series of bedding trenches which had formed a long enclosure, terminating at the eastern end in a massive flattened crescentic façade. Successive phases for the enclosure are claimed, but this might only reflect dilapidation and subsequent repair. The bedding trench of the façade was some 3 ft in width and depth and trunks some 2 ft in diameter had stood in it. The more massive trunks were concentrated in the straight centre section and at each end. A most striking feature was the connected returns to the enclosure trenches from each extremity, a feature recalling the façade of the Nutbane long barrow, which is discussed below. One of these returns had been destroyed by a chalk quarry.

All the trunks of the façade, excepting four at the north-eastern end, had been burnt down to their bases, as had those of certain parts of the enclosure bedding trenches. Had there been the remains of a burnt mortuary house and burials behind this façade, they would have been destroyed by the quarry.

Three façaded (fig. 27) mounds form the 'heaped' series. One, Nutbane, had a sequence of timber structures at its proximal end, of which the façade was but the final stage. They were contained within a mound which revealed no trace of its initial retaining elements. The other two, Hanging Grimston and Heddington 3, have yielded evidence of façades and, indeed, mortuary houses, but again nothing to suggest the original method of retaining the mound.

A seemingly solid façade terminated the Nutbane complex and mound. A sequence of timber structures had been concentrated at the 75 ft broader, proximal end of an apparently unretained mound which narrowed to 25 ft at the distal end of its 170 ft length. The initial structure [Morgan, 1959, 21, fig. 3] appears to have been four posts

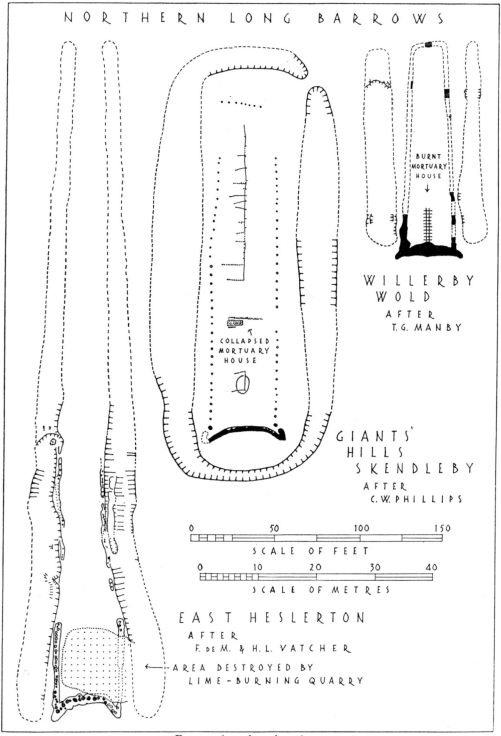

BURNT
MORTUARY
HOUSE
↓

WILLERBY
WOLD
AFTER
T. G. MANBY

COLLAPSED
MORTUARY
HOUSE

GIANTS'
HILLS
SKENDLEBY
AFTER
C. W. PHILLIPS

0   50   100   150
SCALE OF FEET

0   10   20   30   40
SCALE OF METRES

EAST HESLERTON
AFTER
F. DE M. & H. L. VATCHER
←—AREA DESTROYED BY
LIME-BURNING QUARRY

28. Excavated northern long barrows

in a roughly rectangular setting. One hole of this setting (no. 2) disclosed traces of three posts, suggesting replacement of rotted wood. A causewayed rectangular ditched area, some 18 ft long and 14 ft broad, was later but with no clearly demonstrable relationship. This seems to be a small version of a long mortuary enclosure [Vatcher, 1961a]. It was entered at its eastern end between two flanking posts, and enclosed the remains of a pitched mortuary house and burials, to be discussed below. The third phase involved reconstruction of what was termed 'the first forecourt building' and an aisled building, some 40 ft by 20 ft with palisade trenches and triple intermediate post-holes, was set across the axis of the enclosure. Next a palisade of vertical dug-in posts with clearly detectable halved-jointed horizontals surrounded the ditched enclosure. The blocking of the fenced area from the larger structure across its end is adduced as a separate phase. At some stage, extensions were made to the outer wall of the large transverse structure, which gave it its final plan. The entire complex was finally covered with a mound.

At some time after the completion of the Nutbane barrow, the transverse structure was fired. Many of the posts seem to have burnt well down into their sockets, leaving a mass of wood charcoal, and scorching the surrounding packing. Finally while this transverse structure, which was not a mortuary house in the sense of those described below, was still burning, it is alleged that chalk was 'tipped' into the interior. The collapse of an enmounded structure would account for the indiscriminate mingling of burnt and unburnt lumps of chalk, while such material filling cylindrical post-voids could have been the result of long-term decay, collapse and settling of the slighted structure.

It is curious, in view of the considerable conflagration, the temperatures involved and the proximity of consumed timbers, that the fenced burial area, even though enmounded, was unscathed. The excavator [Morgan, 1959, 26] is adamant regarding the clean white chalk which filled the narrow gap between them.

A trench running from side to side beneath the proximal end of the wedge-shaped mound of Heddington 3, immediately behind which there seems to have been a mortuary house, could well have housed a façade. The 'whole of the mound was thrown over' but no other structural feature was recorded.

The Hanging Grimston mound, 78 ft long and 50 ft wide, had a transverse trench beneath its eastern end. This was nearly straight, deep in the middle and shallow at its extremities. The middle was joined to a large pit, one of an axial pair which were the basis of a mortuary house. This was interpreted as a pit-dwelling [Mortimer, 1905, 103, fig. 249] but was clearly a façade bedding trench. Mortimer's description makes this clear, for 'many streaks of burnt and decayed matter ran obliquely—and in some places almost vertically—into the pit dwelling, reaching in places nearly to the bottom'.

Eight earthen long barrows in the southern region have proved, after intensive excavation, to have been of the 'heaped or stacked' kind, i.e. there was no direct evidence either of mound retention or of timber enclosures or façades, although single, or modest numbers of standing posts occurred beneath the ends of one or two mounds.

I Prospect of Julliberrie's Grave, 11th October 1724

II The Wor Barrow after excavation: A,B,C, bedding trench of timber palisade; D,E,F,G, quarry-ditch of barrow; H, causeway

III The Gran's long barrow,
Rockbourne, Hampshire

IV The Martin's Down,
Dorset, bank barrow from
the air

V The Giant's Grave
(Milton Lilbourne 7) from
the air

VI The Danebury barrows
from the air

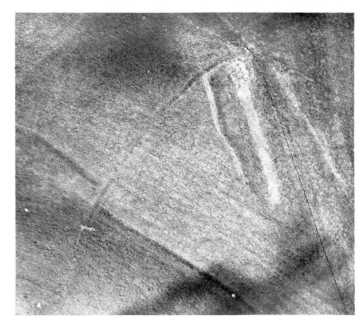

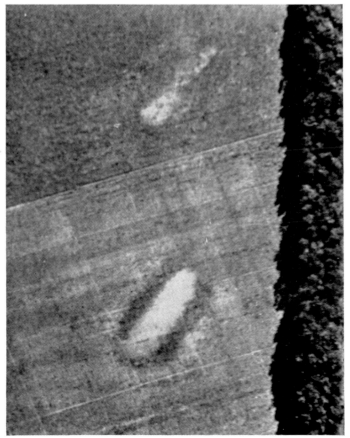

IX Overton Down Experimental Earthwork:
a three-year accumulation of
silt in the ditch

VII The Dorchester (Oxon)
long mortuary enclosure

VIII A Scottish long barrow:
Cairn Catto, Aberdeenshire

x The excavated Fussell's Lodge long barrow from the air

XI Silting of the ditch of the Fussell's Lodge long barrow

XII Fussell's Lodge long barrow: the posts

XIII Wor Barrow, details of construction: A,B,C, bedding trench of timber palisade with packing stones; D, timber upright visible in section; E,F, ancient soil outside and inside palisade

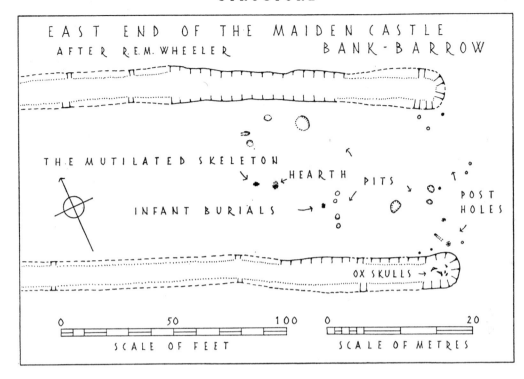

29. The eastern end of the Maiden Castle bank barrow

The bank barrow at Maiden Castle was shown, by trenching at its eastern end (fig. 29), to have had a turf core enveloped in chalk rubble. As only ditch sections were used to demonstrate its great length, and since little of a mound remained at the western end, it has been suspected of being a cursus [Stone, 1948, 11]. The section dug by Atkinson [1953] showed that it was indeed a barrow. Four post-holes, with a fifth that might have held a strut, set across the easterly end, might have held a light façade. The surface was much denuded and other post-holes may have disappeared [Wheeler, 1943, 88]; occasional ones along the inner margins of the ditches could not be considered to indicate a retaining structure.

The Gussage St Michael II (Thickthorn Down) mound was roughly parallel-sided, 100 ft long and 60 ft broad, and had been thrown up from a causewayed U-ditch (fig. 30). It had been built of top-soil piled along its axis, enveloped in chalk. Three pits, filled with chalk rubble, flint and charcoal, seem to have been sealed by the ancient soil. Post-holes on the main ditch causeway may have been those of a porch. While the Holdenhurst mound, also U-ditched (fig. 30), had been built round a series of roughly conical dumps of top-soil piled along its axis and covered by gravel, it had been finished as a stack of turves, 240 ft long and 35 ft wide. Beneath the mound was a pit containing burnt flints, and a large block of local sandstone had been set into the side

41

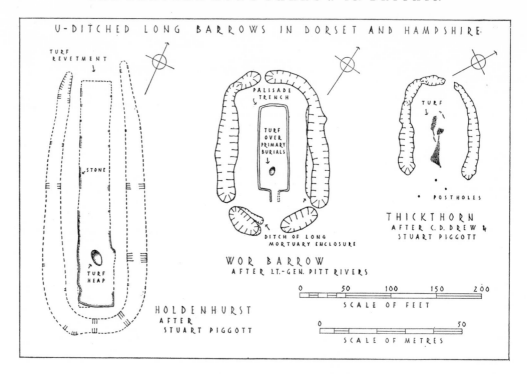

30. U-ditched long barrows in Dorset and Hampshire

of the turf stack. This block recalls that by the entrance to the Wor Barrow enclosure [Pitt-Rivers, 1898, pl. 255, F]. Julliberrie's Grave, possibly another U-ditched mound, truncated at one end by a river meander and damaged by ploughing at the other, was entirely of axial dump construction. There was no trace of any other feature except a pit.

A wedge-shaped mound at Barton Stacey (Moody's Down Southeast) was razed without record during the construction of a rifle-range in 1940. The inspection of incidental trenches [Grimes, 1960, 248] revealed no trace of any structure which might have involved slots or trenches cut into the ancient surface. Witnesses of the destruction indicated that it was built of soil mantled with chalk rubble. When the nearby ploughed out Windmill Hill Horslip barrow (fig. 31) was completely examined in 1959, no trace was found of either stone or timber structure. Two small axial pits were the only features, although a series of quarry-scoops suggested that the work was incomplete. The mound of the Badshot long barrow had been completely eradicated and is known only from the character of the ditches.

Two heaped mounds in East Anglia, West Rudham and Therfield Heath, are of note. Both may have been surrounded by almost continuous ditches. The infiltration veining at the interfaces of the West Rudham mound gave the appearance of sods. Its proximal

42

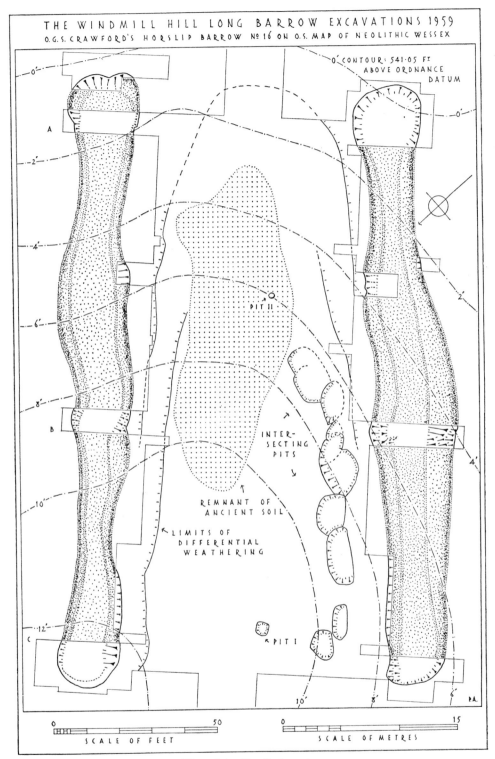

31. Plan of the Horslip long barrow

43

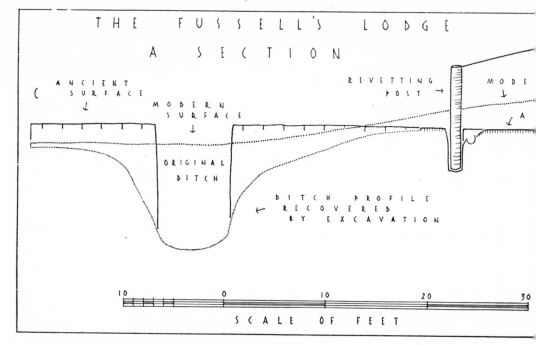

32. A restored section of the Fussell's Lodge long barrow

end seems to have had an additional, lightly ditched, enclosure attached to it. The Therfield Heath mound was also of soil, described as decayed turves, covered by chalk.

The notes [Scott, W. L., 1936, 1937] describing the excavation of the Whiteleaf mound refer to a rectangular structure of trunks opening onto a crescentic forecourt, and assert that it was delimited by posts set at 2 ft intervals in a trench. As far as can be seen from Scott's posthumously published plan the structure, perhaps a mortuary house, was axial, but the 'crescentic forecourt' may be no more than soil-slip [Toms, 1922, 158, fig. 1; Crawford, 1928, pl. II, the long barrow]. This phenomenon produced the frequently mentioned kidney shape of the mound.

Two medium-sized long barrows, near Avebury [Smith & Evans, 1968], by Beck-hampton Road (Bishop's Cannings 76) and at South Street (Avebury 68), were built by methods closely related one to another to very similar designs. No evidence of burials was found nor do they seem to have been intended as funerary structures. Spoil dug from the side ditches had been dumped into a framework of hurdles. In each barrow this hurdling (pl. XIVa, b) had been set out as an axial line with pairs of offset lines. This arrangement sub-divided each longitudinal half into a series of bays.

The outer limits of the bays of the Beckhampton Road long barrow were closed by further hurdles which effectively delimited its flanks, producing a trapezoid plan, which was reflected in the ditches. At the eastern end such hurdling had been used to form a spurred convex end or façade. It was possible to see, during excavations, that dumping of the vari-coloured silts and marls of which the barrow was built had taken

44

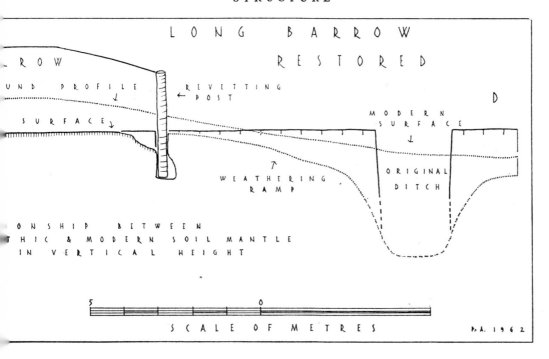

place progressively in the bays. This structure was 138 ft in length. The ditch was coextensive with the convex façade at the proximal end but at the distal end the ditches ran on for another 37 ft. Fine chalk may have washed from the mound to form a concreted revetment-like mass about it.

South Street's long barrow, thought for long to have been stone-built [Stukeley, 1743, Tab. XXIV], was rectangular in plan. There was no delimitation and this has been thought to suggest that it was unfinished. Like its fellow it had been built by progressively infilling the hurdled bays; indeed, a sequence of construction has been adduced. In two bays there was a core of small boulders while towards the proximal end there was a cluster of large sarsen stones, considered to form no significant pattern. A capping of chalk rubble may have heightened the structure, for the remains of such were found.

The incidental observations made during the 'extensive' operations of the nineteenth-century pioneers should be added to the evidence of mound structure from modern 'intensive' excavations. Colt Hoare's and Cunnington's work was almost entirely restricted to the Salisbury Plain West group, and it comprises a whole body of knowledge regarding it. The same might also be said of the work of Greenwell in Yorkshire.

Colt Hoare noted the ancient soils beneath certain barrows (Tilshead 2, 4; Warminster 14; Knook 5; Sherrington 1) and observed that black loam forming the lower and middle parts of mounds was a constant structural feature (Bratton 1; Tilshead 2,

45

5; Heytesbury 4). As the nature of this black soil, clearly natural in his view, was uncertain to his friends, one of them had a sample analysed [Colt Hoare, 1810, 92ff.]. Its vegetable content was detected and ideas involving body decomposition and burning were thereupon rejected. Construction by dumps of soil along a selected axis is clearly described in his account of the Tilshead 2 mound: 'The different *strata* bore the appearance of a circular barrow within the long one.' He mentions the gravel construction of Sherrington 1 [Colt Hoare, 1810, 100] and the inclusion of quantities of flints, sarsen and marl stones in other mounds (Heytesbury 1, 4). Among the stones which were the core or base of Heytesbury 1 (The Bole's Barrow) was the celebrated block of bluestone [Cunnington, B. H., 1920; 1924; Cunnington, M. E., 1935]. A great sarsen stone was found standing in the mound of Warminster 1.

Thurnam was concerned almost exclusively with the character of the human remains from the earthen long barrows. His summary accounts contain only the barest mention of structure, e.g. '*Stratum* of black earth' or, with regard to Norton Bavant 13, 'Chiefly of chalk rubble'.

In the north, the long barrow described by Bateman·[1861, 227–8] as 'four miles N.W. from Pickering', was clearly built of earth and stones. From Greenwell's accounts [Greenwell, 1877] a few more details can be gleaned. Trenches beneath the proximal ends of Westow, G.ccxxiii, Rudstone, G.ccxxiv, Kilburn, G.ccxxv, and Market Weighton, G.ccxxvi, might, with the re-examination of Willerby Wold, G.ccxxii, in mind, be considered as those of end façades, and walling beneath the mounds at Kilburn, G.ccxxv, and Gilling, G.ccxxxiii, may be of enclosures, perhaps of trapezoid plan. Indeed, recent work has disclosed a stone enclosure beneath the Seamer Moor long barrow [Vatcher, 1961b], but full details are not yet to hand. Shallow 'trenches' apparently flanking the mortuary house beneath Kilham, G.ccxxxiv, may also have housed the posts of an enclosure.

Greenwell's account of his investigation with Rolleston (who excavated the Market Weighton, G.ccxxvi, mound) of Crosby Garrett, G.ccxxviii, gives fuller structural details than others. The mound, a trapezoid 179 ft long, 62 ft wide at the proximal end and 36 ft wide at the distal end, was a cairn, 'composed of limestone and sandstone, some of the stones being of large size'. A trench, just within the proximal end, full of burnt earth, stones and charcoal, may have been that of a façade. At the distal end and upon the axis of the structure was a large pointed sandstone block recalling those recorded, in the south, from Warminster 1 and Wor Barrow.

Apart from closed cists, few structural features have been noted in the northern long cairns. The cist beneath the 'bottle-shaped' cairn on Bradley Moor [Raistrick, 1931, fig. 3; Butterfield, 1939] had upright stones by it and another such stone on the axis. Bellshiel Law [Newbigin, 1936] had been carefully stacked and was boulder demarcated. Another long cairn in Northumberland, the so-called Devil's Lapful, has smaller stones at its core than in its outer cover. Across the Border, a long cairn, the Mutiny Stones in Berwickshire, was investigated by Craw [1925]. It was built of stones 'of which few required the strength of more than one man to lift' and was much mutilated, although the regular broad end and northern side may be original. Excavation revealed a stretch of walling lying transversely to the axis, and two groups of upright slabs parallel to each other and at right angles to, though at a distance from, this wall. A Scottish long cairn or mound of the Balnagowan Class, at Caverton Hillhead south of Kelso, of approximately trapezoid plan but long since destroyed, was recorded as consisting 'of fine loose mould, intermixed with large stones, covered over with heath'. Others in this region seem to have been of similar composition [Atkinson, 1962, 12].

DITCHES

The mounds of the earthen long barrows were thrown up from their ditches, and in general reflect the soil profile in inverted order.

Three forms of earthen long barrow ditch can be distinguished on a basis of ground plan: the flanking ditches (fig. 26) associated with the trapezoid mounds in both south and north and, in the south, also with bank barrows; U-ditches (fig. 30), i.e. ditches that circle one end of rectangular mounds, apparently a localized form mainly in Cranborne Chase and Dorset [Grinsell, 1959, 9, fig. 1] in the southern region; ditches which effectively surround rectangular mounds.

As far as can be seen from the partial excavation of the few examples of the first type, these are normally continuous, whereas both U-ditches and those which return about both ends are broken by causeways. Only two earthen long barrow ditches have been completely excavated: at Wor Barrow and Gussage St Michael II, Thickthorn Down.

It seems probable, judging from the vertical sides at their bottoms (which would have been quickly covered, thus arresting the weathering process), that long barrow ditches originally had vertical sides (fig. 32). Their present-day profiles as recovered by excavation (pls. XV, XVI) are the product of weathering and denudation [Cornwall, 1958, 58, fig. 3; Ashbee, 1963, 8–11, figs. 1, 2], as are their infills. They were either comparatively narrow and deep or broad and shallow.

U-ditches are known in Cranborne Chase and Dorset and suspected at Whiteleaf and Julliberrie's Grave. The Wor Barrow ditch, although returning around both ends, had axial causeways and two more at its proximal end, the central proximal causeway coinciding with the entrance to the enclosure. The ditch was markedly larger at the proximal end of the mound. The ditch round the Giants' Hills at Skendleby was relatively large on each side, and smaller round the façade (pl. XVII). At one corner of the distal end excavation disclosed a causeway, but it was not possible to investigate the ditch at the other distal corner to see if there was a balancing causeway there. Both the Therfield Heath and West Rudham mounds may have been surrounded by almost continuous ditches in the manner of Wor Barrow, but unfortunately both were incompletely examined, and little of the former's ditch was visible before excavation, so their full character is problematical.

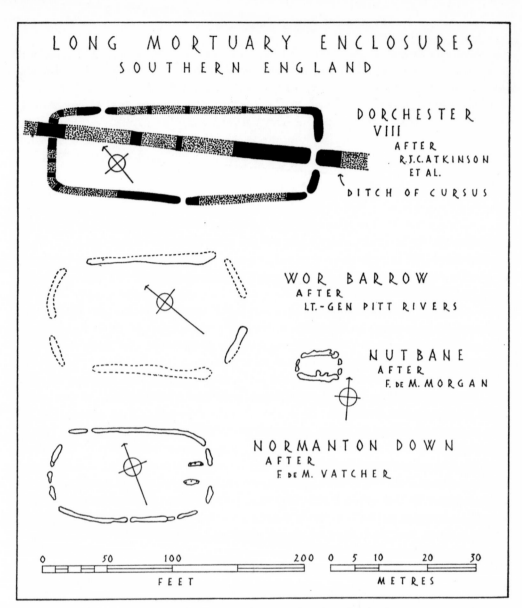

LONG MORTUARY ENCLOSURES
SOUTHERN ENGLAND

DORCHESTER VIII
AFTER
R.J.C.ATKINSON
ET AL.
DITCH OF CURSUS

WOR BARROW
AFTER
LT.-GEN PITT RIVERS

NUTBANE
AFTER
F. de M. MORGAN

NORMANTON DOWN
AFTER
F. de M. VATCHER

0   50   100   200   0   5   10   20   30

FEET   METRES

33. Long mortuary enclosures in southern England

The West Rudham ditch [Hogg, 1940, pl. III], described as of 'blunt V-section', may perhaps have been only partially examined to the top of its coarser silting, which in its weathered state would have been difficult to differentiate from the local natural gravel. On the other hand, on both flanks it was cut through sand which would, again, have been hard to distinguish from the weathered fill.

The flanking ditches of the Fussell's Lodge trapezoid enclosure were exactly parallel to its sides; the ends of the Wayland's Smithy I barrow were inturned round an ovoid

48

enclosure, and U-ditches, as at Thickthorn Down and Holdenhurst, point to rectangular mounds. It thus seems that the character of the ditches may give some indication of the character of mounds and structures. The localized nature of U-ditches and the small number of ditches of Wor Barrow type contrast with the greater frequency of the flanking ditches.

LONG MORTUARY ENCLOSURES

In certain circumstances, long mortuary enclosures (fig. 33) may have been the initial stage in the construction of long barrows with ditches of Wor Barrow type. Such an enclosure preceded Wor Barrow itself [Pitt-Rivers, 1898, pl. 249], for its slight ditch survived in part on the inner flank of the great ditch of the northern side, and as almost a segment on the southern side of the eastern axial causeway. That this pilot ditch might have been an enclosure was suggested by Atkinson after his examination of the Dorchester long mortuary enclosure [Atkinson, Piggott & Sandars, 1951, 60, fig. 2]; this was of similar general plan and sections showed that, with its sub-rectangular internal banks, it antedated the cursus which may have been deliberately aligned to pass through it. Furthermore, the cursus ditch was broken by a causeway coinciding with the causewayed entrance to the enclosure. This inclusion of a long mortuary enclosure in a cursus recalls that of a long barrow in the Dorset Cursus [Atkinson, 1955, fig. 1] and is a further link between the two sites. A diminutive long mortuary enclosure forms part of the complex of structures in the Nutbane long barrow.

A plough-razed long mortuary enclosure on Normanton Down [Vatcher, 1961a] has been examined in some detail. The ditch, dug in some ten segments, had silted naturally and only weathered chalk indicated the site of the destroyed internal bank. Inside the broad, easterly, terminal causeway were two trenches with vestiges of three posts, joined at their bases by horizontal timbers. It was thought that these might have formed an entrance passage or porch leading to a further enclosure which either had left no trace or was never completed. The general characteristics of this monument closely resembled those of Wor Barrow, although there the spoil from the slight ditch is thought to have been banked round the timbered enclosure [Vatcher, 1961a, fig. 5]. In view of the evidence from these two sites it seems likely that long mortuary enclosures were the first stages of long barrows and later were abandoned for some reason; their relative rarity might also support this view. Few instances of uncompleted long barrows can be cited. The inter-connecting scoops on the south side of the proximal end of the Horslip Barrow on Windmill Hill [Ashbee & Smith, 1960] might have been holes which never housed stones for which they were intended, and this might explain this apparent earthen barrow in a group of tombs which are otherwise almost all stone-chambered.

MORTUARY HOUSES

The accounts of the long barrows dug into by Cunnington and Colt Hoare record a number of such phenomena as, for example, the 'pyramid of loose flints, marl stone, etc.' found beneath the proximal end of Boyton 1: beneath these stones were the burials, which lay on the ancient surface between 'two excavations in the native soil, of an oval form, and seven feet apart'. The contents of such pits were sometimes described [Colt Hoare, 1810, 83, 91, 117]. One, beneath Knook 2, had in it 'only vegetable mould, charred wood, and two bits of bone'. Another, beneath Tilshead 2, 'cut with as much exactness in the chalk as if it had been done with a chisel [*sic*]' contained 'nothing but vegetable mould and charred wood'. Under Winterbourne Stoke 53, there were 'two deep cists containing an immense quantity of wood ashes, and large pieces of charred wood'. In the north, Greenwell [1877, 507] described 'trenches' which were found filled with 'burnt chalk, charcoal, and black sooty matter'. It was thought that bodies had been burned in them and that 'provision for keeping the fire alight was apparently made by excavating hollows at intervals along the line of the deposit'. In one instance it was alleged that 'flues had been formed. . . . These rose from the level of the deposit of bones through the overlying limestones up to the surface of the mound'.

Until relatively recently Colt Hoare's flints and stones were considered as cairns covering burials [Morgan, 1959, 39], although the 'cists' (pits), termed 'ritual' by classical analogy [Phillips, 1936, 88], have been thought of as post-holes [Piggott, S., 1954, 56]. Greenwell's observations have always been taken to denote 'flue cremations' [Grinsell, 1953, 34]. However, Childe [1925, 288] and Crawford [1928, 12; 1932, 5] long ago considered that earthen long barrows had timber chambers, and that the 'crematorium trenches' were such chambers that had caught fire [Childe, 1940, 63]. The recent excavation of the Nutbane building disclosed traces of burnt posts and burning phenomena [Morgan, 1959, 26] very reminiscent of some of Greenwell's descriptions of burning and apparent collapse [Greenwell, 1877, 486, 511]. Since it emerges from the descriptions of burials [Greenwell, 1877, 506] that this burning was most intense at the proximal ends of the deposits, the 'cremation trench' idea is clearly untenable, and the suspicion arose that here was evidence of collapse, in some ways comparable with that observed in certain round barrows [Ashbee, 1957a, 148].

Excavation of Wayland's Smithy I, the 'earthen' first phase, has disclosed the positive remains of an axial mortuary house (pl. XVIIIa) [Atkinson, 1964a; 1965]. Two large D-shaped pits were found bracketing the burials, and it was clear from the dimensions of the softer replacement material with harder packing about it that they had housed massive half tree-trunks, their flat sides inwards. At the proximal end, two considerable flat-sectioned sarsen stones had been pitched together, an arrangement which was apparently continued by timbers set against a ridge supported at each end by the trunks, which seem to have projected above the barrow. Four wooden principals had left shallow depressions at the four corners of the sarsen pavement (pl. XVIIIb) upon which the burials lay. Small sarsen stones, of the same character as those which formed the base of the ovoid enclosure's infill, were found over and flanking the burials. It is uncertain whether these supported or delimited the bottoms of the pitched timbers, but the latter is suspected.

In the excavator's own words [Atkinson, 1965, 130]:

As finally revealed, the evidence leaves no doubt that the burials were deposited within a wooden chamber resembling a low ridge-tent, with a massive post at either end, between which a ridge-pole was supported by mortised joints. The combined sides and roof were presumably formed of close-set timbers resting at their inner and upper ends on the ridge-pole, and at their lower and outer ends on the ground immediately outside the lateral banks of sarsen stones, where there is on each side a significant linear gap separating the base of these banks from the basal sarsen cairn.

It is possible that these lateral banks of sarsen stones represent the erstwhile cover of the pitched timbers which fell when the timbers decayed.

A feature frequently revealed in earthen long barrows has been the axial pits, normally at the proximal end and sometimes termed 'ritual'. These, which often seem to have held timber remains, are listed by Phillips [1936, 88]. They were usually associated with irregular banks of turf or cairns of flints or stones, sometimes mixed with charcoal or carbonized wood, lying upon the burials. It is thought that wherever such pits, turf, flints or stones have been encountered and described, they are to be explained as the collapsed, and thus distorted, remains of the mortuary housing of burials (fig. 34). It will be readily appreciated that many of the earlier excavations were only partial and their records are correspondingly fragmentary, but there is such remarkable conformity in the evidence (Appendix 6) that the mere record of axial pits leads one to suspect some former structure.

The Fussell's Lodge axial pits contained weathered flint nodules with dirty chalk which seemed, particularly in the distal pit, to be joined to the covering cairn. Similar material only partly filled the middle axial pit, which was topped and covered by bones of the burial complex. At the proximal end the cairn filled and covered another pit, which had slighted the trapezoid enclosure entrance. Parts of a pot were found both deep in the infill of the distal pit and beneath the bone-stack beside it. No trace of timbers was noticed in the cairn, and it is thought that they might not be particularly obvious among tumbled flints. The ridged, irregular mass of flints (pl. XIX) lying on the burials, the smashed bones and 'exploded' skulls among them, and the pits and their contents, as well as the circumstances of the pottery, all point to a collapsed structure (fig. 34).

Inside the rectangular enclosure at Nutbane, two holes, in which the remains of posts were detected, straddled the burials, upon which lay the remains of turf, covered with chalk blocks. Here again, a former pitched mortuary structure seems likely. At Wor Barrow two pits straddled the turf-covered burials, and such a structure can be envisaged here also. At Wexcombe, in the Tow Barrow, Crawford detected traces of a large vertical post, but recorded nothing more.

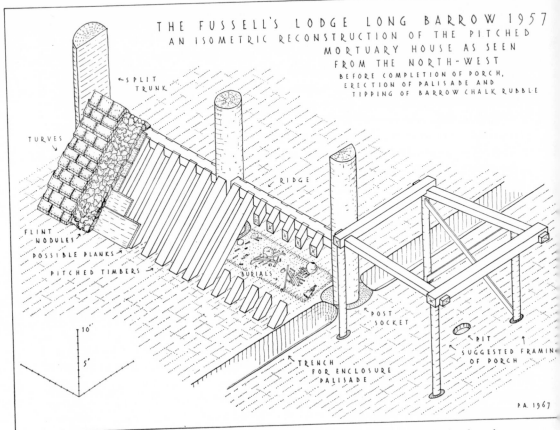

THE FUSSELL'S LODGE LONG BARROW 1957
AN ISOMETRIC RECONSTRUCTION OF THE PITCHED
MORTUARY HOUSE AS SEEN
FROM THE NORTH-WEST
BEFORE COMPLETION OF PORCH,
ERECTION OF PALISADE AND
TIPPING OF BARROW CHALK RUBBLE

34. An isometric reconstruction of the mortuary house under the Fussell's Lodge long barrow

Many of the details recorded by Colt Hoare and Thurnam are clearly those of former pitched mortuary structures of the Wayland's Smithy type. For example, the flints and marl stones in Boyton 1 are described as 'ridged' while the mass was of triangular section and lay between 'two excavations in the native soil, of an oval form' which, 'with the skeletons, were covered with a pyramid of flint and stones'. Beneath Heytesbury 1 there was 'a ridge of large stones and flints, which extended wider as the men worked downwards' while 'a floor of flints regularly laid' had the burials upon it. It was 'in form like the ridge of a house' and by the skeletons Cunnington found 'a large cist'. Stones and earth had covered the structure in Heytesbury 4, and the fill of 'a large circular cist' was 'nothing but black earth intermixed with stones and marl'. The bones were 'on a pavement of flints' in Tilshead 2, the 'black earth, ashes, and remains of bones' presumably denoting the collapsed structure, while 'an oval cist' had 'nothing but vegetable mould and charred wood' in it. The upright sarsen stone in Warminster 1 may have been one part of a structure of which 'a pile of large loose stones' was another.

Some axial pitched mortuary houses in the north may have been longer, with more uprights, than others. The burnt structure in Kilburn, G.ccxxv, had three posts standing in oval pits into which burnt material had fallen, presumably to replace the remains of the finally decayed structure. Five pits, each described as a 'transverse trench', lay beneath 'a deposit of chalk rubble down the mesial line' of Market Weighton, G. ccxxvi. Among this rubble was much charcoal and burnt matter as well as traces of fire. In Willerby, G.ccxxii, 'a large quantity of charcoal in lumps' was 'covering some burnt bones' while 'the mesial deposit of chalk and flint . . . was perfectly distinct from the general material of the barrow', though the chalk round the most marked signs of burning had been affected 'only in the slightest degree'. Recent excavation has recovered the outline and apsidal distal end of the structure [Manby, 1963, 181, fig. 5]. In Westow, G.ccxxiii, Greenwell met clear traces of a well-built structure, some of which had fallen, still in order, into one of the pits. He refers to 'a pile of oolitic slabs, arranged in a sloping fashion from the middle to the outside, forming a roof-shaped ridge'. The burials lay beneath, on 'a pavement of flagstone $2\frac{1}{2}$ ft wide'. Also 'quantities of charcoal were found all along the outside of the burnt matter and underneath the pile of stones arranged roof-fashion'. At Crosby Garrett, G.ccxxviii, in which a standing stone appears to have been part of the burned structure, a series of posts had been employed, which, after burning, left traces called 'flues' by Greenwell.

The axial pit, $6\frac{1}{2}$ ft in depth, which was joined to the Hanging Grimston façade together with the other axial 'oblong grave', could have held the posts of a pitched mortuary house. The façade and, presumably, part of this structure appear to have been destroyed by fire, of which there was 'much evidence'. Pits, in two groups separated by 'a considerable area covered with wood ashes', beneath the Helperthorpe mound, also point to an axial structure of the pitched class. Those at the proximal end were of great size and could have housed enormous timbers comparable in size, for example, to those erected in the Woodhenge C holes [Cunnington, M. E., 1929, 23]. Evidence for burning was found by Greenwell at Helperthorpe at an earlier date [Greenwell, 1877, fn.].

Not all timber mortuary houses beneath earthen long barrows were of the pitched variety, nor were they all at the proximal ends of their barrows. A rectangular structure built round four posts may have stood beneath the middle of the Whiteleaf mound; the nature of the walls and roof is uncertain, but horizontal timbers are to be suspected and flints may also have been used. A similar slight rectangular building, apparently of 'hurdles' secured by stakes, enclosed the 'Empty Hole' feature beneath the Giants' Hills, Skendleby.

Certain mortuary structures were not built with posts at all. At Thickthorn Down, two short parallel walls had been built of turf; the form of their vertical inner faces, 3 ft in height, had been preserved by the collapse of a roof and an inrush of chalk rubble filling the space between them (pl. xx). Beneath lay turf, apparently from the roof, but no burials were found. The sides of a mortuary house beneath the Giants'

Hills, Skendleby, seem to have been built of turf, one on a stone foundation. The burials had been packed into the distal half of the space between these three walls, and the open end may have been blocked with chalk when the mound was constructed. Fall-in, in the form of chalk blocks, rested 'directly on the bodies' and filled the space between what were the walls of the structure [Phillips, 1936, 54]. These blocks had spread and partly covered the burials on one side, and a marked depression in the barrow's profile denoted the site of this burial complex. The possibility must also be entertained that the amorphous heap beneath the Holdenhurst turf-stack was a crushed turf structure [Piggott, S., 1937a, pl. VII, upper].

All these turf and rectangular mortuary houses were axial like the pitched ones, but unlike them, they stood at a distance from the proximal end of the barrow. They also tend to be associated with rectangular, or nearly rectangular, barrows.

Chapter 4

BURIALS

CONDITION · NUMBER, SEX AND AGE · ARTICULATED SKELETONS
ARTICULATED SKELETONS AND DISARTICULATED BONES
DISARTICULATED BONES · BURNED BURIALS · MUTILATION
SUBSEQUENT BURIALS · SMALL AND OVAL LONG BARROW BURIALS

Burials beneath earthen long barrows occupy a modest axial area out of all proportion to the massive mounds that cover them. Excavation has shown that while for the most part they were concentrated beneath the higher, easterly ends, in certain instances they had been sited, still axially, at some distance from what was considered the proximal end. The bones usually lay on the surface of the ancient soil under the mound, but were sometimes laid on a pavement of flints, stones or chalk blocks. Over and around them lay the tumbled remains of the mortuary houses defined above (chapter 3), while astride and beneath them were the sockets which had held the timber principals of these. Exceptionally, some bones might have been in graves, while at least one long cairn covered a large cist for their reception.

Broken pots were unambiguously associated with the burial rituals in only two instances, while flint artifacts in similar contexts were almost as rare. A few burials in the south had ox skulls and feet by them: a bone pin is unique in the north. Any form of furnishing (chapter 5) is exceptional.

Knowledge of earthen long barrow burial, as of other internal features, is based primarily on recent intensive examination of a distressingly small number of mounds, supplemented by the accounts of the early antiquaries. Since grave furnishings, or sometimes bones, were the objectives of these early operations, the burials received more than incidental attention; thus the rite can often be determined from their records.

The individuals buried beneath earthen long barrows are represented by articulated skeletons (pl. XXI) or disarticulated bones (pl. XXII). Articulated skeletons can result only from the interment of corpses, but assemblages of wholly or partly disarticulated bones point to disintegration prior to burial, and previous burial or storage before interment seems likely. A few apparent single burials are known, but they are normally of several persons and hence have frequently been termed *collective*. These multiple

55

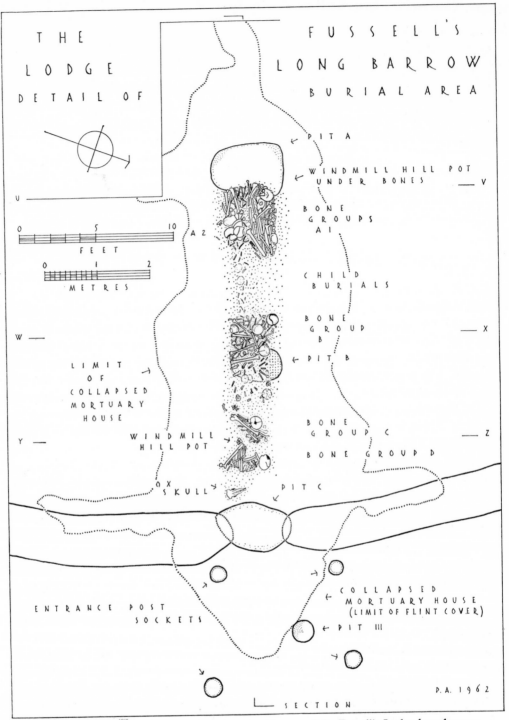

THE
LODGE
DETAIL OF

FUSSELL'S
LONG BARROW
BURIAL AREA

← PIT A

← WINDMILL HILL POT
UNDER BONES ___ V

BONE
GROUPS
A1

U ___

0   5   10
FEET

0   1   2
METRES

A2

CHILD
BURIALS

BONE
GROUP
B   ___ X

W ___

← PIT B

LIMIT
OF
COLLAPSED
MORTUARY
HOUSE

Y ___

WINDMILL
HILL POT

BONE
GROUP C   ___ Z

BONE GROUP D

OX
SKULL ↙

PIT C
↙

ENTRANCE POST
SOCKETS

COLLAPSED
← MORTUARY HOUSE
(LIMIT OF FLINT COVER)

← PIT III

D.A. 1962

SECTION

35. The burials beneath the collapsed mortuary house of the Fussell's Lodge long barrow

56

burials comprise either *articulated skeletons* alone, *articulated skeletons and disarticulated bones,* or *disarticulated bones* alone.

Another basis on which earthen long barrow burials can be studied is whether they were *unburned* or *burned.* This division has a geographical origin for, although burned burials were early recognized in Wiltshire, extensive knowledge of them stems from Greenwell's [1877, 506] examination of Yorkshire long barrows. He encountered remains which led him to believe that

> the bodies, . . . either entire or in a greater or less degree dismembered and incomplete, appear to have been placed under and partly amongst chalk rubble and wood, the former so arranged as to enable a draught to carry on the fire from the place of ignition to the other end of that part of the mound sought to be subjected to its action. Further provision for keeping the fire alight was apparently made by excavating hollows at intervals along the line of the deposit . . .

These accounts have led to the term *cremation in situ* [Piggott, S., 1935, 124] and the division into two categories [Hogg, 1939, 325; Grinsell, 1953, 33–4], *platform cremations* and *flue cremations.* The first allegedly involved burning upon a hard surface, a practice, with one exception, confined to Wessex, the second a procedure, as described by Greenwell, with arrangements of flues or vents to stimulate combustion. It has been possible to demonstrate that these 'flue cremations' are the remains of burned mortuary houses (chapter 3); when the structures burned the burials housed within them were also burned. In every instance it was observed that the signs of burning were more pronounced at the proximal end of the complex, decreasing inwards to the distal end. Bones at the outer proximal end were sometimes intensely burned, the chalk round them turned to lime, in a manner far beyond that of normal cremation, graduating to the innermost which were sometimes unscathed.

Mingled with and beneath the unburned burials in the Fussell's Lodge long barrow (fig. 35) were other bones, burned and scorched but by no means cremated [Ashbee, 1966; Brothwell & Blake, 1966]. In the tumble of flints which had been built up over the pitched mortuary house was a small quantity of chalk almost turned to lime and large pieces of charcoal. This is the only example of the 'burning' phenomenon encountered in a modern southern excavation, but it is suspected that one or two early accounts in this region reflect such an incorporation. Scorched and burned bones have been regularly observed side by side with unburned bones in collective burials in stone chambers contained in long mounds and cairns [Piggott, S., 1962a, 68].

Unburned burials conform to the three categories enumerated above, but the accounts of the burned burials allow the recognition of four variations. Thus there were *unburned articulated and burned disarticulated bones* together and *unburned disarticulated bones* together as well as *burned articulated skeletons and disarticulated bones.* However, each of these categories is represented by one single site, and the third may represent merely an incidental accident of circumstance, for this and the last category, that of *burned disarticulated bones,* observed at nine sites, correspond to the rite of the unburned burials. It is apposite to observe at this point that the excavation of an undisturbed burned burial is a research priority, for the recent re-excavation of the Willerby, G.ccxxii, mound disclosed only a part.

The rites have been tabulated below (Appendix 7), where a synopsis of burials on a basis of region and rite is given together with a list of Numbers of Individuals, Age and Sex, as well as Neolithic and Bronze Age Secondary Burials, their Rites and Furnishings.

Colt Hoare's descriptions have been classified on a basis of his terminology, for two usages recur. His use of the term 'skeleton', for example Knook 5: 'an entire skeleton' or Wilsford 30: 'four other skeletons', has been taken to mean that recognizable articulated skeletons were encountered. The phrase 'the remains of several human bodies', which is his description of the burial beneath Heytesbury 1, 'the remains of a great many human skeletons' found beneath Heytesbury 4, of the laconic 'remains of several skeletons that had been disturbed before' which describes the Maiden Bradley 8a burial complex, should, in contrast to the recurring use of the term 'skeleton', denote disarticulated bones. Thurnam uses the term 'skeletons' for what are clearly articulated remains, but his descriptions of what were clearly disarticulated bones are much more detailed. Bateman's references to burials in Yorkshire long barrows are similarly direct and the term 'skeleton' is clearly used.

CONDITION

Under some long mounds no visible trace of burials was present. Acid soil conditions, in which burials by inhumation might not have survived, were encountered at Holden-hurst, and were probable at West Rudham and possible at Gilling, G.ccxxxiii, while incomplete excavation might account for some apparent absences of primary burials, for example in Amesbury 42. This could not apply, however, to the intensive total examination of the Thickthorn Down mound, for chalkland conditions normally ensure good preservation of bones, and had burials been set beneath this mound, some part would presumably have survived, even if exposure in the turf mortuary house had hastened decay.

Inhumation burials in acid, and thus lime-hungry, soils sometimes survive as anthropomorphic silhouettes to be defined by careful anticipatory excavation [Ashbee, 1957a, 149; Piggott, S., 1956, 182; Scott, J. G., 1958, 31], though not upon every occasion [Piggott, S., 1937a, 7]. Difficulties are also presented by the permeable character of certain chalks and chalk soils [Brothwell, 1963, 9]. Optimum preservation depends upon the exclusion of air. Conditions comparable to the non-oxygenated soils of the Alpine regions [Pittioni, 1955, 104] could well obtain beneath large compact clay or sod-built long mounds in high rainfall regions. This is supported, for example, by the birch bark and branches found by Greenwell [1877, 337, 724] beneath a round barrow on Kepwick Moor in the North Riding of Yorkshire, the condition of the burial beneath the clay-built Gristhorpe barrow [Williamson, 1872] and others of its kind [Gomme, 1886, 94–5; Elgee, 1949]. Well-burned bones, normally termed

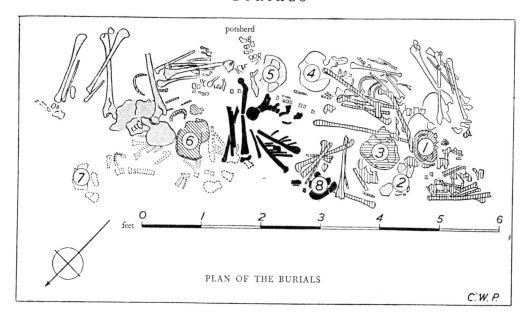

36. The burials beneath the Skendleby long barrow

cremated [Wells, C., 1960, 35], whether unurned or inurned, survive in good condition
in acid soils, as the careful excavation of heathland round barrows during the past
three decades has shown [Piggott, C. M., 1938, 173; 1943, 4; Thompson, Ashbee &
Dimbleby, 1957, 126].

Cornwall [1956, 206] and Brothwell [1963, 18] have adduced criteria which may
indicate that flesh and blood covered certain bones when they were exposed to fire.
They should be borne in mind if a 'burned' burial is ever examined by modern intensive excavation. Thus the bones with the 'black coloured glaze', thought by Camps
[1953, 48–9, 128] to show that blood was still present at the time of the fire, might be
equated with Thurnam's bones from the Tilshead 1 long barrow which were 'unequally
burnt, and many merely charred were quite black'. Mortimer [1905, 41] similarly
described a humerus from a round barrow.

Thurnam [1868, 185] was much concerned with what he termed 'Cleft Skulls:—
Evidence as to human sacrifice'. He claimed to have found such 'Cleft Skulls' in the
burials from no fewer than five mounds, namely Amesbury 14, Netheravon 6, Tilshead
2, 5 and 7, besides those noted by Cunnington in Heytesbury 1, the Bole's barrow.
There was no trace of such wholesale cleavage of the skulls from the Fussell's Lodge
burials. Most of the long barrows in which this 'cleavage' was encountered housed
disarticulated burials, and it is therefore possible that these marks may represent
damage sustained during disinterment or collection before burial. Other possible
causes are the edge pressures of stones from collapsed mortuary structures or even

unwitting damage during excavation. It must be emphasized that the collapse of mortuary houses could well account for much of the bone breakage observed in both southern and northern regions. Keith's [1916, 272] comments on the matter of pre- and post-mortem fracture are relevant in this context.

When commenting on the Giants' Hills, Skendleby, bones (fig. 36), Cave [1936, 95] drew attention to their eroded and weathered condition. This weathering, considered together with the skull containing the egg-case of a species of land-snail which never goes underground to lay its eggs, was thought to point to the exposure of bones in the open air before their burial in the barrow [Phillips, 1936, 83]. However, relatively 'open air' conditions might have existed in the mortuary house which enclosed the burials, before its collapse. Shells of the same species of snail have been found with the bones in the Wayland's Smithy I mortuary house [Atkinson, 1964a].

At Nutbane the excavator commented on the relative freshness of one skeleton, contrasting it with the apparently weathered condition of the others. On this account, and because it appeared to overlie a pit, it was considered to be a later insertion. Differential exposure in the diminutive long mortuary enclosure prior to the construction of the pitched mortuary house might account for the difference of condition. Differentially weathered bones were also noted in the Wayland's Smithy I burial deposit. Colt Hoare's [1810, 72] observation regarding 'the decayed state of the bones' might denote heavily weathered bones, since the comment seems to be exceptional in his narrative, and Thurnam remarked on the eroded character of the bones from the Figheldean 31 barrow primary burial.

The tooth-marks of rodents were noted on the edges of four crushed skulls from Fussell's Lodge [Brothwell & Blake, 1966], and have frequently been observed upon bones from round cairns in Derbyshire [Bateman, 1848, 61; Ashbee, 1963, 5]. These need not represent the depredations of former carrion feeders: rodents could well have chewed at bones to redress calcium deficiencies.

NUMBERS, SEX AND AGE

In all, thirty-nine unburned burials have been found beneath earthen long barrows, only five of which were in the northern region. Against this total there are only thirteen burned burials, of which eight are concentrated in the northern region.

Of the unburned burials known at the time of writing, sixteen were of articulated skeletons, twenty of disarticulated bones, and only three of articulated skeletons and disarticulated bones together. Of the first, thirteen are in the south and three in the north; of the second, nineteen are in the south and only one in the north, while of the third, two are in the south and one is in the north.

Numbers of individuals (Appendix 7, 2) in earthen long barrow burials vary considerably. A single articulated skeleton seems well attested from Heddington 3; four were found in the Nutbane mound and Colt Hoare's account of the Boyton I burials, 'eight skeletons lying promiscuously in various directions', would seem an amplification of the Nutbane rite, while at Kilham, G.ccxxxiv, Greenwell apparently found at least nine skeletons, either flexed or contracted, lying on the ancient surface along the axis of the mound.

Burials of articulated skeletons and disarticulated bones are well documented. There were six adult males, three with 'their bones in sequence' (i.e. articulated) and three 'put in as bones' (disarticulated), beneath the Wor Barrow (pl. XXIII) and four, perhaps five, articulated skeletons with disarticulated bones in the Giants' Hills, Skendleby, including two males, five females and one child. In the mortuary house of the Wayland's Smithy 1 long barrow, the bones of fourteen individuals lay at the proximal end and a single articulated skeleton at its inner end.

Numbers of persons represented by the burials of disarticulated bones, both unburnt and burnt, range from perhaps fifty-three to fifty-seven beneath the Fussell's Lodge mortuary house to single individuals as at Whiteleaf. The average, however, is ten!

Any comment on the numbers of disarticulated burials must raise the problem of the discrepancy between the numbers represented by the bones found at Fussell's Lodge and the modest totals estimated for similar burials elsewhere. At Fussell's Lodge there were bones of at least fifty-three, perhaps fifty-seven people [Brothwell & Blake, 1966], this total being arrived at after scrutiny in the laboratory of every piece of bone from the burial complex. Burials of disarticulated bones, even in the Salisbury Plain region, have never been attributed to more than fourteen (at Heytesbury 1) or perhaps eighteen individuals (from Norton Bavant 13), both from early excavations. Thurnam and others, on encountering a single stack of bones, may well have considered that the whole burial had been found. At Fussell's Lodge four such stacks were uncovered before the total was reached. Indeed, the West Kennet long barrow, where Thurnam was misled by filling and blocking into thinking that there was only one chamber, could be a similar circumstance [Piggott, S., 1962a, 5]. In their report on the Fussell's Lodge bones, Brothwell and Blake [1966] drew attention to the low estimate of numbers of persons made at the time of excavation on a basis of skulls and long bones [Ashbee, 1958, 109]. A similarly low initial estimate of the numbers in a collective burial was made when the bones in the second Mournouard Seine-Oise-Marne chalk-cut 'grotte' were first observed [Leroi-Gourhan, Bailloud & Brezillon, 1962, 78]. Field estimates can thus today be wide of the mark, giving grounds for the re-examination of such earthen long barrows as Tilshead 7, beneath which close-packed disarticulated bones have been found. It would seem that the same arguments also apply to disarticulated burials in stone-chambered tombs [Daniel, 1950, 103].

The differentiation of sex and age of individuals in earthen long barrow burials poses special problems. While adolescents are readily distinguishable from adults, men, even at the present time, cannot always be separated from women. For while differences exist they are diffused and only matters of degree [Cornwall, 1956, 228], and it is only by noting variability among a large assemblage that any measure of certainty can be achieved [Brothwell, 1963, 51]. It follows that early accounts should be treated with extreme caution.

The considerable quantity of bones from Fussell's Lodge [Brothwell & Blake,

1966] included fourteen or fifteen adult males, fifteen or sixteen adult females and between twenty-two and twenty-four children. It was claimed that there were six males in the Wor Barrow, three males and one child at Nutbane and two males, five females and one child in the Giants' Hills at Skendleby. There was a single mutilated male, accompanied perhaps by two children, in the Maiden Castle bank barrow. The disinterment and re-examination of the bones described and presumably reburied by Colt Hoare and, indeed, re-excavation of selected examples of his long barrows, coupled with a re-examination of such bones as are preserved in the Thurnam Collection (Duckworth Laboratory, Cambridge), might aid the vexed question of sex.

Knowledge of skeletal ageing is still far from complete [Brothwell, 1963, 57], and it is often difficult to go beyond the basic differentiation of adults from adolescents. The Giants' Hills bones were seen as representing a middle-aged man, perhaps a youth of between seventeen and twenty, a child, and five women, the eldest between thirty and thirty-five, two between twenty-five and thirty and two about eighteen or nineteen years of age [Cave, 1936, 94]. The male from the Maiden Castle bank barrow was in 'the prime of life', namely between twenty-five and thirty-five years of age at death [Morant & Goodman, 1943, 344]. Two of the Nutbane males were assessed at between thirty and forty years of age, the other at between forty and fifty, while the child was between twelve and thirteen [Bunting, Verity & Cornwall. 1959]. With regard to the Fussell's Lodge bones, Brothwell and Blake [1966] suggested that most adults were under fifty years of age at death.

ARTICULATED SKELETONS

Articulated burials were normally contracted, that is the thigh bones made an angle of 90° or less with the spine. Colt Hoare's expression 'strangely huddled' (Wilsford 30) might denote contracted burials; Thurnam (Tilshead 5; Winterbourne Stoke 1) is more explicit and writes of 'a skeleton in the contracted position' or remarks of another that it had 'the knees drawn up', while Cunnington (Heddington 3) notes a single 'crouched' skeleton. Although skeletons are frequently described in early accounts as 'lying' this does not necessarily imply extended burial in the now accepted sense. Of the burials under the Maiden Castle bank barrow and at Nutbane some individuals had been laid along and some across the axes of those barrows. A degree of precision is apparent in this procedure, especially at Nutbane.

Apart from early accounts, e.g. Warminster 6 and Winterbourne Stoke 1, the only direct evidence we have for single burials, in the form of articulated skeletons, beneath earthen long barrows, is from the Heddington 3 excavation and the Barton Stacey destruction, with their shortcomings. Bearing in mind all the factors surrounding the early enterprises, the possibility that other burials were not found cannot be overlooked: at Heddington most of the mound was 'turned over', while at Barton Stacey it was destroyed.

ARTICULATED SKELETONS AND DISARTICULATED BONES

The Wor Barrow burial complex, of articulated skeletons and disarticulated bones, allegedly contained six males. Two contracted skeletons were at the proximal end of the former timber and turf pitched mortuary house, and lay along the mound's axis, as also did another articulated individual. Behind these, at the distal end, were the bones of three more individuals with their long bones laid out beside the skulls. Like the Wor Barrow burials, those beneath the Giants' Hills at Skendleby were at some distance from the proximal end of the barrow but, unlike them, they lay in the fallen remains of their mortuary house, across the axis. Four skeletons were complete and articulated, another less so; many of the bones had been crushed and broken by the chalk that had fallen in on them, while others were soft and decayed. The disarticulated bones, as in Wor Barrow, occupied a separate area and were either 'scattered' or in a 'closely packed pile'. There were also bones not belonging to any of the skulls set with them, and amongst these was the atlas of an ox. In the remains of the pitched mortuary house beneath Wayland's Smithy I, the disarticulated bones occupied pride of place between the principal posts; among them were differentially weathered bones, some in articulation, and they were considered to be the contents of a charnel house. At the distal end, apart from the rest, lay one articulated skeleton.

DISARTICULATED BONES

From the available evidence, disarticulated burials can be resolved into two types. First, there are examples of the disarticulated bones of single individuals, scattered as at Therfield, Whiteleaf, and perhaps Wexcombe, or bundled up as in Figheldean 31. Second, there are the masses of (mainly) broken bones of many persons, stacked together. The best example is at Fussell's Lodge where the bones, beneath their pitched mortuary house, had been set into four clear stacks, the remains of each person being confined to a specific stack. Another version of this procedure was encountered, in the north, at Over Silton, G.ccxxvii, where each skeleton was apparently disarticulated but had been arranged in an individual pile.

Regarding the first category, it would seem from Nunn's description [Phillips, 1935, 101] of the Therfield burial that the single individual represented there had been buried as a collection of bones and not as a body. At Whiteleaf the left foot and a tooth were within the confines of the four post-holes, but the skeleton was scattered. Scattered fragments of a skull and other bones were found in the burial under the Wexcombe Tow Barrow.

A prominent feature of the Fussell's Lodge burial complex (fig. 35) (second category) was the separation of skulls and long bones within the stack. This practice was most apparent in the innermost bone heap (pl. xxiv). In his description of the Chute earthen long barrow, Passmore [1942] emphasized the 'circular arrangement of human skulls with long bones within the circle, the long bones showing evidence of having been tied up in bundles'. Pitt-Rivers [1898, 82] describes the three disarticulated burials in the

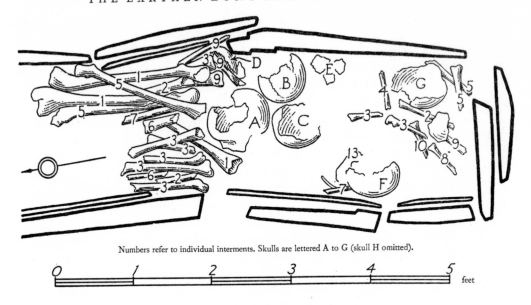

Numbers refer to individual interments. Skulls are lettered A to G (skull H omitted).

37. The burials in the Millin Bay long cist

Wor Barrow as 'put in as bones and not in sequence, the limb-bones being laid out by the side of the skulls'. Yet another feature of the arrangement of the Fussell's Lodge burials was noted in the central burial group. Here the more robust bones had been laid diagonally across the axis of the barrow, while the skulls were to one side. Most of the bones here were broken, but the lower part of the mass had comprised weathered and broken pieces of bone. A group of unrelated bones seemed to have been laid out in semblance of articulation, a circumstance recalling the lower jaws supplied, not always correctly, to the arranged skulls in the Lanhill stone-chambered long barrow [Keiller & Piggott, 1938, 127]. At Millin Bay [Collins & Waterman, 1955, 13, fig. 6 and pl. V,A] it was considered that the bones in the long cist (fig. 37) which, in its oval retained cairn, recalls in a general sense the arrangements of Wayland's Smithy I, had 'clearly been subject to deliberate sorting and grouping at the time they were introduced into the burial structure'.

No early account specifically describes such separation and sorting of bones as noted above. Those of Colt Hoare's and Cunnington's which clearly relate to disarticulated burials stress such characteristics as 'no regular order' (Heytesbury I), 'skeletons crossing each other in every direction' (Heytesbury 4), or 'very much broken, and interred in complete confusion' (Fittleton 5). Thurnam emphasized the small volume into which the remains had been packed. What were claimed as the remains of eight individuals were concentrated into 'a space of less than 4 ft in diameter, and about 18 in. in depth' (Tilshead 7), while possibly eighteen skeletons were spread in a 'confused mass' over an area 'about 8 ft long and 3 ft broad' (Norton Bavant 13).

64

XIV The South Street long barrow: above, the reconstructed hurdling; stakes in original holes; below, the infilled bays

xv Fussell's Lodge long barrow: the cleared end of the ditch

xvi The Horslip, Windmill Hill, long barrow: the cleared end of the ditch

xvii The Skendleby long barrow: the ditch and façade trench at the eastern end

XVIII Wayland's Smithy 1: above, the mortuary house with burials *in situ*; D-shaped axial post-hole and post-holes of porch in foreground; below, the mortuary house from above; showing pitched sarsen stones, sarsen stone pavement and depressions for pitched timbers

XIX Fussell's Lodge: the mass of flints which covered the mortuary house

xx Thickthorn Down: collapsed turf structure in section

XXI The Lambourn long
barrow: an articulated
supplementary burial

XXII The burials of the
Fussell's Lodge long
barrow

xxiii The burials and remains of the mortuary house beneath the Wor Barrow

xxiv The Inner Bone group of the Fussell's Lodge long barrow

Detailed evidence pointing to disarticulation before burial appears to have been obtained by Thurnam when, in 1864, he re-examined the Bole's Barrow (Heytesbury 1), initially dug into by Cunnington [Piggott, S., 1954, 57]. One of the skulls which had a severed neck vertebra must, perhaps, be treated with reserve, but three were found resting on their lower mandibles and occiputs, suggesting that they were separated from their trunks when placed in position. A mandible was also found with the condyle encircled by a vertebra, pointing to the absence of flesh before burial. Even more spectacular evidence of the disarticulated condition before burial was observed at Wayland's Smithy 1 [Atkinson, 1964a], where separated and much weathered bones were mixed with articulated spines and limbs in the mass of bones in the mortuary house.

An observation regarding the Fussell's Lodge bones which illustrates the mode of burial emerged after their examination under laboratory conditions [Brothwell & Blake, 1966]. It was seen that remains from all parts of the skeleton were represented, with no clear predominance of any particular bone or area. There was, however, a lack of ribs, small bones of the extremities, patellæ, clavicles and scapulæ, long bones were unevenly represented, and the most regularly recognized part was the skull. Besides this detailed analysis, there is Thurnam's [1868, 185] comment on the absence of limb-bones from the Norton Bavant 13 burial, but here the theories about the extraction of limb-bones from burials, discussed below (chapter 6), should be borne in mind. There were bones that were not associated with any of the skulls in the disarticulated section of the Giants' Hills, Skendleby, complex (fig. 36), while pieces of skull and bone, perhaps taken at some stage from the burials, were in the make-up of the Wor Barrow mound.

BURNED BURIALS

The majority of *burned burials* are concentrated in Yorkshire and these appear, before burning, to have been burials of disarticulated bones in mortuary houses (chapter 3). As noted above, these burials have hitherto been referred to as 'cremations *in situ*' [Piggott, S., 1935, 124; 1954, 109], i.e. carried out within the barrow during its construction, or as 'platform' or 'flue cremations' [Hogg, 1939, 325; Grinsell, 1953, 33–4].

In all instances in Yorkshire, burning was intense and largely confined to the proximal end of the axial assemblages. The remains at the distal and innermost ends were unscathed. Thus the term 'cremation' has been abandoned, for it is considered that, had cremation been the primary object, every endeavour would have been made to ensure that all the bones were equally burnt by the fires. Indeed, in his account of the Market Weighton, G.ccxxvi, burials, Greenwell notes burnt chalk and charcoal with bones among them, but he does not say that the bones were burnt: a point that he emphasizes in other descriptions. These disarticulated burials were burned incidentally in the burning of a structure and were covered in by its collapse (chapter 3). The alleged Yorkshire 'trenches' seem to have been formed by contrast between the relatively solid barrow material and the looser collapsed material above the burials [Manby, 1963, fig. 4. Section J–I].

A problem which cannot be resolved without modern intensive excavation is that of the incorporation of burnt bones and burnt material into what seem to be essentially unburnt burials. This is almost entirely a southern phenomenon.

Under the eastern end of Tilshead 2, Thurnam found a skeleton, perhaps that of an adolescent, with partly burned, broken and disarticulated bones close by. It is by no means certain that this burial was investigated in its entirety, but the presence of burned flints points to the bones having been in contact with fire. Thurnam also found partly burned bones beneath Bratton 1, but could find no bones at all in Knook 2, in spite of Cunnington's claims to have found some, assumed to have been burnt, in 1802. Burned bones, flints, chips of sarsen stone and chalk seem to have mingled to form a breccia in the make-up of Tilshead 1; Thurnam notes that 'this substance was very abundant and would probably have filled a bushell'. Several pieces of burnt bone and 'mortar' were also found under Winterbourne Stoke 53.

Subsequent consideration of these accounts has been somewhat conditioned by Greenwell's description of 'Platform cremations' [Hogg, 1939, 325; Grinsell, 1953, 33–4], but the traces of fires do not seem to have been so extensive in the southern barrows as in the northern. This may be only the result of partial excavation of large burned structures which originally had floors, although, as some burnt materials and bones have been observed in the mound and burial at Fussell's Lodge [Ashbee, 1966] and in certain stone-chambered long barrows [Piggott, S., 1962a, 24, 68], these early accounts may well reflect similar incorporations. At Rudstone, G.ccxxiv, there are grounds for thinking that unburnt bones and skulls were put into a burnt mortuary house, when the others were already burnt and cold but before the ultimate collapse.

An area of reddened sand beneath the southern end of the enigmatic West Rudham mound has been put forward as a burnt burial [Hogg, 1940, 322] on the grounds that the reddening was iron oxide which, with splintered sand grains, had resulted from fire, while any wood ash and bones had dissolved away. It must be noted that while ash might be assimilated into a soil profile, wood and charcoal frequently have survived in acid soil conditions beneath comparable mounds [Piggott, C. M., 1943, 25] and, as noted above, cremated bone regularly survives in such conditions [Preston & Hawkes, 1933, 420; Cornwall, 1956, 206]. While such iron oxide could have been evidence of burning, the fire need not have been more than that occasioned by site clearance [Ashbee, 1960, 58]. In most earthen long barrows the burials are at the end which is easterly and where the ditch [Hogg, 1940, fig. 2] is most massive. This end was unexamined at West Rudham, except for slight trenching, and it is possible that the burial area here still lies untouched.

Unburned and burned disarticulated bones were found together in the cist under the Bradley Moor long cairn, and there were burned articulated skeletons and disarticulated bones together in the deposit beneath Westow, G.ccxxiii. The latter is, of course, comparable with the small unburned series in Wor Barrow, Wayland's

Smithy 1 and Giants' Hills, Skendleby. At Westow in the mortuary house which was burned there were, first, disarticulated bones set in an area 5 ft in length and 2½ ft across, then two skeletons laid along the axis and then two across (one incomplete). All, except the innermost part-skeleton, were burned by the conflagration.

From Greenwell's description [Greenwell, 1877, 484–510, 550–6] of the burials of burned disarticulated bones in Yorkshire, it emerges that they were in mortuary houses which were longer and had more uprights than their counterparts in the south. Further, it would seem from his observations (e.g. Market Weighton, G.ccxxvi; Rudstone, G.ccxxiv), that the bones were set in more circumscribed groups, namely the bones of individual bodies, rather than in sorted assemblages.

MUTILATION

The eastern end of the Maiden Castle bank barrow covered three individuals [Wheeler, 1943, 20; Morant & Goodman, 1943, 344]. The principal burial (pl. xxv), set on the axis, was the skeleton of a man described as '25–35 years old, with an extremely long skull (cephalic index about 70), and a height about 5 ft 5 in.'. Furthermore, 'although all the significant bones were present and the elbow-, knee-, and ankle-joints were in articulation, the limbs and the head had been roughly hacked from the body shortly after death, and three fruitless attempts had been made to obtain access to the brain by circular incisions'. It is not possible to cite another example of such wholesale dismemberment among earthen long barrow burials, although trepanation is not unknown in Britain at this time [Piggott, S., 1940a] and was twice suspected among the Fussell's Lodge skulls [Brothwell & Blake, 1966]. Somewhat similar unsuccessful treatment had been accorded to skulls found beneath a round barrow in Saxony, Germany [Gerhardt, 1951]. When describing the Maiden Castle burial, Wheeler referred to Thurnam's words on 'cleft' skulls commented on above, as well as to Mortimer's discovery of broken and dismembered human bodies [Mortimer, 1905, xxiv, 21, 41, 127]. These early observations are, however, more relevant to the general problems of damaged disarticulated bones.

The skull, long bones of arms and legs and pelvis of this Maiden Castle skeleton showed clear signs of 'having been hacked with considerable force by a sharp instrument' (pl. xxvi). That much of the skeleton was in articulation was put forward as indicating that the mutilation was carried out while the body was flesh-covered. Indeed, a sequence was suggested: 'decapitation probably being the preliminary gesture—the legs next, and the arms last'. It was observed that all cuts on the long bones were at right-angles to them [Wheeler, 1943, pl. XLIII].

While 'hammer and chisel' was suggested as the means of trepanation there is still the question of the tool used to hack the long bones, which left prominent marks. Such bones are massive when green and have to be sawn when an amputation is carried out, and it would seem that flesh removal must have preceded the hacking if a stone axe was used. However, judging from the marks, which could only have been

67

made with a slender-profiled and well-sharpened axe, the possibility that it was a metal one must be seriously considered (discussion on this point with D. R. Brothwell, 1963). Even with a metal axe, a considerable amount of flesh and sinew would presumably have had to be hacked away from, for example, the femurs, before the edge could have been applied to the bones. It would not be uninstructive to investigate this matter by experiment! Alternatively examination of animal bones from prehistoric sites, with methods of butchery in mind, might yield useful comparative evidence.

SUBSEQUENT BURIALS

Subsequent or secondary burials are those put into, or immediately around, a barrow at any time after its completion. In earthen long barrows, these were either set in the mound or dug into the ditch silt. All are single-grave burials [Ashbee, 1960, 69–94] and a few are furnished. Two unmistakable inhumation rites have been encountered: of contracted or flexed skeletons and of extended skeletons. Cremations, with one indeterminate exception, were all inurned. The contracted skeletons, on account of their furnishings and the associations of the rite, can be regarded as of broadly Beaker and Food-vessel affinity (Appendix 7 (4b)); the extended skeletons, again by virtue of rite, furnishings and associations, emerge as Roman or Saxon (Appendix 7 (5)). The cremations were in or beneath cinerary urns.

Not all accounts of subsequent burials say exactly where in the barrow they were situated. One well documented barrow, Thickthorn Down, may have had no burials in the collapsed turf mortuary house beneath it, but there were Beaker burials, some furnished, diagonally across the highest part of the mound; the presence of one was denoted by the shallow depression in the top of the barrow. At least five Beaker burials, some furnished, lay along the axis of Wilsford 34, examined by Thurnam. He remarked that 'altogether sixteen holes have been sunk into this barrow without meeting the primary interment, the hope of which must be abandoned Oct. 20th 1866'. This apparent absence of a primary burial recalls the arrangements of Thickthorn Down. Greenwell's Rudstone, G.LXVI, has recently been shown to be part of a cursus [Dymond, 1966]. The circumstances here might, from what is known of them, be compared with these two southern sites. A Beaker grave here may well be secondary, inserted by digging down through the mound. Two feet from the surface of the top of Winterbourne Stoke 1, Thurnam found the crouched skeletons of what he considered to be a man, a woman and four children; with them were a food-vessel and flint scraper. It will be remembered that a single flexed male skeleton with a flint core has been put forward as the primary burial from this earthen long barrow. In the top of Figheldean 31 was a Beaker burial. Thurnam described this as 'about a foot below the surface ... the skeleton was in a moderately contracted posture ... near the hips a fine drinking cup of red-ware much broken but since restored'. Here, again, the remains considered to be the primary interment were 'a skeleton doubled up ... within a space not more 1½ ft square. There was reason for thinking that the bones had been separated in part before interment'. This was 'much nearer the centre than usual, and was only found (after making four distinct excavations) about 55 ft from the east end, the entire length being 150 ft'. Thurnam also found the skeletons of an adult and an infant in the top of Amesbury 42, and although the head and hooves of an ox (chapter 5) were recovered from the mound no primary burial was unearthed [Thurnam, 1868, 180], perhaps because the excavation was incomplete. This series of contracted inhumations of Beaker and Food-vessel affinity, axially placed and in the tops of sparsely-occupied mounds, provides grounds for postulating that such barrows comprise a distinct class of monument.

Thurnam [1868, 195] was careful to note that secondary interments were 'not infrequently met with in the upper strata, or near the summits of long barrows'. He thus had them in mind when conducting his investigations. That he seems to have excavated a larger part of each mound than did his predecessors may have some bearing upon the fact that it was from his activities among the Salisbury Plain East (Stonehenge) group that the largest number of secondary contracted inhumations is recorded. Such burials were found in five mounds, each of which contained from two to six graves. One burial in each of three was furnished with a distinctive beaker or food-vessel.

The secondary burials encountered by Colt Hoare and Cunnington in the Salisbury Plain West group totalled two inurned cremations from Boyton 1 and Warminster 14, and a small vessel, apparently not with a burial, in Warminster 6. An inurned cremation lay in the southern lobe of the Whiteleaf mound on the Chiltern Hills.

Subsequent burials were also found by Greenwell in the mounds of Yorkshire's long barrows. Here cists [Ashbee, 1960, 91–2] had been used to house contracted burials, two of which were furnished with food-vessels. One such cist lay in the side of the mound at Kilburn, G.ccxxv, as did others at Westow, G.ccxxiii. At Kilham, G.ccxxxiv, the site of a secondary burial was denoted by 'what looked like a small round barrow placed upon the end of the existing long mound' at the western end. Inurned cremations from the Hill of Foulzie, an Aberdeenshire long cairn, seem to have been in rather similar circumstances.

The only early burial from an earthen long barrow ditch was found as the direct result of the total excavation of the Wor Barrow. Here, at the top of the rapid chalk rubble silting [Pitt-Rivers, 1898, pl. 250, 71], lay skeletons thought to be of an adult male and a child. This would, perhaps, be an odd association, and the possibility of a female tending to male characteristics [Brothwell, 1963, 51] should not be overlooked. Among the ribs of the adult was a leaf-shaped arrowhead. As Pitt-Rivers [1898, 63] observed, this interment must have been made 'not long after the construction of the Barrow, and before any mould had time to accumulate in the Ditch'.

Romano-British burials (Appendix 7 (5)), some decapitated, lay in the ditch silts at either end, and in the top, of Wor Barrow: such burials were confined to the ditch at the southern end of Julliberrie's Grave at Chilham, Kent. Saxon burials (Appendix 7 (5)) are known only from the mounds of earthen long barrows. These apparent trends may be due only to the rarity of fully explored ditches. At Maiden Castle, at the proximal end of the bank barrow, the bones of a 'strongly built man in the prime of life', furnished with iron scramasax and small knife, lay roughly on the axis, just below the turf. A skeleton, presumed to be Saxon, occurred just below the ground at the eastern end of Wilsford (S) 30. Saxon burials in Sherrington 1, Tilshead 5 and Warminster 14 were furnished with swords, shields and spears and, in one instance, a bucket. The Therfield Heath 'human skeleton with its legs crossed' was found on subsequent excavation to have had with it a spearhead and ferrule. In Rudstone, G.ccxxiv, Greenwell found Anglian pottery, some at quite a depth, in 'the south of the Northern limb, at its eastern end'.

SMALL AND OVAL LONG BARROW BURIALS

The burials recorded from the small and oval earthen long barrows (Appendix 11 (b)), Colt Hoare's xii, Long Barrow No. 2, were contracted inhumations and cremations. Winterbourne Stoke 35, a large oval mound, covered two axially placed contracted inhumations, one with a long-necked beaker, the other with four leaf-shaped and lozenge-form arrowheads. Beneath one of the small long barrows on Oakley Down, in Cranborne Chase, lay two axial cremations, one with an incense cup [Thurnam, 1870, 373]; beneath the other were three axial cremations, one unurned, one with an urn and bone tweezers, and one inurned and with a single amber bead. At Huish (Wilcot 3) the sites of two burials were seen before excavation as depressions in the barrow, as though they had been dug into, and not placed beneath it; there was also a third depression which had no underlying burial.

Chapter 5

ARTIFACTS AND ANIMAL REMAINS

Such artifacts as have been found in earthen long barrows (Appendix 8) are mostly pieces of pottery and the debris of flint knapping. They occur with or by burials, in the material of mounds, and in the silts of ditches.

The absence of burial furnishings in long barrows has been commented on from the first [Colt Hoare, 1810, 21; Thurnam, 1868, 193; Greenwell, 1877, 482; Mortimer, 1905, xx], and also by subsequent writers [Kendrick, 1925, 13; Piggott, S., 1935, 119; 1954, 61].

Sherds, single or in quantity, are recorded in close proximity to burials at Nutbane and Skendleby, as well as with the Yorkshire 'burnt' burials [Newbigin, 1937, 195 and pl. XIV]. Vessels, normally with their basal parts missing, were intimately associated with burials in the Maiden Castle bank barrow [Wheeler, 1943, fig. 29, 50], in Norton Bavant 13 (pl. XXVII) [Piggott, S., 1931, 89, fig. 5, below; 1954, 69, fig. 10, 2] and at Fussell's Lodge (pl. XXVIII) [Ashbee, 1965]. Parts of four bowls were found at the proximal end of the Hanging Grimston long barrow, and of one bowl at Kilham, G.ccxxxiv (fig. 38).

Crawford recovered sherds from the ancient surface beneath the Tow Barrow on Wexcombe Down [Piggott, S., 1931, 142; Crawford, 1955, 108]. At Whiteleaf (pl. XXIX; fig. 39) a mass of pottery, 24 lb. in weight and representing fifty-five to sixty individual vessels, was recorded as scattered throughout the 'inner mound' [Childe & Smith, 1954, 216]. Sherds were in and beneath the Beckhampton Road and South Street long barrows [Smith & Evans, 1968]. Colt Hoare recorded 'rude pottery' from the mounds of Bratton 1 and Warminster 14. As well as fragments of Neolithic wares scattered in the loamy deposit in the Giants' Hills, Skendleby, two sherds of cord ornamented bell (B) beaker were found in small chalk rubble there; both were weathered and it is thought that they could only have been incorporated in the mound during its construction [Phillips, 1936, 53].

The ditches of eight earthen long barrows have provided consistent series of stratified sherds [Clark, 1937, 174: add Maiden Castle, Fussell's Lodge and Nutbane].
Early Neolithic wares occurred almost exclusively on ditch bottoms or in primary
silts. A later Neolithic sherd allegedly from the Lamborough ditch bottom [Grinsell,
1939, 202] can perhaps be disregarded [Piggott, S., 1954, 61]. From the middle and
upper silts come mainly later Neolithic (Ebbsfleet and Mortlake) pottery but beaker
and rusticated sherds are also found. Fragments of Ebbsfleet-Mortlake pottery and of
an all-over-cord beaker were recovered from the upper part of the primary silt of the
South Street long barrow [Smith & Evans, 1968, 142]. The pottery with the earlier
secondary burials (Appendix 8 (4)), Beaker, Food-vessel and Cinerary Urn forms a
sequence broadly comparable with that provided by the sherds from the ditches.

Flint artifacts with burials were either discarded materials, or such tools as cores,
flakes and hammerstones from Fussell's Lodge, nodules from Norton Bavant 13,
Winterbourne Stoke 1 [Thurnam, 1868, 194, fig. 2], and Tilshead 2, arrowheads from
Milton Lilbourne, Wayland's Smithy 1 (without points), Heslerton, Cropton and
'near Pickering', and a scraper (the only tool) from Kilham, G.ccxxxiv. Mounds
have yielded flint material of the same character. Whiteleaf yielded more than six

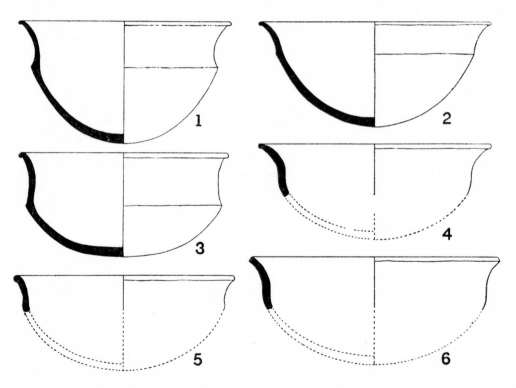

38. Pottery from the Yorkshire long and round barrows ($\frac{1}{5}$)

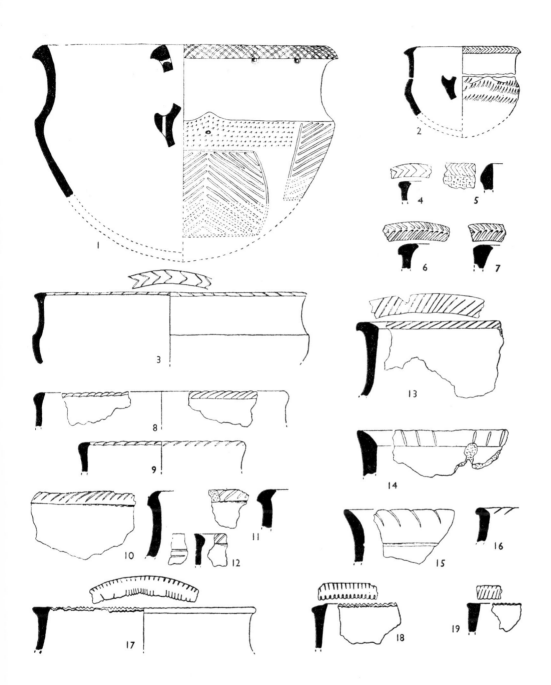

39. Pottery from the Whiteleaf long barrow ($\frac{1}{3}$)

hundred pieces. Of special note are the polished flint axe with squared sides (fig. 40) from the loam core of Julliberrie's Grave at Chilham [Jessup, 1939, 268, fig. 1, 2] and the hoard of the Duggleby Group (fig. 41) from Seamer Moor [Smith, 1926, 104, fig. 100]. Similar material has been recovered from ditch silts: nests of flakes which could be reconstructed were a feature of Fussell's Lodge, and the flakes (pl. XXXI) here, at Thickthorn Down and Julliberrie's Grave were coated in calcium carbonate [Drew & Piggott, 1936, 89; Jessup, 1937, 131].

A probable broken celt of fine-grained rock has been recorded from Warminster 14 [Colt Hoare, 1810, 73] and a stone bead from Bratten 1 [Colt Hoare, 1810, 56]. Fragments of sandstone and other pieces from alien geological solids were noted from Wor Barrow [Pitt-Rivers, 1898, pl. 249, 67] and the ditches of the Windmill Hill Horslip Barrow [Ashbee & Smith, 1960, 299]. Carved chalk objects from Thickthorn Down [Drew & Piggott, 1936, 86] included possible figurines broadly comparable with that from the Giants' Hills, Skendleby, ditch [Phillips, 1936, 76, fig. 18, pl. XXIV].

Bone pins, akin to the Dorchester and Skara Brae series [Piggott, S., 1954, 118, 357, fig. 62, 4, 5; Childe, 1931a, 115] have been found in Willerby Wold, G.ccxxII, Market Weighton, G.ccxxvI, and Whiteleaf. A bone point from the Windmill Hill Horslip Barrow was of the Upton Lovel type [Stone, 1958, pl. 13; Piggott, S., 1962b]. A chisel-ended bone tool from the Giants' Hills, Skendleby, has counterparts at home and abroad [Phillips, 1936, 58, fig. 8, 1–4]. Other bone and antler artifacts from Thickthorn and the Windmill Hill Horslip Barrow have the character of industrial debris.

The upper silts of Wor Barrow and the Giants' Hills, Skendleby, produced a selection of later prehistoric and Roman material [Pitt-Rivers, 1898, pl. 250; Phillips, 1936, 69, fig. 13]. Quantities of Romano-British sherds, coins and other objects have come from six earthen long barrows (Appendix 8 (5)).

Artifacts from earthen long barrows are notable for their sparseness and above all their predominantly broken or waste character, in marked contrast to the vessels furnishing the secondary burials. The broken and seemingly discarded materials tend to be associated with disarticulated burials. Two articulated burials had finished tools with them.

ANIMAL REMAINS

From the first, animal bones (Appendix 9) have excited the attention of those who have dug into earthen long barrows [Colt Hoare, 1810, 83]. Thurnam [1868, 182–3] recognized 'Remains of Funeral Feasts: Bones of Oxen' and 'Remains of other animals'. Pitt-Rivers [1898, 127–33] collected, identified and listed by layers all the bones that he recovered from the Wor Barrow ditch. Animal bones from earthen long barrows have been studied more recently by Jackson [1936a; 1936b; 1937; 1939a; 1939b; 1943]. Cornwall [1956, 243] has emphasized the potential information in animal remains, while Jewell [1962; 1963] has given special attention to the bones of cattle.

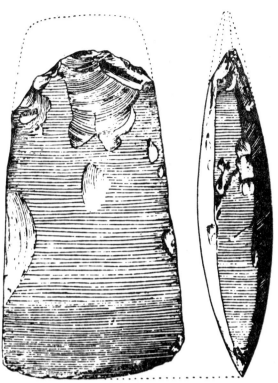

40. Flint axe with squared sides from
Julliberrie's Grave ($\frac{1}{2}$)

Two categories of animals occur: domesticated and wild. A general statement regarding Neolithic domesticated species made by Stuart Piggott [1954, 89] has been amplified by Zeuner [1963]; Piggott [1954, 10] has also noted the wild species contemporary with the Neolithic of Britain. A basis for the study of these in terms of history, environment and economic potential has long existed in the work of Harting [1880], Ritchie [1920] and Matheson [1932]. The scope and methods of economic exploitation have been detailed by Clark [1952, 5], and theories concerning winter feeding [Watson, 1931, 201] have recently been questioned [Higgs & White, 1963].

The animal bones, like the artifacts, from earthen long barrows must be considered under three headings: those with or about the burials, those in or beneath the mounds and those in the silts of ditches.

When Thurnam [1868, 182] wrote on bones with burials (Appendix 9 (1)) he remarked that the parts of oxen most frequently met with were 'those of the skull and feet'. He hazarded that the carcases of the beasts were eaten and that the heads and hooves, perhaps held together by the skin, were buried. Grinsell [1958, 25] has listed such remains. They are confined to the two groups of Salisbury Plain barrows and our knowledge rests almost exclusively on early observations. Their general validity was confirmed by the excavation of the Fussell's Lodge burial complex. Ox foot bones were found at the top on the axis of the collapsed mortuary house (pl. xxxiib) while beneath, by the first bone group, was an ox skull. The problem of Neolithic ox heads and bones in graves as a European phenomenon has recently been discussed by Gandert [1953] and Piggott [1962c]. Antlers lay near burials in Knook 2 and Tilshead 5, as did 'the entire skeleton of a goose' in Amesbury 14. Ox heads and hooves with burials seem absent in the north, judging from the 'extensive' work of Greenwell and others. However, pigs' jaws representing at least twenty beasts, besides scapulæ, leg bones, deer antler and an ox vertebra, lay at the proximal end of the Hanging Grimston mound [Mortimer, 1905, 103].

Ox bones are the most frequent finds in mounds (Appendix 9 (2)) in the south, and they seem mostly to have been split and broken: such limb-bones were found at Thickthorn Down, more pig than ox bones were noted at Whiteleaf, while pig was

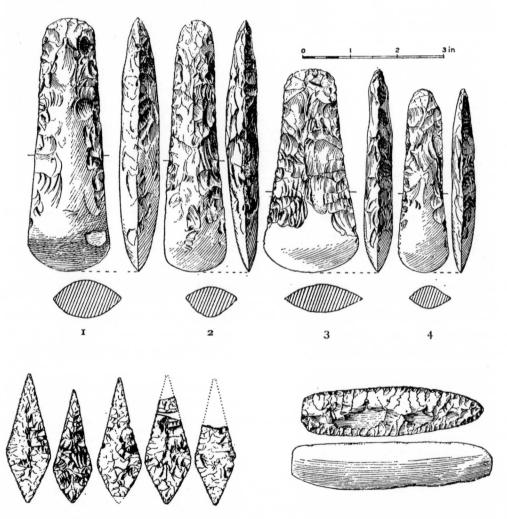

41. Flint axes, adzes, arrowheads and knife from the Seamer Moor long barrow ($\frac{1}{2}$)

predominant in Warminster 14. Three ox skulls were at intervals beneath the mound of the Beckhampton Road long barrow as well as the well-preserved bones of other animals [Smith & Evans, 1968]. Red deer is the commonest wild species represented, and this by antlers or pieces of antler. Roe deer, birds and horse also occur. In the north, ox as well as dog bones were observed at Helperthorpe, and ox, pig and sheep or goat bones in the Crosby Garrett cairn, G.ccxxviii, as well as those of horse, polecat, water vole and grouse.

Ditches (Appendix 9 (3)) contain two kinds of animal remains. There are those which suggest deliberate deposition at a given point and those, almost all split, broken and fragmentary, which occur throughout ditch silts. Both could, when considered in terms of ditch silting [Jewell (ed.), 1963], have been put in immediately after the ditch was dug or perhaps as much as a millennium later. Reminiscent of the ones with burials were the ox heads from the proximal ditch ends of the Maiden Castle bank barrow (pl. xxx) [Wheeler, 1943, 88]. Other deposits were piles of bones at Fussell's Lodge (pl. xxxiia) and on the ditch bottom of the Windmill Hill Horslip Barrow. In the ditch of the Giants' Hills, Skendleby, an ox skeleton was associated with long-necked beaker sherds. The bones from the ditch of the Wor Barrow (noted as almost all broken) [Pitt-Rivers, 1898, 127–33] are the best recorded, and ox humeri were the most frequently represented. Jackson [1936b], as well as calling attention to the broken bones from Thickthorn, remarked that the greater proportion were concentrated in the east end of the northern ditch. Broken bones obtained at all levels at Badshot, Julliberrie's Grave, Chilham, in the upper silt at Therfield and throughout the Giants' Hills, Skendleby, ditch.

Although animal bones from earthen long barrows have been recorded from the first, the methods of presentation of the evidence only exceptionally allow precise and reliable conclusions regarding their character and the proportions of species represented. Most writers, however, have indicated the frequency of the species represented by the bones that they had examined. The overwhelming quantity of ox is apparent, while other domestic animals were sheep or goat and perhaps pig. The few horse bones found are normally thought to represent wild creatures. Red deer is the most frequent wild species. Certain bones, such as those of the Wor Barrow badgers, probably represent the remains of creatures that subsequently inhabited the barrow.

Whatever the significance of the heads and hooves associated with the fallen mortuary houses and the burials beneath them, the masses of split, splintered and broken animal bones do recall and resemble the heterogeneous assemblages of pottery, broken tools and waste materials that comprise the artifacts from the earthen long barrows.

Chapter 6

STRUCTURE AND THE WORK ENTAILED

FORM, RITE AND USAGE

Stukeley, in his description of Stonehenge [Stukeley, 1740, 20], appears to have been the first to reconstruct a monument and to compute the work entailed in its erection. This site lends itself admirably to such consideration, and E. H. Stone [1924, 99] continued Stukeley's work while Atkinson [1956, 107], by further experiment, has considerably amplified the knowledge to be gained by these methods.

Reconstructions based upon a study of the structural problems in the light of materials, quantities and work involved, and supplemented by specific experiment [Ashbee, 1963, 12] or the results of other experiments, differ fundamentally from those that, in the past, have been attempted without due attention being paid to these factors. Many of the latter are impossible [e.g. Glasbergen, 1955, 3] and many more demand extreme caution [e.g. Reinerth, 1928; Kersten, 1936]. Conversely, for example, the timbers of the Leubingen mortuary house [Höfer, 1906] were in a good state of preservation, and the reconstructions seem reasonably justified. Of relevance here are the calculation of the volume of soil and stones in the mound and the comment on construction [Höfer, 1906, 15].

A few estimates have been made of the quantities and labour involved in the raising of long cairns and barrows, both stone-chambered and earthen. Childe [1944, 91] observed that a great Caithness cairn had sufficient stone in it to build five reasonably-sized parish churches. Clifford [1950, 35] considered that the building of the Rodmarton long cairn, which contains at least 5,000 tons of stone, would have involved the labour of 100 men for two years. Hogg [1940, 323] calculated the volumes of the turf and gravel dug from the ditch of the West Rudham earthen long barrow and suggested that originally it was probably higher than when dug into.

The Overton Down Experimental Earthwork [Ashbee & Cornwall, 1961; Jewell (ed.), 1963] provided information concerning not only the expansion factors of chalk but also the methods of use and the relative efficiency of primitive tools. The time and

78

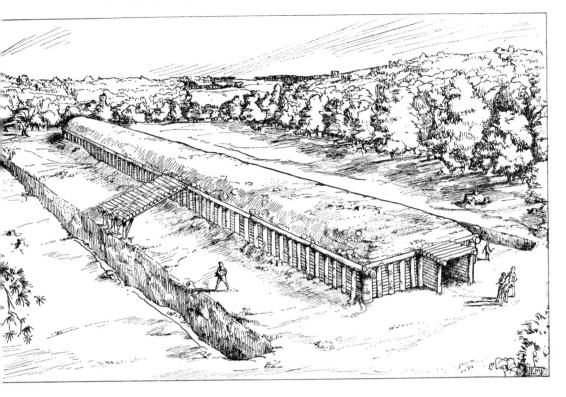

42. A reconstruction of Fussell's Lodge long barrow

man-power required for the two interdependent operations, first of digging and filling receptacles in the ditch and then of transporting and tipping them on the bank, would be a major part of any such operation [Atkinson, 1961, 295].

Many have contended that early digging methods are reflected in the resulting ditches. Hawley [1928, 165] claimed that the Stonehenge ditch was dug by progressive enlargement of segments which he termed 'craters', and so denoted gang labour. Phillips [1936, 65], from the haphazard piling of the Skendleby mound, postulated ditch digging by undercutting. Grinsell [1941, 90; 1953, 59], quoting round barrow ditches, in which short straight portions were detected, suggested incorrect joining of sections. Tips of turf down the axis of the Fussell's Lodge long barrow could point to continuous work, in both ditches, from the top downwards.

The volume of chalk dug from the Fussell's Lodge ditches was calculated on the assumption of more or less vertical ditch sides and allowing for side weathering and overall differential weathering [Ashbee, 1966]. A modest expansion factor [Jewell (ed.), 1963, 28], and a greater height at the proximal, broad end than at the distal, narrow one, and from the sizes of timbers computed from their impressions in the palisade trench, were considered and the product was some 28,000 cu. ft. Following upon this, it was estimated that there must have been a run of some 2,163 ft of timbers, both massive and modest, supplemented by at least 2,070 ft of scantling set behind it (fig. 42). This excludes the erstwhile mortuary house (fig. 34), for which at least another 150 ft of timbers, some massive, could have been used.

The selection, felling, trimming, preparation and transport of suitable timbers would have been a considerable factor in the raising of certain of our earthen long barrows. Experiment with flint axes [Nietsch, 1939, 70; Klindt-Jensen, 1957, 38] has shown that trees of modest proportions can be cut down in less than an hour, and small pine trees of about 7 in. diameter in as little as seven minutes. Massive trunks would take a disproportionately greater time. Long straight timbers, such as the trunks found in the silts of East Anglian rivers, would have been readily available under natural forest conditions [Edlin, 1958].

In Neolithic times [Clark, 1952, 7] supplies of freshly cut timber of modest but regular diameter could have been available with no more labour than collection and cutting to length. There is no reason to suppose that the timber felling propensities of the European beaver (*Castor fiber*) were less than those of the New World beaver (*Castor canadensis*): thus their little realized but formidable activities [Retzer, Swope, Remington & Rutherford, 1956] may have been exploited by early man. The trunk of the larger tree forming part of the Star Carr platform [Clark, 1954, pl. IV] had an end reminiscent of a sharpened pencil, which is a characteristic of beaver felling by gnawing [Retzer, Swope, Remington & Rutherford, 1956, front.]. However, the bases of trees cut down by means of polished axes in Denmark [Jørgensen, 1953, figs. 28, 29] also have this form. The recovery of well-preserved cut ends, coupled with observation and experiment, is now needed.

Great trunks such as those that formed the Fussell's Lodge façade would have presented a transport problem. Such a trunk, some 13 ft in length, might weigh some 67 lb. per cu. ft when green, a total of about 2⅓ tons. Organization and a labour force comparable with that required for the Stonehenge Bluestones [Atkinson, 1956, 109] would have been needed. Indeed, timber and stone handling and working were probably interchangeable and carried out side by side, as is attested by the composite character of the Sanctuary [Cunnington, M. E., 1931] or the celebrated Stonehenge mortices, tenons, tongues and grooves [Atkinson, 1956, 25–6].

Earthen long barrow structures provide indirect evidence of competent planning and building methods. As in the Dorset Cursus [Atkinson, 1955, 9], the straight northern side of the Fussell's Lodge trapezoid enclosure contrasted with an irregular southern side. The southern side of the Wor Barrow enclosure is straighter than the northern side. This could suggest that they were laid out by offsets and that these, at least at Fussell's Lodge, were not all equally accurate. The Fussell's Lodge mortuary house post-sockets lay exactly on the axis of the enclosure and in line with the entrance causeway, which was precisely in the centre of the slightly convex proximal façade. The distance of the ditch from the enclosure, taking all weathering and change into consideration, was remarkably constant. The breadth of the proximal end of the

xxv The mutilated burial beneath the Maiden Castle bank barrow

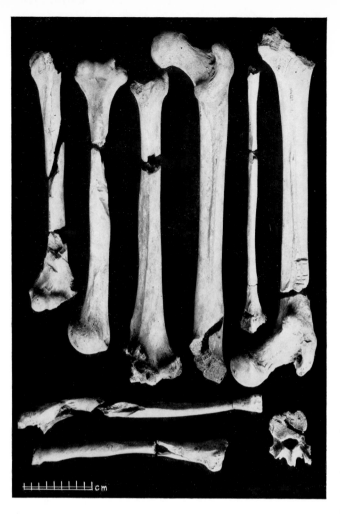

XXVI Maiden Castle: the cut
bones of the mutilated Neolithic
skeleton

XXVII Neolithic pot from beneath
the bones of the Norton Bavant
13 long barrow burial
XXVIII Neolithic pot from beneath
the bones of the Fussell's Lodge
burial

XXIX Pottery from the Whiteleaf long barrow

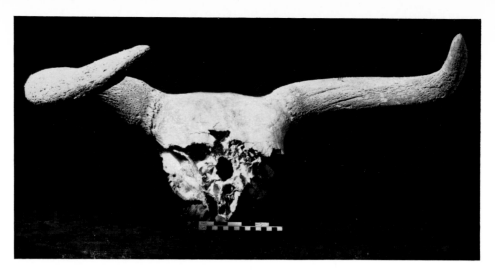

XXX Maiden Castle: horn cores of *Bos primigenius* from the infill of
the south ditch of the bank barrow

XXXI Fussell's Lodge: a nest of flint flakes in the ditch silt

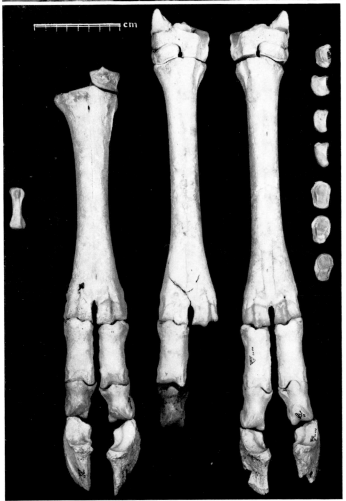

XXXII above, ox bones in the ditch silt of the Fussell's Lodge long barrow; below, ox feet from the collapsed mortuary house

XXXIII Barkaer: below, long houses; above, long house with outlines of divisions visible on the original earth floors

XXXIV A North German boulder-bounded long barrow, Tarbeck, Kr. Segeberg

XXXV Putlos, North Germany: reconstruction of rectangular boulder-bounded long barrows on the river bank

xxxvi Reconstruction of a Kujawish Grave in the Forest of Sarnowo, Włocławek District, Poland

enclosure was twice that of the distal end, while the length was roughly three-and-a-half times the proximal width. This is *not* intended as proof of a unit of measurement such as Stukeley's *Druid Cubits* [Stukeley, 1743, 11, 19, 31]. Nonetheless it seems hard to avoid the conclusion that a reasoned system of proportional gradation lies behind the concept.

At Fussell's Lodge it was observed that the trunks had fitted into the palisade trench with fair precision. The post impressions showed that such pains had been taken to ensure that they stood vertically as to presuppose a plumb-line. The use of horizontal lines might explain how timbers of disparate dimensions had been lined up with fair accuracy.

We may tend to underestimate prehistoric constructional capabilities [Ashbee & Cornwall, 1961, 134]. These aspects of earthen long barrow structures, like others of Neolithic engineering [Atkinson, 1961], point to organization and direction in Earlier Neolithic society.

FORM, RITE AND USAGE

Colt Hoare [1810, 21] perceived 'a singularity of outline' in the construction of earthen long barrows as well as 'a singularity in the mode of burial' and later [Colt Hoare, 1819, 110], on account of the absence of grave furniture, supposed 'that they were appropriated to the interment of the lower class of people'. Thurnam [1868, 177] expressed the hope that he would be able to show 'that they were the tombs of Chieftains'. Greenwell [1877, 479–83] felt unable to fit them into the European scene of his time on account of differences of skull form. Mortimer [1905, xx] saw that they differed from round barrows but was unconvinced that they were older. Grinsell [1936, 32; 1953, 33] has endeavoured to express the varied evidence in terms of a series of actions connected with the dead. Stuart Piggott [1954, 367] envisaged initial successive burial, preceding the erection of the barrow, which was 'the final and irrevocable sealing of the burial deposits', on either the same or a different site. While the raising of the mounds may well have been the final structural undertaking, there remains the question of continued access to, at least, the pitched mortuary houses.

Modern excavation has shown that earthen long barrows in many ways resembled the broadly contemporary long houses found in diverse parts of north-western Europe (for the details of this relationship see below, chapter 7). A hurdlework fence system, giving an impression of compartments, at the distal end of Giants' Hills, Skendleby, brings to mind the divisions in the rectangular long houses in the Neolithic village at Barkaer (pl. xxxiiia, b) [Gløb, 1949; Bibby, 1957, 296–301, pl. xix lower]. Somewhat similar arrangements in stone were encountered in the Randwick long barrow [Crawford, 1925, 129–133], Upper Swell, Pole's Wood South long barrow [Greenwell, 1877, 521–4; Crawford, 1925, 125–8] and Burn Ground [Grimes, 1960, 65, fig. 28]. It seems unlikely that these sectors at Skendleby were intended as guidance for tipping parties [Phillips, 1936, 89] since they lay on one side only of the axis; they appear to have had no structural significance within barrow or cairn. The pitched timber and turf mortuary houses would seem, ultimately, to have affinities with Advanced Palaeolithic and Circumpolar structures (for details see chapter 7). Indeed, there emerges from long barrow together with mortuary house the curious principle of a house within a house.

Both Childe [1925, 288] and Crawford [1928, 11] thought that earthen long barrows had in them turf or timber chambers and that these reproduced the stone chambers of Megalithic tombs. Crawford [1932, 5] felt that division into chambered and unchambered denoted only geological conditions. This may be an oversimplification, but the problem of the function and usage of the mortuary house remains.

The evidence, mainly structural, points to the simultaneous deposition of bones, but nevertheless there could have been subsequent access to them and thus 'Successive Burial' [Daniel, 1950, 110]. Although the 'Ossuary' theory [Daniel, 1950, 109] goes far in explaining the principles involved, no one contention appears to fit the diverse evidence.

Childe [1940, 63] considered that successive burials were made in turf or timber chambers in earthen long barrows in the manner that was believed at that time to have obtained in stone-chambered tombs. Two well-documented excavations of earthen long barrows were available to him in 1940, the Wor Barrow and Giants' Hills, Skendleby. The burials beneath both were compounds of disarticulated bones and articulated skeletons. It was believed that in certain chambered tombs, earlier interments, already skeletonized, were pushed aside or re-arranged to make space for later ones [Keiller & Piggott, 1938, 128].

The Wor Barrow articulated skeletons were at the proximal end of the complex and it might be thought that the remains 'put in as bones and not in sequence' [Pitt-Rivers, 1898, 82] had been pushed to the rear. The skull of no. 6, like no. 2 [Pitt-Rivers, 1898, 82], was too decayed for restoration, but that of no. 1, which could be considered as the last corpse to be put into the mortuary house, was in good condition. At Skendleby [Phillips, 1936, 83] the egg-case of a land-snail which never goes underground was adduced as evidence of exposure of the bones before burial. Presumably such a snail could enter into a mortuary house before barrow collapse rendered it 'underground'. Bones which could not be associated with skulls, and packing into a small space, were thought to indicate simultaneous deposition. However, certain disarticulated bones lay above articulated remains [Phillips, 1936, 83, fig. 25, 3 above 4]. At Nutbane it was considered that the clean, hard condition of the most distal skeleton, beyond the distal post of the mortuary house, pointed to a later deposition than that of the three other disturbed ones [Morgan, 1959, 24]. Here, however, as the skeletons lay within an attenuated version of a long mortuary enclosure, differential exposure rather than successive burial might account for this condition. The Fussell's Lodge bones were in specific groups, those of no individual being in more than one group. They can be considered successive only in the presumed order of their packing into the mortuary house. At Wayland's Smithy 1 there was an articulated burial beyond the bone mass.

Although a pitched mortuary house might seem ill-designed for the packing of bones and corpses, ingenious experiment [Keiller & Piggott, 1938, 128] has shown how such might be manœuvred within a comparable space.

At Fussell's Lodge, Hanging Grimston and Willerby Wold, G.CCXXII, the proximal posts of the mortuary houses were in the façades and would thus, seemingly, have precluded entrance once all was complete. In the Wor Barrow and the Giants' Hills, Skendleby, however, the mortuary houses lay within the body of the mound.

Articulated skeletons clearly point to the interment of corpses, while disarticulated remains can only have been bones when set into the barrows. To account for assemblages of articulate skeletons (if the possibility of a series of deaths within a brief period be ruled out), the 'Human-Sacrifice Chieftain' theory [Daniel, 1950, 109] might be applied to the Nutbane males, or the possibility of preservation along the lines suggested by Lethbridge [1950, 23] or Herodotus [Penguin Classics, 1954, 264].

During the excavation of the Fussell's Lodge earthen long barrow it was not possible to account for all the decayed and admixed soil, nor could the collapse of the mortuary house be held responsible for all the bone breakage. The disarticulated bones might represent exhumations from such locations as the post-marked Early Neolithic single graves, in one of which some bones had remained [Piggott, S., 1929; 1936; Pitt-Rivers, 1898, 49; 42, pl. 243]. Broken pottery might to some extent be explained by this theory.

The separation and stacking of long bones and skulls was a feature of the Fussell's Lodge burial complex and was recorded from Chute 1. Stuart Piggott [1962a, 68] commented on the importance of skulls and thigh bones in connection with the West Kennet stone-chambered long barrow, whence some had evidently been deliberately abstracted [Wells, L. H., 1962, 80–1], and drew attention to their emblematic qualities in classical antiquity. At Fussell's Lodge many individuals were represented by only a few bones [Brothwell & Blake, 1966], as was elsewhere noted regarding limb bones by Thurnam [1868, 185]. Long barrows may have been the source of the human bones in the Windmill Hill causewayed camp ditches [Smith, I. F., 1959, 161]. Bones in similar circumstances were noted at Knap Hill [Cunnington, M. E., 1912] and Abingdon [Leeds, 1928, 476], and burials as well as bones at Whitehawk [Curwen, 1934, 124–6; 1954, 78]. It seems not impossible that the traffic between the camps and the long barrows was reciprocal.

The Maiden Castle butchered skeleton [Wheeler, 1943, 21] is unique, for there is no other positive evidence for such treatment. Morant [Morant & Goodman, 1943, 346] was able to show that decapitation was followed by an assault, first on the legs and then on the arms. Cannibalism was originally suspected [Wheeler, 1943, 21], but there is little evidence for this practice [Brothwell, 1961], and a slighting of the aura surrounding these members may possibly be implied [Onians, 1954, 123–167, 174–186].

It has long been claimed that the Yorkshire burned burials were remains cremated within the barrow [Greenwell, 1877, 506; Hogg, 1940, 328; Grinsell, 1953, 34; Piggott, S., 1954, 109; Manby, 1963, 192]. It has emerged (chapters 3 and 4) that these were almost entirely burials of disarticulated bones housed in pitched mortuary houses which had been burned. The intense burning was largely confined to the proximal ends, although at Willerby Wold, G.ccxxII, [Manby, 1963, 181, fig. 5] the entire structure had been consumed. Comparison should be with the recent burning of an experimental house [Hansen, 1962, 141, fig. 11]. It is not easy to account for the concentration of burnings: accidental ignition has been considered [Childe, 1925, 288; 1940, 63] by the medium of purificatory and other fires [Piggott, S., 1954, 110]. Charred and scorched bones have been encountered in a number of stone-chambered tombs in Britain and abroad [Wace, 1932, 141; Daniel, 1950, 99; Piggott, S., 1962a, 68]. Beliefs associated with the drying, scorching or burning of bones are not unknown [Onians, 1951, 254-70]; but this pattern of structure burning is somewhat reminiscent of later fort-slighting [Childe, 1940, 216; Wheeler, 1952, 78], and a lingering echo may remain in the recurrent burning house motif of early heroic literature [Dillon, 1946, 4].

Collective burial might betoken a family relationship [Childe, 1951, 57-8]. This has been postulated by Keith [1916, 271; 1925, 8], Wace [1932, 121] and Cave [1938, 147-8] for burials in stone-chambered tombs. Cave [1936, 95] examined the bones from the Giants' Hills, Skendleby, and considered that if archaeological evidence suggested a family group this would not conflict with the osteological data.

Broken pottery at chambered tomb entrances has been considered as representing forecourt offerings [Piggott & Powell, 1949, 135], but this would not account for what has been observed in earthen long barrows where vessels with burials were never complete. Could it be that portions of pots were taken out in a manner similar to that suggested for bones?

With regard to the heads and hooves [Thurnam, 1868, 182; Piggott, S., 1962c] that may betoken hides, there is a mass of early European beliefs connected with oxen [Johnson, 1912, 481-87; Onians, 1951, 239-46; Behrens, 1953, 99], and there are also horned deities [Sjoestedt, 1949, 17], but no direct connection with these can be shown. The possibility that heads, antlers and even stuffed carcases [Herodotus, Penguin Classics, 1954, 264-5] were set up over mortuary house or barrow should also be considered, or the great mass of split, splintered and broken ox bones might suggest that beef eating at earthen long barrows had at times [Powell, T. G. E., 1958, 157] a more than practical purpose.

It emerges that at least the collective burial tradition has much in common with, but does not precisely follow, that rite in stone-chambered tombs, and since the recognition of the pitched mortuary house, the relationship is perhaps closer than has been hitherto thought. The occurrence of articulated burials is a definite trait, perhaps from the first, but a Middle Neolithic re-introduction from Single Grave groups [Ashbee, 1960, 160] must not be discounted. No single explanation can account for the complexities of form, rite and usage.

Chapter 7

AGE

In the years following the First World War absolute estimates of the duration of the Neolithic moved from the aeonic utterances of Dr Sturge to that of a 1200-year period of vigorous change [Kendrick & Hawkes, 1932, 56], beginning *c.* 3000 BC after a Mesolithic of some four millennia [Clark, 1932, 4], which was disrupted by the intrusive Beaker communities in about 1800 BC. From then onwards later estimates for the beginning of the Neolithic gained ground [Hawkes, J., 1934, 41; Piggott, S., 1934, 375]. Childe [1940, 8], fully conscious of the shortcomings of dating by archaeological estimate and supported in some measure by the sequences of palaeobotany, set down for British prehistory a system of dated periods designated I–IX. It was intended that the evidence should be referred impartially to this system, which was linked with his European scheme [Childe, 1929, 418, Table], and ultimately to contacts with the historic civilizations of the Near East [Childe, 1932]. Attention was drawn to a vague horizon in the Wessex culture marked by segmented faience beads [Beck & Stone, 1936; Stone, J. F. S., 1943–8; Fox, A. & Stone, 1951; Stone & Thomas, 1956] and the arguments that could be built upon the gold-bound amber disk from Knossos [Childe, 1940, 145; 1948]. Two European chronological systems, long and short, were adduced and defended by Childe [1939; 147, 330–6] and, even when the first radio-carbon datings were available, he felt unable to decide between the two competing systems [Childe, 1957, 342]. In a final essay [Childe, 1959], he considered that a reliable absolute chronology was prehistory's most urgent need.

When Stuart Piggott [1954, 380] estimated the duration of Neolithic culture in Britain he started from the date of the Wessex culture [Hawkes, 1948; de Navarro, 1950]. The Wessex culture was an amalgam with Late Neolithic components, and perhaps not far removed from it; one or one and a half centuries were seen as the length of a Middle Neolithic phase and with an Early period, a time span of about four centuries was postulated, the Neolithic cultures of the British Isles thus being contained within the first half of the second millennium BC.

The radio-carbon revolution, which had begun a decade before [Libby, 1955; Aitken, 1961, 88–120; Willis, 1963, conveniently review this rapidly expanding subject], first made full impact upon Neolithic studies in a work by Clark and Godwin [1962]. This was a re-examination of the classic local sequence of Post-glacial deposits at Peacock's Farm, Shippea Hill, in Cambridgeshire [Clark, Godwin & Clifford, 1935]. It emerged that the Neolithic culture there was at least as old as 3000 BC and this date conformed well to the emerging patterns, for the Neolithic began before 3000 BC in Ireland [Watts, 1960] and early occupation of Windmill Hill was of the same order [Smith, I. F., 1960]; meanwhile Case [1961, 210] has compared a further Irish group with a Continental series and Daniel [1961] has considered the western European chambered tombs. The Neolithic phase in British prehistory had lasted three times as long as had been envisaged a decade before [Piggott, S., 1954, 381] after thirty years of fluctuating estimate. Clark and Godwin [1962, 21] also emphasized that it might even have begun about half a millennium earlier, a thousand years earlier than had been allowed by the arguments based on archaeological estimates.

It emerged from the European pattern [Clark & Godwin, 1962, 22] that the earlier dates lay in the West, and that this could be consistent with a western or south-western origin for our earliest Neolithic. This has been challenged by Case [1962, 214] who feels that we must await developments.

This elongation of the duration of the Neolithic gives considerable validity to the divisions Early, Middle and Late, which had hitherto been contained within a mere five centuries [Piggott, S., 1954, 373–81 and table]. While, as Clark and Godwin [1962, 22] observed, definitive boundaries cannot as yet be assigned to these, dates from specific sites (fig. 43) can be fitted into them. Case [1962, 214, fig. 1] has set out English Early and Middle Neolithic dates, together with the relevant European range at twice the standard deviation [Piggott, S., 1962d, 233].

Pieces of oak in the mortuary house collapse of the Fussell's Lodge long barrow yielded the date BM–134, 3230–150 BC [Ashbee, 1964], which lies firmly within the range of the Early Neolithic. Remains of oak posts from the second forecourt building at Nutbane [Vatcher, 1959] emerged as BM–49, 2721–150 BC, which is consonant with the Middle Neolithic. However, antler from the bottom of the ditch of the Horslip, Windmill Hill, long barrow [Ashbee & Smith, 1966] gave the date BM–180, 3240±150 BC. At Wayland's Smithy [Atkinson, 1965, 132] it seemed that just before the building of the second barrow the site had been cleared by burning. A sample from a branch or small trunk, some 4 ft long, found on the berm and ditch silt of the first barrow has given I–2328, 2828±130 BC [Atkinson, 1965, 132 and fn. 16]. Two dates have been obtained, from timber out of the burnt mortuary house, and from a pit in the middle of the façade bedding trench, for the Willerby Wold long barrow [Manby, 1967]. The first is BM–188, 2950±150 BC, the second BM–189, 3010±150 BC. A date, NPL–73, 3080±90 BC has come from the Seamer long barrow.

43. Radio-carbon dates of long barrows and other earlier Neolithic sites

With further selective earthen long barrow excavation undertaken with a proper range of concepts and their implications in mind, together with the submission for radio-carbon dating of suitable materials from primary contexts, a spread and more significant range of dates might emerge (fig. 43).

ORIGIN AND AFFINITY

Within the European long barrow province, stretching from Ireland to Poland and from Brittany to the Northern Isles of Britain, it is not possible to indicate a specific group as the source from which all others derive. It remains therefore to examine and comment on possible origins for the various elements of rite and structure.

Articulated contracted burial was practised in Palaeolithic times [Macalister, 1921, 294–99, 248–56, 380–86 for a convenient account], while a skeleton at Téviec was contracted, as were those beneath Tardenosian midden heaps at Muge [Roche, 1960, 109–30] and Hoedic [Pequart, 1954, pl. v, fig. 2]. Reliable excavation has shown the rite in use by a primary village farming group as early as 6000 BC [Rodden, 1962, 286, pl. XLII].

There was until comparatively recently, owing to low standards of excavation and anatomical record, little reliable or relevant comparative material outside the British Isles for the collective burials of mostly disarticulated bones. Where a comparable rite has been recorded [Daniel, 1950, 113, fn. 2] the precise age is not known and, indeed, there is every possibility that eastern examples might post-date those under consideration. Hawkes [1940, 147] considered that Mesolithic burial groups as were at Téviec [Pequart, Boule & Vallois, 1937, pl. v] might have made a contribution to the collective nature of long barrow burials. Indeed, collective burial in natural caves was known in Mesolithic Palestine [Childe, 1957, 219]. Use of caves for collective

87

burial continued current in Italy and southern France, and is not unknown in England [Daniel, 1950, 46].

Assemblages of bones, partly articulate and partly disarticulate, burnt and unburnt, chiefly in fallen mortuary houses, have been encountered many times, mostly in middle Germany. Their associations are mainly the Walternienburg Culture and the Corded Ware series [Feustel & Ullrich, 1965, 129], which is broadly Middle Neolithic [Case, 1962], although the 'vault' at Stein, in Holland [Modderman, 1964], may be earlier.

At Nordhausen [Feustel & Ullrich, 1965, 108] the skeletons of fifty, perhaps sixty, people were beneath the collapsed remains of a pitched mortuary house (fig. 44). Their lack of anatomical order was commented upon and they had been badly broken by the collapse of the stone-covered structure. Another mortuary house at Niederbösa (fig. 45) was found to contain the bones of some sixty-eight persons in an almost precisely similar context. The human remains found in the 'vault' at Stein, which was a long timber-roofed trench, consisted almost entirely of cremations. Modderman [1964] compared it with a collective burial 'vault', examined a decade before, at Bonnières-sur-Seine, in France [Basse de Ménorval, 1953].

In view of the foregoing, a number of sites hitherto treated with some reserve can be reconsidered. A fallen timber building at Gotha [Spiessbach, 1934] had upon its stone-paved floor about a hundred inhumation burials. Its excavator emphasized nests of skulls and six incidences of the wrong skull on a skeleton. To account for this he adduced that when new interments were made older ones were set aside. A multitude of cremations together with numerous charred bones and pottery of the Bernburg Culture were contained within what had clearly been a mortuary house at Aspenstedt, Kr. Halberstadt [Ebert, 1955]. There is also the possibility that the long mound at Krakelbos, Ottembourg, in Belgium [Mariën, 1952, 62, fig. 58] covered a structure of this character, yielding as it did to early excavators layers of sand and charcoal with pottery and burnt stones.

The pitched and turf-built mortuary houses might ultimately owe something to the Circumpolar cultures [Gjessing, 1944], for houses recalling these forms were widespread amongst the hunting and collecting groups beyond the margin of the temperate forest [Gjessing, 1944, 46, 50; Clark, 1952, 133]. Attention must also be drawn to the apparently axial character of Advanced Palaeolithic structures seemingly originally dug into the peri-glacial loess [Childe, 1950; Klima, 1956]; lines of alleged 'hearths' are their most prominent features, and it is a possibility that these were burnt axial posts.

Chronological priority precludes the derivation of trapezoid and rectangular barrows and timber enclosures from known developed house forms of similar plan and dimensions. However, as the Danubian in the Netherlands begins at least as early as 4000 BC [Daniel, 1961, 579] and there are rectilinear house forms in Greece and perhaps the Balkans by 6000 BC [Rodden, 1962, 269], a contribution from here is not impossible.

The trapezoid plan of the earthen long barrows is inherent in certain of the stone-chambered and -surrounded long barrows and cairns. Indeed, it could be argued that

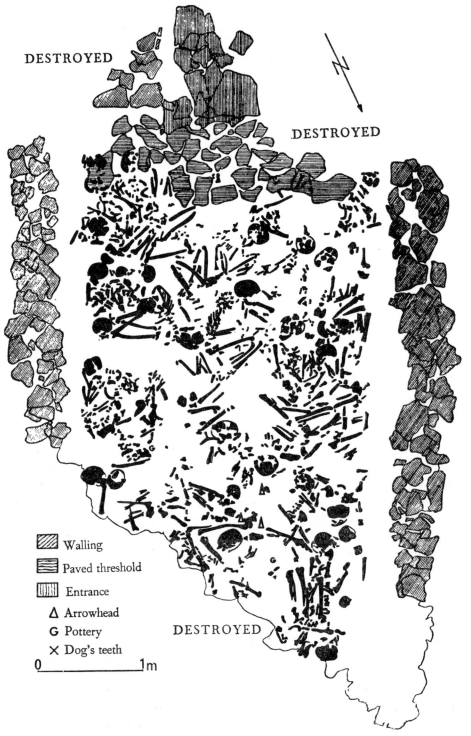

DESTROYED

DESTROYED

DESTROYED

Walling

Paved threshold

Entrance

△ Arrowhead

G Pottery

✕ Dog's teeth

0 _____ 1m

44. Ground plan of the collapsed remains of the Nordhausen mortuary house

89

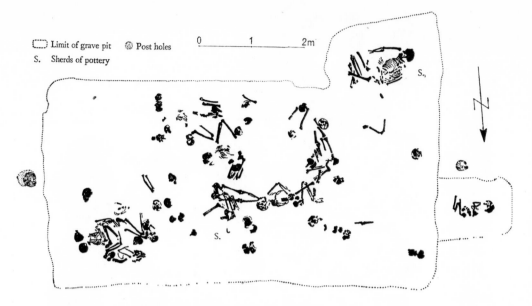

45. Plan of the Niederbösa mortuary house

they are all but variations of one class of monument—long barrows [de Valera, 1960, 82–5; 1961, 234–40]. Trapezoid cairns, limited by wall or boulders, are a feature of the chambered tombs of the Severn–Cotswold group [Grimes, 1960, 90, fig. 37; Piggott, S., 1962a] and Clyde [Piggott, S., 1954, 152; de Valera, 1960; Corcoran, 1960; Scott, 1962], while this tendency is also marked in certain Irish Court Cairns [e.g. de Valera, 1960, 87, pl. 1, 2] as well as in the Wedge Cairns [Ó Ríordáin & de Valera, 1952; de Valera & Ó Nualláin, 1961, 112], and indeed among the Orkney–Cromarty long cairns [Henshall, 1963, 45]. The enclosed courts of such full court cairns as Creevykeel [de Valera, 1960, 87, pl. 1, 2] and Malin More [de Valera, 1960, 108, pl. XVII, 19] are not unreminiscent of the principle of the timber enclosure, while the segmented chambers recall, at least in their ground plans, the massive-posted mortuary houses. This is emphasized by the stone chamber of Doey's Cairn, Dunloy [Evans, E. E., 1938], of which the timber roof, supported by three axial posts, had been burned in a manner recalling the Yorkshire mortuary houses.

More or less rectangular cairns, containing stone chambers and comparable with such pronouncedly rectangular earthen monuments as the Wor Barrow and Holdenhurst, are not unknown [Henshall, 1963, 82]. The scrupulously excavated and recorded Millin Bay cairn [Collins & Waterman, 1955], in the long cist of which was a collective burial which had been brought from another place, is the first example.

These general relationships between earthen long barrows and certain of the stone-chambered and -surrounded long barrows and cairns, inherent in plan and principle, may be seen to continue into specific aspects of construction [Daniel, 1967]. Indeed,

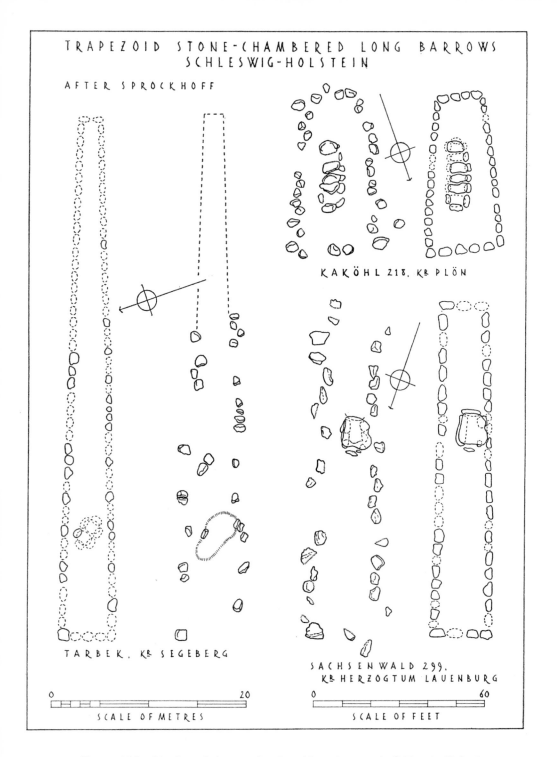

46. Trapezoid boulder-bounded stone-chambered long barrows in Schleswig-Holstein

91

the contentions of Childe [1940, 64] and Crawford [Crawford & Keiller, 1928, 11] concerning the architectural character of earthen long barrows must be seriously reconsidered.

Owing to the varied techniques that differences of material imposed upon long barrow builders, much escaped notice until total, careful excavation allowed the recognition and recovery of detailed features. The great trunks that formed the façades of Fussell's Lodge [Ashbee, 1966] and Nutbane [Vatcher, 1959] have their counterparts in the stone façades of lithic long barrows such as West Kennet [Piggott, S., 1962b, 17–18, fig. 7]. The walling between such stones is matched by the lighter timbers behind trunks which would have retained chalk rubble. Walling delimiting a lithic long barrow [Grimes, 1960, fig. 28] can be compared with the trench-set retaining timbers of Fussell's Lodge or the Wor Barrow. Stone slabs flanking the proximal end of the Wayland's Smithy 1 pitched mortuary house [Atkinson, 1965, 128, fig. 1] and the stones remaining about it demonstrate the use of the two traditions, lithic and timber, while there seems to have been a timber mortuary house within a cairn at Pitnacree, in Scotland [Coles & Simpson, 1965].

Daniel [1965, 86] has recently suggested that the so-called classic European Passage Graves might be stone funerary versions of wooden dwelling houses. While, as observed above, the compartment principle in certain stone tombs does recall the groups of burials in timber mortuary houses, it is not easy to point to specific stone counterparts of any timber mortuary house. In this respect the simple, divided, rectangular chambers of the Medway Tombs [Evans, J. H., 1948; 1950; Alexander, 1961], and their fellows, come to mind. Indeed, a characteristic of their structure is the manner in which side-stones have been leaned against middle stones. A recently excavated divided chamber at Monomore, in Scotland [Mackie, 1963–4, 23], led, after comparison of its ritual with that of earthen long barrows, to the comment that the orthostatic chambers of the lithic monuments ought to be the equivalent mortuary structures in areas with different resources of building materials: both they, it was said, and the wooden structures seem to have been the receptacles for a series of burials made over a long period of time. Green Low, in Derbyshire [Manby, 1965, 38], carefully excavated and claimed as a passage grave, could also be considered in like manner.

With the foregoing in mind it must also be considered how closely such stone structures as the west chamber at Dyffryn Ardudwy [Powell, T. G. E., 1963, 20, pl. 11, b], a 'portal dolmen', and perhaps the Pentre Ifan [Grimes, 1948] portal and chamber, as well as other tombs of this character, recall the combinations of timber porch and mortuary house which are a feature of Fussell's Lodge, the Wor Barrow and Wayland's Smithy 1. Indeed, wooden porches which have been effectively blocked by posts, as at Fussell's Lodge, recall also the so-called 'false-portals' of the Severn–Cotswold laterally-chambered stone long barrows [Daniel, 1950, 74; Piggott, S., 1954, 136] as well as, perhaps, the enigmatic coves [Piggott, S., 1947–8, 113]. With these could also be considered the box-like structure, open to the front, which had been built over a contrived slot in the roof of the passage of the renowned New Grange [O'Kelly, 1966].

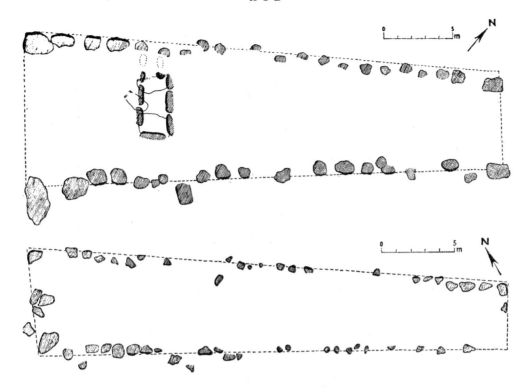

47. North German boulder-bounded long barrows: Dwasieden and Lupow

The excavator of Wayland's Smithy 1 was able to show [Atkinson, 1965, 128, fig. 1] that the verticals of the pitched mortuary house there had been half-round in section and had most probably projected above the spine of the barrow. Like the posts of the later timber circles [Piggott, S., 1940b, 215] it would seem unlikely that they were but naked posts. For it must be remembered that it was observed [Powell & Daniel, 1956, 48] with regard to mural art that its main canvas was probably perishable materials. The flat surfaces of great timbers could have carried designs normally seen only in embryo as scratchings on chalk in flint mines or, for example, doubtfully on the Ty Illtyd Severn–Cotswold tomb [Crawford, 1925, 64]. Comparison could, however, be considered with anthropomorphic schemes as developed on the similarly flat surfaces of Stone 22 at Barclodiad y Gawres [Powell & Daniel, 1956, 29, pl. 16] and Stone 7 at Four Knocks, Co. Meath [Hartnett, 1957, 222]. Something of the ability of Earlier Neolithic woodworkers is shown by the long known assemblage of objects from Ehenside Tarn [Darbishire, 1874], while insight into Later Neolithic woodworking is afforded by the pieces from the Essex Coast [Warren et al., 1936, 184].

In recent years attention has turned to northern and northern central Europe where

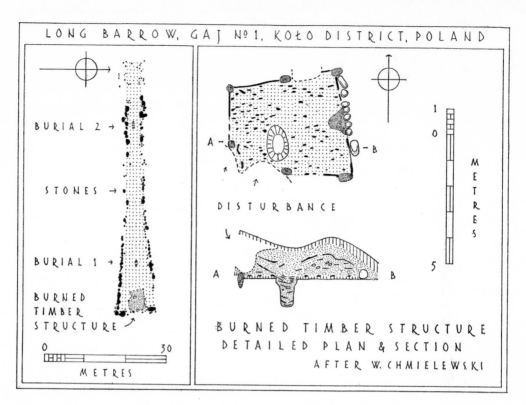

Text within the figure:

LONG BARROW, GAJ Nº 1, KOŁO DISTRICT, POLAND

BURIAL 2 →
STONES →
BURIAL 1 →
BURNED TIMBER STRUCTURE ↗

0   30
METRES

A —
— B
DISTURBANCE

A   B

1
0
5
METRES

BURNED TIMBER STRUCTURE
DETAILED PLAN & SECTION
AFTER W. CHMIELEWSKI

48. Long barrow, Gaj no. 1, Koło District of Poland

long cairns and barrows (pls. XXXIV, XXXV), as well as long houses, comparable to our earthen long barrows have been recognized. Childe [1949a, 135] drew attention to the comments of Sprockhoff [1938, 10] and Gløb [1949], who had compared their local long barrows with long houses, and posed the question whether similar ideas had influenced our insular long barrow builders. It should be noted that M. E. Cunnington [1938, 73] had made this comparison at an early stage, quoting Schuchthardt [1919] while Stuart Piggott [1955, 101; 1961a, 564; 1967] has since amplified and qualified the earlier parallels.

Trapezoid boulder-bounded long barrows (fig. 47) at Dwasieden on Rügen and Lupow, Kr. Stolp, in Pomerania [Sprockhoff, 1938, 31], are similar in form to the Fussell's Lodge and Willerby, G.CCXXII, enclosures, while a shorter version occurs at Kahkol, Kr. Plön [Sprockhoff, 1938, 33], Holstein, and on the Dölauer Heide, near Halle [Behrens, 1957]. Also relevant are the trapezoid and tapering Kujawish (pl. XXXVI) long barrows (fig. 48) [Chmielewski, 1952], some of which had burned structures at their ends [Piggott, S., 1961a, 564, fig. 76] similar to the Yorkshire series and to Nutbane. Long barrow-like structures of similar plan are known also from Brittany [Piggott, S., 1937b] and have for long been considered as the Breton equivalents of English long barrows.

94

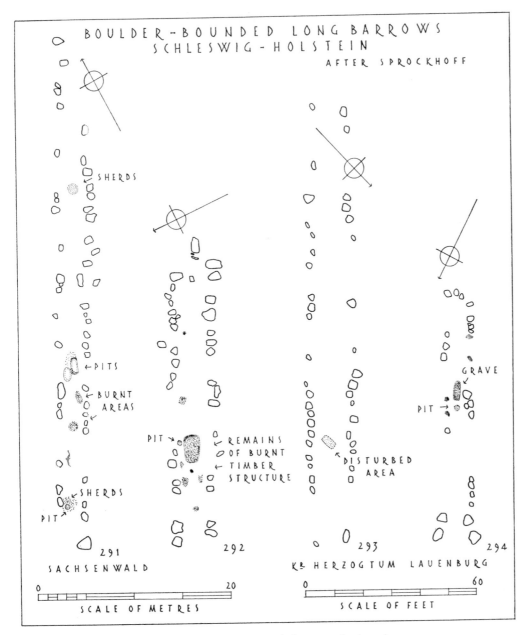

49. North German boulder-bounded rectangular long barrows

Of special note are rectangular long barrows (fig. 49) such as those in the Sachsenwald [Sprockhoff, 1952; 1954; 1966] and their counterparts in Sweden documented by Kaelas [1956, 9, Abb. 4]. Their stone-framed burials are more or less central to the monument and recall the mortuary house siting at, for example, Wor Barrow and Skendleby.

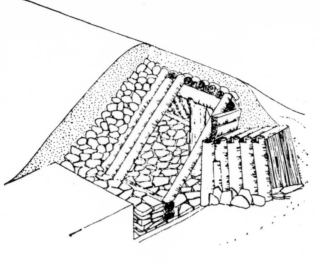

50. A reconstruction of the Nord-hausen mortuary house

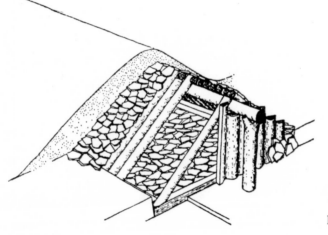

51. A reconstruction of the Nieder-bösa mortuary house

The burned buildings found beneath the trapezoid Kujawish long barrows recall the English pitched series. That at Gaj (fig. 48) was rectangular, and, judging by the axial posts, ridged, while the sides may have been vertical, although their height is not known. Burned timber structures were also a feature of certain of the North German boulder-bounded long barrows, notably those in the Sachsenwald [Sprockhoff, 1966, Atlasblatt 120]. Very closely resembling the English pitched mortuary houses are those, seemingly soil-covered, but not beneath barrows, of the Middle German Walternienburg Culture, the burials of which have been noted above. That at Nord-hausen (fig. 50) [Feustel & Ullrich, 1965, 105], some 17 ft in length and 12 ft in breadth, housed about sixty persons. Like those in the Fussell's Lodge mortuary house [Ashbee, 1966], the bones had been broken and crushed by the fall of the stone-cased roof.

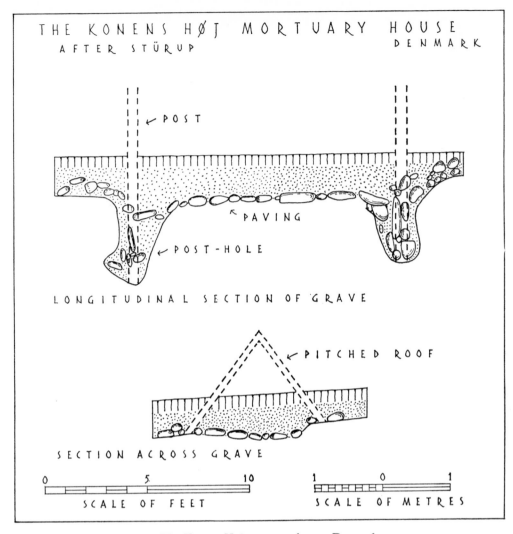

←POST

←PAVING

←POST-HOLE

LONGITUDINAL SECTION OF GRAVE

←PITCHED ROOF

SECTION ACROSS GRAVE

0   5   10
SCALE OF FEET

1   0   1
SCALE OF METRES

52. The Konens Høj mortuary house, Denmark

Another mortuary house at Niederbösa, Kr. Sondershausen (fig. 51) [Feustel & Ullrich, 1965, 112], 23 ft in length and about 12 ft in breadth, which had in it the bones of, in all, seventy-eight people, had two substantial axial posts to carry the ridge. The roof timbers had been stone covered. Both of these essentially 'pitched' mortuary houses had been built into, or about, rectangular grave-pits which corresponded closely to their interior dimensions. Both had end-entrances, that at Nordhausen being in the form of a passage recalling the Fussell's Lodge plan.

Ullrich compared these Walternienburg mortuary houses with the well-preserved and well-known examples in the great Saxo-Thuringian royal barrows [Höfer, 1906] those described by Reinerth [1928], besides citing numerous structures which have come to light in recent years under barrows and in other circumstances [Behm-Blancke,

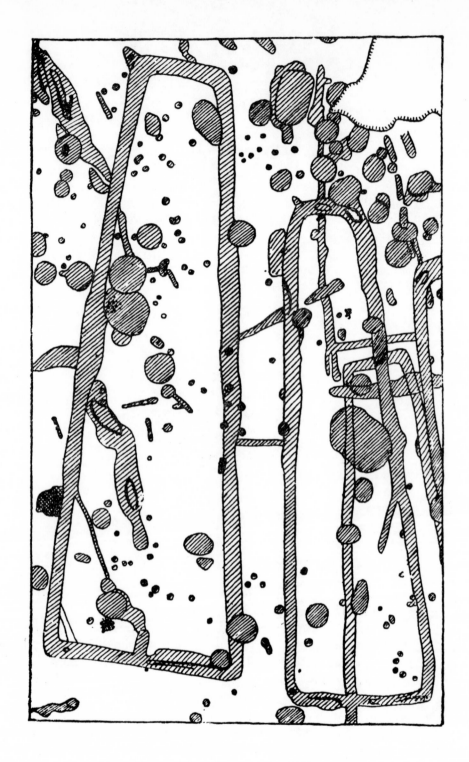

53. Plans of trapezoid long houses at Brześć Kujawski, Poland

98

1953–4; Wiegand, 1953–4]. He also considered that mortuary houses yield valuable evidence regarding the constructional methods employed in building the houses of the living.

A recent excavation on a sandbank called the Konens Høj, in Denmark [Stürup, 1965] (fig. 52), disclosed, adjacent to an extensive settlement site, a grave which had been constructed with a paved floor and a wooden superstructure carried, apparently, on two massive timber gables connected by a ridge. Roofing was supplied by pitched timbers the bottoms of which had been held in place by rows of stones. This mortuary house, of a character closely resembling the German examples, had been burned and as a result of this had fallen in towards the middle of the paved area. Here also there was no trace of a covering barrow. Tooth enamel and pieces of bone attest a skeleton etched away by the lime-hungry sand. This single burial had been furnished with, besides other things, a copper spiral ring, an amber belt-slider and a small pot. Charcoal in the sand covering the paving gave a radio-carbon date (K–919) of 2900 ± 100 BC. Stürup compared this structure with the Wayland's Smithy pitched mortuary house [Atkinson, 1965] and its dating.

European long houses which are comparable with our earthen long barrows are, like them, of two forms: trapezoid and rectangular [Childe, 1949a; Piggott, S. (ed.), 1961b, 350, figs. 2, 3 conveniently illustrate them]. Fussell's Lodge and Willerby Wold, G.ccxxii, recall the longer trapezoid houses at Brześć Kujawski (fig. 53) [Jaźdżewski, 1938] and Biskupin [Rajewski, 1958] in Poland, Postolprty (fig. 54) [Soudsky, 1955] in Czechoslovakia and Bochum am Hillerberg, in Germany [Brandt & Beck, 1954], which were built in palisade trenches. Shorter houses of the same character at Deringsen-Ruploh [Buttler, 1938, 17, Abb. 12] and Trebus [Radig, 1930, 124, Abb. 54] in Germany should also be taken into consideration. This last may be an incompletely excavated longer house. Giants' Hills, Skendleby, the enclosure of which was nearly rectangular but slightly tapering, has its counterpart in a trapezoid house, built of posts set into sockets, recently examined at Yonne-et-Cure (fig. 56) in France [Carré, Dousson & Poulain, 1958].

The returned façade of the Nutbane structure in its final form and the absence of timber delimitation to the mound recall the compound plans of bedding trench and post-socket which characterize such houses as at Sittard in Holland (Building 45, Modderman, 1958–9; Waterbolk, 1958–9) and Bylany in Czechoslovakia [Soudsky, 1962]. Pronouncedly rectangular house counterparts for the Wor Barrow, for example, have been recorded at Aichbühl [Schmidt, 1930; 1936; Childe, 1949b, 80, fig. 2 and pl. XXII] and Köln-Lindental [Buttler & Haberey, 1936, Bei. 1; Taf. 28, 1; 29, 12].

The earthen long barrows may well employ variations on both eastern and western traditions, perhaps basically long barrows with single graves and stone-chambered tombs with collective burials.

CONTINUITY

When the first concepts of the British Neolithic emerged, via its pottery, R. A. Smith

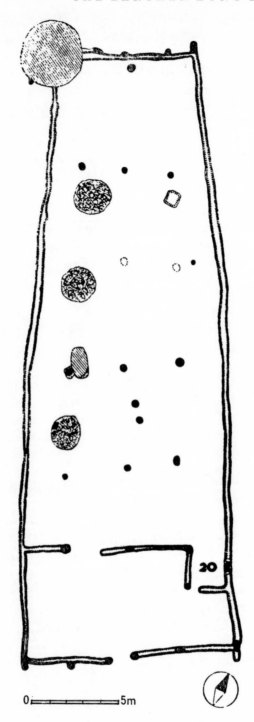

54. Plan of a trapezoid long house at Postolprty, Czechoslovakia

0 ⊨⊨⊨⊨⊨⊨ 5m

[1910] followed by Kendrick [1925, 13–14] defined a duality of wares and hinted at an origin in north-eastern Europe for the second category. Leeds [1927, 459] coined the eponymous term 'Windmill Hill' for that pottery and gave precision to Menghin's [1925, 717–18] 'Grimston- and Peterborough-keramik'. Stuart Piggott [1931], following Childe [1925, 289; 1931], was able to expand the basic theories with material from the causewayed camp excavations [Curwen, 1930]. In the post-war period, the Windmill Hill culture and the Peterborough culture were still seen as separate groups [Piggott, S., 1954, 95], although two complicating elements had emerged, namely Grooved Ware [Warren et al., 1936, 191] and Ebbsfleet Ware [Burchell & Piggott, 1939]. These, and the Peterborough culture, were grouped with others as the Secondary Neolithic Cultures [Piggott, S., 1954, 279]. Peterborough pottery was considered as intrusive to England, and settlement from the Baltic lands was envisaged [Piggott, S., 1954, 315]; the remainder were thought of as ultimately Mesolithic, as suggested by Clarke [1932, 12].

Examination of the pottery from Whiteleaf [Childe & Smith, 1954] emphasized that the identities of 'Western' Neolithic required reconsideration. I. F. Smith subsequently showed (unpublished thesis, University of London, 1956) that certain 'Secondary Neolithic' wares formed a sequence, namely Ebbsfleet, Mortlake and Fengate in that order [Childe, 1957, 332; Smith, I. F., 1966]. They had developed from evolved Windmill Hill pottery of the Abingdon and Mildenhall series [Piggott, S., 1962a, 32] with influences from other styles, in particular Beakers in the later stages. Chronological inferences in the manner of Abercromby [1912, I, 85] were not made.

Longworth [1961] recently has been able to demonstrate in detail what had long been generally suspected [Abercromby, 1912, II, 9; Piggott, S., 1938, 91; Fox, 1952, 40; Ashbee, 1960, 126, 154], that the Bronze Age collared urns developed from the Peterborough ceramic tradition, with contributions from other sources. It follows *sine dubio* that there is established ceramic continuity from the Earlier Neolithic to the Middle Bronze Age. This theme has, recently, been discussed in detail by Clark [1966].

Side by side with the ceramic continuity a series of traits of distinctively Neolithic character, sometimes deriving directly from earthen long barrows, can be seen in the round barrows of the Bronze Age. There is also the contiguity of long and round barrows as well as coincidence of distribution, not only of these but also of other monuments, both of which factors demonstrate continuity of social tradition [Ashbee, 1960, 173].

The impact of Beaker communities in the Middle Neolithic phase, demonstrated by Stuart Piggott [1954, 374] in respect of the Essex coast, is supported by the appearance of a bell-beaker sherd in the mound of the Giants' Hills long barrow [Phillips, 1936, 53, pl. xxvii, fig. 2]. Case [1959, 44] has contended that bead-rimmed beakers, comparable to the heavy rims of Abingdon–Whitehawk–Mildenhall Neolithic pottery, also illustrate this thesis.

Two long barrows, Thickthorn Down and Wilsford 34, may have been raised to house the beaker graves set along their axes; they could conveniently be called

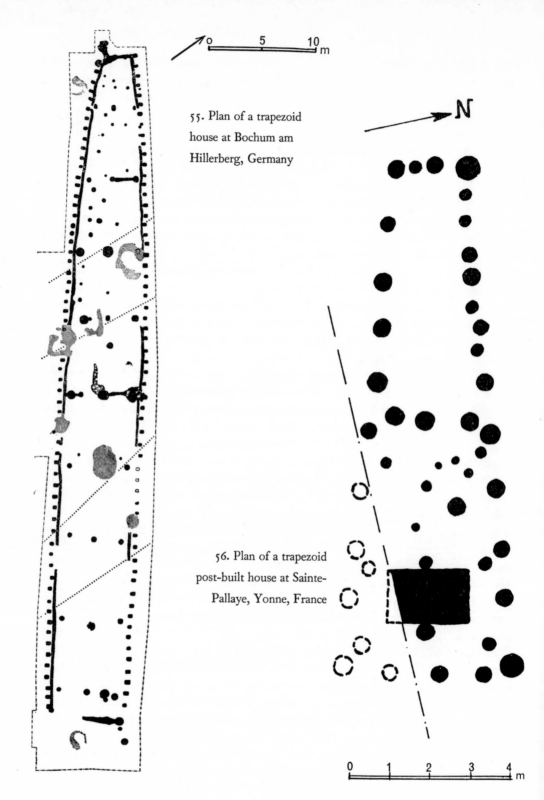

55. Plan of a trapezoid
house at Bochum am
Hillerberg, Germany

56. Plan of a trapezoid
post-built house at Sainte-
Pallaye, Yonne, France

'over-grave' long barrows (Appendix 11, a). A series of small and oval long barrows (Appendix 11, b) [Colt Hoare, 1810, 22 (XII, Long Barrow no. 2); Cunnington, M. E., 1914, 411], embody this principle of dug-in axial burials. Two small wedge-shaped mounds in the Oakley Down round barrow cemetery are good examples [Colt Hoare, 1810, 241–2, pl. XXXIII, 4; Crawford, 1928, 174–83; Grinsell, 1959, pl. 11, B]. A development might be the enditched multiples of round barrows, particularly those of the bell and disc series (Appendix 11, c). Round barrows with causewayed ditches (Appendix 12) which are intimately associated with beaker burials, may also be associated with or derived from inturned-end or causewayed long barrow ditches such as those flanking Wayland's Smithy 1 or round Wor Barrow. In the same way penannular round barrow ditches [Grinsell, 1941, 106, App. VIII; Case, 1952] could be connected with the restricted series of U-ditched long barrows.

All the techniques and types of timber circles found round and beneath round barrows [Ashbee, 1957b] were present in the timber architecture of the long barrows. For example, the palisades round the Letterston turf barrows which contained collared urns [Savory, 1948] stood in trenches like that of the Fussell's Lodge enclosure. It is perhaps more than coincidence that the majority of such circles are associated with cinerary urns.

Sherds of pottery, charcoal, struck flints and artifacts, as well as bones, apparently discarded, have been found incorporated in some round barrows [Bateman, 1848, 14; 1861, 298; Greenwell, 1877, 10–11; Ashbee, 1957a, 157, fn. 1]. This could be a survival of the phenomenon noted by Phillips [1936, 57, 87] and others in the earthen long barrows.

Pitched mortuary houses resembling the collapsed structures in earthen long barrows were explored beneath two round barrows at Wrangworthy Cross, Devon [Radford & Rogers, 1947; Ashbee, 1960, 54]. An elaborate pitched mortuary house lay beneath a great Saxo-Thuringen round barrow at Leubingen [Höfer, 1906, Taf. 1; 9, fig. 4; 10, fig. 5; Ó Ríordáin, 1937, 204; Childe, 1929, 242–4; 1957, 199–202] and a structure beneath a similar great barrow at Helmsdorf [Grössler, 1907, Taf. III] should also be considered in this context. Bronzes may link this series with the British continuum [Ó Ríordáin, 1937, 300; Childe, 1957, 200; Coghlan & Case, 1957, 103; Evans, J. D., 1958, 66, fn.; Piggott, S., 1963, 80; Campbell, Scott & Piggott, 1960–61, 58]. Pitched structures have also been alleged beneath Corded Ware barrows at Sarmenstorf in Switzerland [Reinerth, 1928, 202–20; Kersten, 1936, 79, Abb. 20, 22].

Material in mounds, grave furniture and burials, in some round barrows are of pronouncedly 'Neolithic' character (Appendix 13) and would suggest fusion and continuity of the native elements as well as a period of impact. Such evidence is sparse in the south but in the north the process can be seen in detail. Not only is Earlier Neolithic material in mounds and with burials, but disarticulated bones, perhaps in collapsed structures, are regularly found. These seem to have led on the one hand to a multiple articulated Beaker-Food-vessel rite and on the other to disarticulated single burial. The distinctive Later Neolithic burials of the Duggleby Group (Appendix 13) also

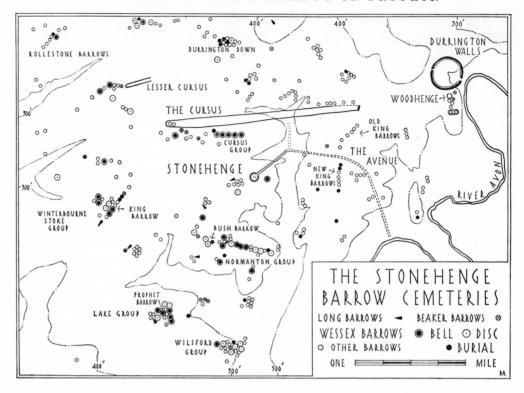

57. Long barrows and successive barrows around Stonehenge

appear to have developed in this region. These arguments have been developed in part by Manby [1963, 195]. The Neolithic round barrow at Pitnacree, in Scotland [Coles & Simpson, 1965] which may have covered a pitched mortuary house seems also to conform to this pattern.

Further evidence of continuity of tradition from the Early Neolithic into the Bronze Age [Clark, 1966, fig. 3] is to be seen in the regular association of long and round barrows (fig. 57). Outstanding examples of this are the Dorset Ridgway Group, twelve miles in length and bracketed by bank barrows [Prehistoric Society, 1962, 24], the small mounds by, and the round barrow cemetery adjacent to, the Wor Barrow [Pitt-Rivers, 1898, 244] and the dynastic round barrow cemeteries, such as Winterbourne Stoke, Lake and Normanton, developing from long barrows, in the Stonehenge region [Piggott, S., 1951, fig. 61; Ashbee, 1960, 33]. Round cairns also cluster round the stone-chambered long barrow at Burn Ground [Grimes, 1960, 45, fig. 18] and elsewhere in Gloucestershire [O'Neil & Grinsell, 1961, 15, figs. 1, 31, 63].

Groups of earthen long barrows have a causewayed camp amongst or by them in almost every instance [Crawford, 1932; Piggott, S., 1935, 121] while round barrows can be clearly shown to cluster round henges [Ashbee, 1960, 32, 130; RCHM, 1960,

25, fig. 2]. Indeed, in certain areas [Dorset: Grinsell, 1959, maps 1–4; Wiltshire: Grinsell, 1957, maps II–V] it is reasonable to suggest that henges developed from the causewayed camps (Appendix 14), with which they share factors of siting, and that groups of long and round barrows, causewayed camps, henges and other monuments were entities which developed during the third and second millennia BC [Ashbee, 1960, 133]. Robin Hood's Ball, with Stonehenge and its Avenue, the Cursus, Woodhenge and Durrington Walls, and Windmill Hill with Avebury, the Avenue and Sanctuary and Silbury Hill, together with their barrows, would be the premier examples of such continuing complexes.

It is no chance coincidence that certain of the physiographic and apparently territorial regions that emerged by the Iron Age [Hawkes, C. F. C., 1959, 172; Rivet, 1962] coincide with what were nodal regions at an earlier time. For example, the focus at Stonehenge could have changed to Vespasian's Camp or at Avebury to Oldbury. The factors determining the changes from causewayed camp to henge, from henge to hill fort, may remain obscure, but it seems undeniable that Roman conquest and subsequent political settlement determined moves such as from Maiden Castle to Dorchester [Wheeler, 1943, 66].

Much, both tangible and intangible, continued through the palimpsest of prehistory to Roman times and beyond [Piggott, S., 1941; Greenfield, 1963]. That the earthen long barrows were throughout of significance in the countryside is attested by much later secondary burials (Appendix 7 (4)) and the later prehistoric wares followed by Roman coins, pottery and other objects from them [Piggott, S., 1962a, 55; Ashbee, 1966]. It seems that our prehistoric past has determined more of later Britain than is normally conceded [Jones, 1961].

Chapter 8

IN CONCLUSION

From the foregoing review of our knowledge of earthen long barrows certain positive indications, as well as a series of problems, obtrude. The latter range from those which further excavation of selected sites might in part resolve, to others which the present limitations of archaeological evidence make it impossible to solve.

Perhaps the most significant advance in our appreciation of Neolithic structures has been the recognition of mortuary houses, pitched and otherwise. The report on the excavation of the burned and collapsed Nutbane building has thrown new light on earlier narratives concerning sites in the north. These can now clearly be seen as having within them structures which had burned and collapsèd with incidental burning of the burials.

Careful examination of what at first appeared as a tumbled mass of stones over the Wayland's Smithy I burials revealed the remains of a structure such as could be reconstructed from the hitherto unexplained amorphous heaps of flints, stones and turf found at the heart of earthen long barrows in both south and north. Here the underlying pits, similar in general outline to those beneath many earthen long barrows, were seen originally to have held split trunks, the uprights of the structure. This is not to say that all mortuary houses were identical, but there seems to be a recognizable uniformity of principle. Similarly, many of the barrow mounds which now appear as arcuate slopes were once timber-retained, often with impressive façades. It can also be seen that there are two forms of enclosure, the trapezoid and the rectangular, the first with and without entrances, while other mounds were without timber-work at all.

In spite of general affinities with other long mounds and cairns, earthen long barrows are clearly a distinct class, when structure is considered. Nowhere is this clearer than at Wayland's Smithy, where the initial phase, the composite monument with pitched mortuary house, was succeeded by a stone-chambered tomb of different plan. The earlier monument must, however, have had a specific significance to those who built the later.

The only series of stone-chambers in tombs that resembles, in a general sense, the pitched mortuary houses is that of the variously named group, seen predominantly in Northern Ireland. One of these seems to have had a timber roof and was burned in a manner reminiscent of those in Yorkshire. This association is substantiated by Case's [1963, 4, 8] comparison of the developing Early and Middle Neolithic Irish pottery styles with those of Yorkshire. It remains to stress that, on the basis of structure and in spite of numerous similarities, no wholly satisfactory origin can be traced among either stone-chambered or other long barrows or the houses of the period. They can only be considered as a component of the widespread European tradition of long tombs and houses (fig. 58), the interrelationships of which remain to be defined with precision.

The modes of burial are mainly those of disarticulated bones or contracted articulated skeletons. Disarticulated burial appears to be the basic rite, but articulated skeletons appear too frequently to be dismissed as exceptional. Two disparate traditions, first of the deposition of a mass of bones and secondly of individual interment, seem to be combined here. Contact with a single-grave tradition does seem to have taken place in Middle Neolithic times, or perhaps the incidence of this rite, sometimes side by side with assemblages of disarticulated bones, had a particular social significance? On the other hand, the mixed rite may indicate that there was a predetermined day for entombment in any given long barrow. By that day some bodies would have had so much less time to become disarticulated through decomposition than others. The removal of 'cremations in situ' from the picture has underlined the similarities of rite, as well as structure, between north and south. The reasons for the burning of the mortuary houses remain obscure; although the masses of bones and the structural character of the mortuary houses point to simultaneous burial of bones brought from another place, evidence for procedure is lacking.

A feature of the series is the geographically restricted distribution of the rectangular mounds. This limited class, with partly or wholly surrounding ditches, represents a departure from the quite uniform and widespread trapezoidal plan with flanking ditches. Does this represent the impact of an alien tradition? For in this small series there lies, on the one hand affinity with the long mortuary enclosures, and on the other precursors for a later series of round barrows. This particular problem, the relationships of the differing tomb forms, might in some measure be resolved by a planned series of C.14 dates, for the changes may well have been rapid. Size is another question that might also be investigated in this manner, since it could determine whether the one great barrow of each group was in fact the earliest.

Although the direct associations of earthen long barrows with the Neolithic cultural entity which includes causewayed camps, leaf-shaped arrowheads, pottery and, in its later stages, cursus monuments and flint-mines, are quite tenuous [Atkinson, 1964b, 8], distributional considerations would suggest a firm relationship. For not only does

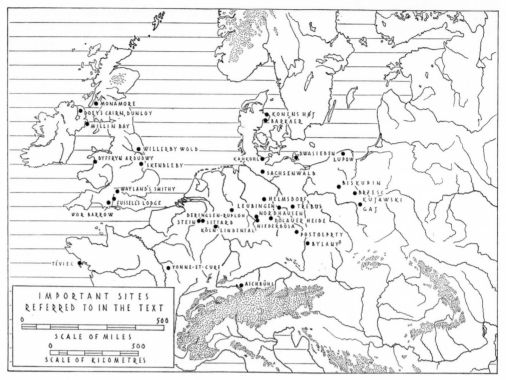

58. Important sites mentioned in the text

one causewayed camp underlie a bank barrow, but each of the southern long barrow groups has one or more associated with it. There are long barrows set into the Dorset Cursus and associated with the Stonehenge Cursus, both in a manner contrary to the local pattern of orientation.

While consideration of the work entailed in earthen long barrow construction might suggest that Neolithic society was stratified and thus organized and directed, we have no real evidence of the social units that were buried in them. Family 'vaults' seem a likely interpretation, and the number of males, females and children buried at Fussell's Lodge would seem to illustrate this idea. However, the groups at Wor Barrow and Nutbane apparently indicate something different. Indeed, these well defined earthen long barrow groups might well have been dynastic and thus, in view of our incomplete knowledge, any attempts to estimate population groups over the long period of time involved would be hazardous in the extreme. There is, too, the problem of the significance of the exiguous fragments of pottery and regularly broken animal bones with the burials from the barrows—funeral and other subsequent feasts seems the only explanation.

Earthen long barrows emerge as carefully planned and often complex structures. It seems likely that their building involved a series of undertakings spread over a considerable period of time. In the more complex examples, the first stage might be an enclosure delimited by timber, sods, stones or ditch. Then there would be the construction of a pitched mortuary house of the Wayland's Smithy variety or a structure of sods and stone as at Skendleby, perhaps with a façade, the absence of which might signify non-completion. Into this, in certain circumstances, might be put corpses which had perhaps lain in the enclosure, or round which the mortuary house might have been built. More frequently bones were exhumed, or brought from another place where they had been exposed, and stacked within the confines of the mortuary house. The filling in of the enclosure with the spoil dug from the ditches, or the raising of a regular mound, would have been the final act.

These structures used materials which, down the centuries, have been particularly susceptible to the decay and collapse which have given them their 'earthen' character. A view has emerged but our knowledge of them is sparse on account of the paucity of modern intensive excavations. Although the resources needed for a comprehensive examination of such a monument exceed those of all but the wealthiest of institutions, the sympathetic excavation of selected earthen long barrows, carried out with the problems of weathering and collapsed structure in mind, is a research priority.

Appendix 1

PRINCIPAL EARTHEN LONG BARROW LITERATURE
EARLY WORKS

SOUTHERN REGION

(a) WILLIAM STUKELEY, *Stonehenge: A Temple restored to the British Druids*, 1740; *Abury: A Temple of the British Druids*, 1743. Use of the term 'long barrow', which barrow he supposed 'The Archdruids who lived at Radfin' (*Stonehenge*, p. 38) and a distinction between 'pyriform barrows . . . some compos'd of earth' and 'others made of stones set upright in that form' (*Abury*, p. 45).

(b) SIR RICHARD COLT HOARE, *The History of Ancient Wiltshire*, Part I, 1810. Accounts of the examination of sixteen earthen long barrows, all but one on the western part of Salisbury Plain. Observations regarding earthen long barrows, in this volume and Part II as well as in the *History of Modern Wiltshire*, are based directly upon his work in the field.

(c) CHARLES WARNE, *The Celtic Tumuli of Dorset*, 1866. He wrote presciently of the difficulties attendant upon earthen long barrow excavation.

(d) JOHN THURNAM, 'Ancient British Barrows, especially those of Wiltshire and the adjoining Counties' (Part I, Long Barrows), *Archaeologia*, XLII, 169–244. He separates unchambered and chambered long barrows and discusses their form and content. This account is based upon all that had been undertaken up to that time together with the results of Thurnam's own excavations.

(e) LIEUTENANT-GENERAL A. H. PITT-RIVERS, *Excavations in Cranborne Chase*, IV (1898), 58–100. The excavation of the Wor Barrow in 1893.

(f) M. E. CUNNINGTON, 'List of the Long Barrows of Wiltshire', *Wiltshire Archaeological Magazine*, XXXVIII (1914), 379–414. A list of earthen and chambered long barrows which utilizes the catalogue compiled by Thurnam of his collection of skulls, now housed in the Museum of Archaeology and Ethnology, Downing Street, Cambridge.

NORTHERN REGION

(a) THOMAS BATEMAN, *Ten Years' Diggings in Celtic & Saxon Grave Hills in the Counties of Derby, Stafford and York, from 1848 to 1858* (1861). Notice of three Yorkshire long barrows contributed by James Ruddock.

(b) WILLIAM GREENWELL, *British Barrows* (1877). Accounts (pp. 484–510; 550–6) of the excavation of nine earthen long barrows in Yorkshire and one in Westmorland.

(c) J. R. MORTIMER, *Forty Years' Researches in British and Saxon Burial Mounds of East Yorkshire* (1905). Contains details of the Hanging Grimston and Helperthorpe earthen long barrows.

Appendix 2

MODERN LITERATURE LISTING
EARTHEN LONG BARROWS

(Numbers refer to list of groups given on page 8)

(1) Dorset Ridgeway and Coast   (2) Cranborne Chase
Dorset Barrows, 77–84 [Grinsell, 1959]

(3) Hampshire Uplands
Proceedings of the Hampshire Field Club and Archaeological Society, XIV, 197–206 [Grinsell, 1939]

(4) Salisbury Plain East (Stonehenge)   (5) Salisbury Plain West   (6) North Wiltshire (Avebury) and Berkshire Downs
Victoria County History of Wiltshire I, Pt I, 137–46 [Grinsell, 1957]
(for Groups 1–6 see also Map of Neolithic Wessex [Crawford, 1932])

(7) Sussex and Kent
(a) *Sussex Archaeological Collections*, LXIII, 157–65 [Toms, 1922]
(b) The Long Barrows and Megaliths in the area covered by Sheet 12 of the ¼-inch Map (Kent, Surrey and Sussex) [Crawford, 1924]
(c) *Sussex Archaeological Collections*, LXXV, 218–21 [Grinsell, 1934]
(d) *The Archaeology of Sussex*, 91–4 [Curwen, 1954]

(8) The Chilterns and East Anglia
The Archaeological Journal, CXVI, 14 [Dyer, 1961]

NORTHERN REGION

(1) Lincolnshire Wolds
(a) Map of the Trent Basin showing the Distribution of Long Barrows, Megaliths, Habitation Sites [Phillips, 1933a]
(b) *The Archaeological Journal*, LXXXIX, 174–202 [Phillips, 1933b]

(c) *Proceedings of the Prehistoric Society of East Anglia*, VII, 423 [Phillips, 1934]

(d) *Archaeologia*, LXXXV, 39, fig. 1, 43, fig 3 [Phillips, 1936]

(2) Yorkshire to Scotland (including long cairns)

(a) *Early Man in North-East Yorkshire*, 40–53 [Elgee, 1930]

(b) *The Archaeology of Yorkshire*, 40–5 [Elgee, 1933]

(c) *The Ancient Burial Mounds of England*, 217–18, 231–2 [Grinsell, 1953]

(d) *The Prehistoric Peoples of Scotland*, 12–13 [Atkinson, 1962]

(e) *The Chambered Tombs of Scotland*, I, 40–4 [Henshall, 1963]   .

Appendix 3

MODERN INTENSIVE EXCAVATIONS OF
EARTHEN LONG BARROWS

(Customary names used)

SOUTHERN REGION

(1) Dorset Ridgeway and Coast
  (a) Holdenhurst (Hampshire) [Piggott, S., 1937a]
  (b) Maiden Castle Bank Barrow [Wheeler, 1943, 20, 86]

(2) Cranborne Chase
  (a) The Wor Barrow [Pitt-Rivers, 1898, 58–100]
  (b) Thickthorn Down [Drew & Piggott, 1936]

(3) Hampshire Uplands
  (a) Badshot (Surrey) [Keiller & Piggott, 1939]
  (b) Nutbane [Morgan, 1959]

(4) Salisbury Plain East (Stonehenge)
  (a) Fussell's Lodge [Ashbee, 1958; 1966]
  (b) Tow Barrow, Wexcombe [Crawford, 1955, 107; Drew & Piggott, 1936, 78; Piggott, S., 1937b, 455]

(5) Salisbury Plain West
  Nil

(6) North Wiltshire and Berkshire Downs
  (a) Avebury 68 [Smith & Evans, 1968]
  (b) Bishop's Cannings 76 [Smith & Evans, 1968]
  (c) Windmill Hill [Ashbee & Smith, 1960]
  (d) Beneath Waylands Smithy [Atkinson, 1964a; 1965]

N.B. Two chambered Long Barrows in this group have been the subject of modern intensive excavation

   (a) Waylands Smithy [Atkinson, 1964a; 1965]
   (b) West Kennet [Piggott, S., 1962a]

(7) Sussex and Kent

   (a) Julliberrie's Grave [Jessup, 1937; 1939]

(8) The Chilterns and East Anglia

   (a) Whiteleaf [Childe & Smith, 1954]
   (b) Therfield Heath [Phillips, 1935]
   (c) West Rudham [Hogg, 1940]

NORTHERN REGION

(1) Lincolnshire Wolds

   (a) Giants' Hills, Skendleby [Phillips, 1936]

(2) Yorkshire

   (a) Bradley Moor (a long cairn) [Raistrick, 1931; Butterfield, 1939]
   (b) Seamer Moor (possibly a round barrow) [Vatcher, 1961b]
   (c) Willerby Wold [Manby, 1963]
   (d) East Heslerton [Vatcher, 1965]

(3) Northumberland

   (a) Bellshiel Law (a long cairn) [Newbigin, 1936]

(4) Scotland
   (a) Mutiny Stones, Berwickshire (a long cairn) [Craw, 1925]

Appendix 4

PIONEER AND EARLY EXTENSIVE DIGGING INTO EARTHEN LONG BARROWS

(References are to published basic and informative accounts; numbers when given follow L. V. Grinsell's list for appropriate areas. NW denotes the O.S. Map of Neolithic Wessex [Crawford, 1932] number)

SOUTHERN REGION

(1) Dorset Ridgeway and Coast (some long barrows in this group are or were stone-chambered)
    (a) Bradford Peverell II. (NW 153) [Acland, 1916, 42]
    (b) Church Knowle II. (perhaps an oval or bell-barrow) [Austen, 1857, 113–15; Warne, 1866, no. 90]

(2) Cranborne Chase
    (a) Chettle I. (NW 161) [Warne, 1866, 2; Shipp & Hodson, 1868, 567]
    (b) Chettle II. (NW 160) [Warne, 1866, 1; Banks, 1900, 144]
    (c) Gillingham I. (NW 132) [Quidam, 1855, 364; Warne, 1866, no. 84; Shipp & Hodson, 1868, 615n, 661; Farrar, 1952, 113; 1956, 96]
    (d) Tarrant Launceston I. (NW 157) [Warne, 1866, Communications from Personal Friends, no. 27]
    (e) Tarrant Rawston I. (NW 156) [Richardson, 1897, lxxxiii, 1]
    (f) Verwood. [Warne, 1866, 7, Communications from Personal Friends, no. 19; Thurnam, 1870, 414; Evans, J., 1897, 377; Smith, R. A., 1927, 85; Piggott, S., 1954, 58, 118]

(3) Hampshire Uplands
    (a) Chute I. [Passmore, 1942, 100]
    (b) Lamborough. (NW 44) [Grinsell, 1938, 15; 1939, 202–3–4]
    (c) Portsdown. [Grinsell, 1938, 16; 1939, 206]

(4) Salisbury Plain East (Stonehenge)
    (a) Amesbury 14. (NW 64) [Thurnam, 1868, 180; Cunnington, M. E., 1914, 382]

(b) Amesbury 42. (NW 69) [Thurnam, 1868, 180, 182: Cunnington, M. E., 1914, 383]

(c) Figheldean 31. (NW 82) [Thurnam, 1867, 41–80; 1868, 180, 184, 197–8; Abercromby, 1912, 1, pl. v, 5; Cunnington, M. E., 1914, 390]

(d) Fittleton 5. (NW 76) [Thurnam, 1868, 180; Cunnington, W., 1895, 172; Cunnington, M. E., 1914, 391, 408]

(e) Milton Lilbourne 7. (NW 35) [Thurnam, 1865b, 170; 1868, 180, 182, 194; 1869, 47; Cunnington, M. E., 1914, 395]

(f) Netheravon 6. (NW 81) [Thurnam, 1868, 180; Cunnington, M. E., 1914, 395]

(g) Tidcombe & Fosbury 1. [Daniel, 1950, 228–9]

(h) Wilsford (South) 30. (NW 62) [Cunnington, M. E., 1914, 405]

(i) Wilsford (South) 34. (NW 65) [Thurnam, 1868, 196, 198; Long, 1876, 93, fn; Abercromby, 1912, 1, pl. v, 8; Cunnington, M. E., 1914, 405]

(j) Winterbourne Stoke 1. (NW 66) [Thurnam, 1865a, 140; 1868, 180, 194, 197; 1870, 379, 420; Cunnington, M. E., 1914, 407]

(k) Winterbourne Stoke 53. [Colt Hoare, 1810, 117]

(5) Salisbury Plain West

(a) Boyton 1. (NW 99) [Colt Hoare, 1810, 102]

(b) Bratton 1. (NW 109) [Colt Hoare, 1810, 102]

(c) Edington 7. (NW 108) [Thurnam, 1868, 180, 194–5; Piggott, S., 1931, 142]

(d) Heytesbury 1. (NW 92) [Colt Hoare, 1810, 87; Thurnam, 1865a, 472; 1868, 180, 183; Piggott, S., 1954, 57]

(e) Heytesbury 4. (NW 103) [Colt Hoare, 1810, 71]

(f) Knook 2. (NW 94) [Colt Hoare, 1810, 83; Thurnam, 1868, 180]

(g) Knook 5. (NW 93) [Colt Hoare, 1810, 86]

(h) Maiden Bradley 8a. [Colt Hoare, 1810, 47]

(i) Norton Bavant 13. (NW 104) [Thurnam, 1867, 71; 1868, 180, 182, 184, 194–5]

(j) Sherrington 1. (NW 98) [Colt Hoare, 1810, 100]

(k) Stockton 1. (NW 96) [Colt Hoare, 1810, 107]

(l) Tilshead 1. (NW 89) [Thurnam, 1870, 297]

(m) Tilshead 2. (NW 87) [Colt Hoare, 1810, 90; Thurnam, 1867, 65; 1868, 175 180, 191–2; 1872, 341]

(n) Tilshead 4. (NW 86) [Colt Hoare, 1810, 91]

(o) Tilshead 5. (NW 88) [Colt Hoare, 1810, 91; Thurnam, 1867, 67; 1868, 182, 184, 196; Cunnington, M. E., 1914, 402]

(p) Tilshead 7. (NW 85) [Thurnam, 1865a, 146; 1868, 180, 184; Cunnington, M. E., 1914, 403]

(q) Warminster 1. (NW 106) [Colt Hoare, 1810, 65]

(r) Warminster 6. (NW 107) [Colt Hoare, 1810, 66; Thurnam, 1868, 180]

(s) Warminster 14. (NW 101) [Colt Hoare, 1810, 72]

(t) Wilsford (North) 3. (NW 84) [Thurnam, 1868, 180]

(6) North Wiltshire (Avebury) and Berkshire Downs

Most long barrows in this group are, or appear to have been, chambered. The status of some of the sites below is uncertain, but it seems that some were earthen although incorporating sarsen stones.

    (a) Bishop's Cannings 65. (NW 27) [Thurnam, 1860, 324; Passmore,1922, 50]
    (b) Bishop's Cannings 76. (NW 24) [Thurnam, 1868, 180]
    (c) Bishop's Cannings 91. (NW 29) [Thurnam, 1868, 180; Passmore, 1922, 49]
    (d) Calne-Cherhill. (NW 25) [Smith, A. C., 1884, 50]
    (e) Heddington 3. (NW 26) [Cunnington, B. H., 1909]

(7) Sussex and Kent

    (a) Alfriston, Long Burgh [Gomme (ed.), 1886, 311, note 17; Toms, 1922, 161]
    (b) Brighton [Bramwell, 1938]
    (c) Julliberrie's Grave, Chilham [Nichols, 1822, IV, 96; re-excavation, Jessup, 1937, 1939]
    (d) Piddinghoe [Toms, 1922, 159–60]

(8) The Chilterns and East Anglia

    (a) Therfield Heath [Fox, 1923, 11; re-excavation, Phillips, 1935]

NORTHERN REGION

(1) Lincolnshire Wolds

    (a) Spellow Hills [Phillips, 1933b, 193–4]

(2) Yorkshire (roman numerals refer to accounts in Greenwell, 1877)

    (a) Cropton (N. Riding) [Bateman, 1861, 211]
    (b) Dinnington (W. Riding) [Thurnam, 1868, 171, fn; Phillips, 1933a, 18]
    (c) Ebberston (N. Riding) Scamridge, G.CCXXI.
    (d) Gilling (N. Riding), G.CCXXXIII
    (e) Hanging Grimston [Mortimer, 1905, 102–5]
    (f) Helperthorpe [Mortimer, 1905, 333–5]
    (g) Heslerton (E. Riding) [Bateman, 1861, 230; Greenwell, 1877, 143, 488–9]
    (h) Kilburn (N. Riding) Wass Moor, G.CCXXV
    (i) Kilham (E. Riding), G.CCXXXIV
    (j) Market Weighton (E. Riding), G.CCXXVI
    (k) Over Silton (N. Riding) Kepwick Moor, G.CCXXVII
    (l) Pickering, 4 miles N.W. from (N. Riding) [Bateman, 1861, 227–8]
    (m) Rudstone (E. Riding), G.CCXXIV (G.LXVI can now be seen as part of a cursus. [Dymond, 1966])
    (n) Seamer Moor (N. Riding) [Londesborough, 1848; re-excavation, Vatcher, 1961b]
    (o) Willerby (E. Riding), G.CCXXII [re-excavation, Manby, 1963]
    (p) Westow (E. Riding), G.CCXXIII

(3) Westmorland

    (a) Crosby Garrett, Raiset Pike, G.CCXXVIII

Appendix 5

STRUCTURAL FEATURES

(Observation of more than one characteristic where possible)

(1) Earthen Long Barrows: Modern Excavation

NAME OF LONG BARROW	Entranced Enclosures	Enclosures	Façades	Aisled Building	Light Post Structure	Heaped or Stacked Mounds only	Incorporation of Large stones	Composite Stone and earthen structure	Hurdle divisions within mound	Flanking Ditches	U-Ditches	Surrounding Ditches	Mortuary Houses (App. 6)
Avebury 68	–	–	–	–	–	–	★	–	★	★	–	–	–
Badshot	–	–	–	–	★	–	–	–	–	★	–	–	–
Bishop's Cannings 76	–	–	–	–	–	–	–	–	★	★	–	–	–
Fussell's Lodge	★	–	–	–	★	–	–	–	–	★	–	–	★
Giants' Hills, Skendleby	–	★	★	–	★	–	★	–	★	–	–	★	★
Heddington 3	–	–	★	–	–	–	–	–	–	★	–	–	★

NAME OF LONG BARROW	Entranced Enclosures	Enclosures	Façades	Aisled Building	Light Post Structure	Heaped or Stacked Mounds only	Incorporation of Large stones	Composite Stone and earthen structure	Hurdle divisions within mound	Flanking Ditches	U-Ditches	Surrounding Ditches	Mortuary Houses (App. 6)
Holdenhurst	-	-	-	-	-	★	★	-	-	-	★	-	-
Julliberrie's Grave	-	-	-	-	-	★	-	-	-	-	?	-	-
Maiden Castle (bank barrow)	-	-	★	-	-	-	-	-	-	★	-	-	-
Nutbane	-	★	★	★	-	-	-	-	-	★	-	-	★
Therfield Heath	-	-	-	-	-	★	-	-	-	-	-	★	?
Thickthorn	-	-	-	-	★	-	-	-	-	-	★	-	★
Wayland's Smithy I	★	-	-	-	★	-	-	★	-	★	-	-	★
West Rudham	-	-	-	-	-	★	-	-	-	-	-	★	-
Whiteleaf	-	-	-	-	★	-	-	-	-	-	?	-	★
Windmill Hill, Horslip Barrow	-	-	-	-	-	-	-	-	-	★	-	-	-
Willerby Wold	-	★	★	-	-	-	-	-	-	★	-	-	★
Wor Barrow	★	-	-	-	-	-	★	-	-	-	-	★	★

(2) Earthen Long Barrows: Early Digging

NAME OF LONG BARROW SOUTHERN REGION	Observation of soils and heaped construction	Possible bedding trenches	Possible enclosures	Composite stone and earthen structure	Standing and large stones	Façade	Stone Structure	Flanking Ditches	Mortuary Houses (App. 6)
Boyton 1	–	–	–	–	★	–	–	–	★
Bratton 1	★	–	–	–	–	–	–	–	–
Figheldean 31	★	–	–	–	–	–	–	–	–
Heytesbury 1 (Boles Barrow)	★	–	–	–	★	–	–	–	★
Heytesbury 4	★	–	–	–	–	–	–	★	★
Knook 5	★	–	–	–	–	–	–	★	★
Norton Bavant 13	★	–	–	–	–	–	–	★	★
Sherrington 1	★	–	–	–	–	–	–	–	–
Tarrant Launceston 1	★	–	–	–	–	–	–	–	–
Tilshead 2	★	–	–	–	–	–	–	★	★
Tilshead 4	★	–	–	–	–	–	–	★	–
Tilshead 5	★	–	–	–	–	–	–	★	–
Tilshead 7	★	–	–	–	–	–	–	★	–
Warminster 1	★	–	–	–	★	–	–	–	★
Warminster 14	★	–	–	–	–	–	–	–	–

NAME OF LONG BARROW NORTHERN REGION	Observation of soils and heaped construction	Possible bedding trenches	Possible enclosures	Composite stone and earthen structure	Standing and large stones	Façade	Stone Structure	Flanking Ditches	Mortuary Houses (App. 6)
Crosby Garrett, G.ccxxviii	–	★	–	–	★	–	★	–	★
Gilling, G.ccxxxiii	–	–	★	★	–	–	★	–	–
Hanging Grimston	–	–	–	–	–	★	–	–	★
Helperthorpe	–	–	–	–	–	–	–	–	★
Kilburn, G.ccxxv	–	–	★	★	–	–	★	–	★
Kilham, G.ccxxxiv	–	★	★	–	–	–	–	–	★
Market Weighton, G.ccxxvi	–	★	–	–	–	–	–	–	★
Rudstone, G.ccxxiv	–	★	–	–	–	–	–	–	★
Westow, G.ccxxiii	–	★	–	–	–	–	–	–	★

(3) Long Cairn Structure

NAME OF LONG CAIRN	Cists	Standing and large stones	Walling	Rock-cut pit	Composite Structure	Boulder demarcation	Upright slabs in cairn
Bellshiel Law	–	–	–	★	–	★	–
Bradley Moor	★	★	–	–	–	–	–
Caverton Hillhead	–	–	–	–	★	–	–
Cropton	★	–	–	–	★	–	–
Great Ayton Moor	★	–	–	–	–	–	–
Hill of Foulzie	★	–	–	–	–	–	–
Knapperty Hillock	★	–	–	–	–	–	–
Long Cairn	★	–	–	–	–	–	–
The Mutiny Stones	–	–	★	–	–	–	★

(4) Long Mortuary Enclosures: Features

NAME OF LONG MORTUARY ENCLOSURE	Setting-out trench for long barrow ditch	Internal post-flanked entrance	Simple entrance	Cursus aligned upon entrance	Internal Bank
Dorchester	–	–	★	★	–
Normanton	–	★	–	–	★
Wor Barrow	★	–	–	–	–

Appendix 6

DETAILS OF MORTUARY HOUSES

(Chalk blocks, flints, stones or turf over burials which, with axial pits, suggest the collapsed remains of pitched mortuary structures of the Wayland's Smithy (pitched) and allied types)

SOUTHERN REGION

(2) Cranborne Chase

Thickthorn Down

Sides of turf with vertical inner faces some 3ft in height. Chalk rubble between them, which had preserved the vertical walls, could have resulted from collapse, while the turf under the chalk and between the walls could have fallen from the roof.

Wor Barrow

Two pits bracketing the burials might well have held posts. The distal pit, 4ft long, 1·8ft wide and 3ft deep, was apparently the larger. The line of flints and the black, 'mould or turf', which was to a height of 2·3ft over the burials, could have resulted from collapse and spread beneath the weight of the mound.

(3) Hampshire Uplands

Barton Stacey, Moody's Down Northwest

The pit could well have held a post, packed about with flints, which fell in as it decayed. There was a mound of 'black soil' covering the skeleton which seems to have been close by the flints. No other post socket was found.

Nutbane

Two posts set in oval holes bracketed three of the burials. A third skeleton lay partly across the distal hole in such a position as to have been outside the space bracketed by the posts. Over the burials lay 'a thick layer of soil' and over this were chalk blocks in a manner 'not substantial enough to form more than a crust to the mound of soil'. The ridged form is suggestive, cf. Morgan, 1959, 27, section O–P.

(4) Salisbury Plain East (Stonehenge)

Fittleton 5

Disordered skeletons beneath a heap of flints at the north-eastern end are the only structural record.

Fussell's Lodge

Bracketing, axial, and partly beneath the great wedge-shaped mass of bones, two pits were found filled in with dirty chalk and weathered flint nodules resembling the covering flints. Stacked long bones protruded uniformly over the inner edge of the distal pit, while parts of a pot, crushed beneath the bones, were in its fill. This might be accounted for by the collapse of a ridged structure, borne between posts in the pits, of which the irregular cairn of weathered flint nodules was the durable remnant. Sections showed, upon each side, that layers had been ruptured and that they dipped in towards the flanks of the cairn. Decay of the vertical posts had allowed flints, and the pottery, to fall into the pits. The broken condition of most of the bones, especially the exploded skulls, might result from fall and subsequent settlement. No traces of horizontal or pitched timbers were seen among the flints although they maintained a roughly ridged form.

Tow Barrow, Wexcombe

A feature strongly suggesting an erstwhile large upright post was observed at one end of the mound.

Winterbourne Stoke 53

'We next observed a rude conical pile of large flints, imbedded in a kind of mortar made of the marly chalk dug near the spot. This rude pile was not more than four or five feet in the base, and about two feet high on the highest part, and was raised upon a floor, on which had been an intense fire, so as to make it red like brick. At first we conceived that this pile might have been raised over an interment, but after much labour in removing the greater part of it, we very unexpectedly found the remains of the Briton below, and were much astonished at seeing several pieces of burned bones intermixed with the great masses of mortar, a circumstance extremely curious, and so novel, that we know not how to decide upon the original intent of this barrow. . . . On exploring this barrow further to the east, we found two deep cists containing an immense quantity of wood ashes, and large pieces of charred wood, but no other signs of interment.'

(5) Salisbury Plain West

Boyton 1

'Mr Cunnington . . . came to a large stone, which required the strength of three men to lift out. This proved to be the top of a pyramid of loose flints, marl stone etc. which became wider near the bottom, where the base of the ridge measured more than twenty feet in length, and about ten feet in width. Beneath the ridge were found eight skeletons . . . they had been deposited on the floor of the barrow, between two excavations in the native soil, of an oval form, and seven feet apart. These oval cists or pits were about four feet long, and two and a half deep; they were cut in the chalk, and, with the skeletons, were covered with a pyramid of flints and stones.'

Heytesbury 1

'The interior parts of the barrow . . . a ridge of large stones and flints, which extended wider as the men worked downwards. At the depth of ten feet and a half, which was the base of the barrow, was a floor of flints regularly laid, and on it the remains of several human bodies deposited in no regular order . . . a great pile of stones raised length-ways along the centre of the barrow over them. This pile (in form like the ridge of a house) was afterwards covered with marl . . . the two ends being level with the plain. . . . At a subsequent period Mr Cunnington made a second attempt on this tumulus . . . a large cist close to the skeletons. . . .'

Heytesbury 4

'The second trial commenced with a section at the broad end. At the depth of eight feet, he came to the black earth, which increased in height as he proceeded, and on working about three feet further, he found it rise into the form of a circular barrow, and the soil was intermixed with large flints, marl and a few sarsen stones, which by their frequent falling down, made a continuation of the operations on this spot dangerous; he therefore made another section immediately over the conical mound of black earth, and after removing a great quantity of earth, found a large circular cist about five feet wide, and two and a half deep, cut very neatly in the chalk, which contained nothing but black earth intermixed with stones and marl. By the side of the cist, and further to the south, lay the remains of a great many human skeletons. . . .'

Knook 2

'Having proceeded to the depth of one foot, they came to a ridge of flints and large marl stones, which widened till, at the depth of five feet nine inches, they found a regular paved floor of flints which extended fifteen feet in length and six feet or more in breadth, but narrowed as it approached the east end. This floor was covered with human and animal bones, and charred wood. . . . At the west end of the pavement, which was near the centre of the barrow, was a cist of semi-circular form, neatly cut in the solid chalk . . . and containing only vegetable mould, charred wood, and two bits of bone.'

Knook 5

'. . . the usual stratum of black earth at the bottom. At the depth of about three feet from the real centre, was an entire skeleton. . . . Four feet further to the east of this skeleton were three others lying in the same direction; and a few feet west from the first skeleton was a circular cist nearly three feet deep, but containing no ashes or bones.'

Norton Bavant 13

'Above these [a confused mass of skeletons (*sic*)] the flints were larger and more numerous, and mixed with an occasional small block of sarsen stone and of the "Warminster Burr" of the upper greensand.'

Stockton 1

Three adult skeletons and one of a young person appear to have been found beneath a 'cairn' of flints while close by was a 'rectangular' pit described as having been filled with flints and marl.

Tilshead 2

'. . . three human skeletons were found lying on a pavement of flints about a foot and a half above the floor; two of them side by side, with their heads to the north, the third lying at the heads of the former, and by its side was an oval cist, cut with as much exactness in the chalk as if it had been done with a chissel (sic). It was three feet long, one foot nine inches wide, two feet and a half deep, and contained nothing but vegetable mould and charred wood. A great deal more of the pavement was examined, and nothing found but black earth, ashes, and remains of bones.'

Warminster 1

'At the south end was a sarsen stone five feet high, terminating almost to a point, and placed in an upright position. Near it lay the bones of three skeletons, which appeared to have been deposited on the south and south east of the stone, with the heads towards the east. They were all placed on a rude pavement of marl, and over them was thrown a pile of large loose stones.'

(6) North Wiltshire (Avebury) and Berkshire Downs

Calne-Cherhill

Small blocks of sarsen stone are variously described as surmounting or surrounding a large shallow grave in which were three skeletons. There appears to have been a considerable quantity of 'charcoal' and 'wood ashes' 'towards the bottom of the cavity, particularly on the north side'. A post could have been housed in Mr Cunnington's 'cist six feet eight inches in depth and about two feet wide, by three feet long'. This had in it 'no traces whatever of human remains, or of human handiwork, indeed, only a few wood ashes, and these may have fallen in accidentally'.

Heddington 3, King's Play

Two axial holes, 15ft apart, bracketed a single contracted skeleton. This was upon the ancient surface and had turf about it.

Wayland's Smithy: primary earthen long barrow

A sarsen pavement, set between two axial sockets which had held massive posts, visible as replacement material in the filling, had upon it the bones of about eleven or twelve people. They had been housed in a pitched mortuary house of stone and timber. Two great sarsen blocks pitched together formed the proximal end of a structure which was of timbers with sarsen blocks stacked against them.

(8) The Chilterns and East Anglia

Therfield Heath

'. . . at the Base of the Hill a bank of flint lying NW.–SE. the portion above described relates to portion No. 1 on ground plan. In portion No. 2 a cyst was found cut in the chalk at the base of the hill about 2 feet depth being 18 to 20 inches, containing ashes, at 6 yards farther west another cyst was found of the same description and dimensions.'

NORTHERN REGION

(1) Lincolnshire Wolds

Giant's Hills, Skendleby

The published section of the burial area (Phillips, 1936, 55, fig. 7) suggests a collapsed walled, roofed, and paved structure. Material described as 'heavy chalk filling' which was 'loosely packed' filled in the interior upon the collapse of the roof. The site of the burials was marked by a pronounced depression in the profile of the mound. Many of the bones had been crushed and broken by the fall-in of the chalk on to them. A collapsed rectangular structure associated with the 'Empty Hole' is also to be suspected (Phillips, 1936, 51, fig. 6).

(2) Yorkshire

Ebberston, G.ccxxi

'. . . loose oolitic rubble which lay in a deposit 3½ft broad, running for about 40ft east and west from the east end of the mound and along the central line of the barrow. This deposit was 3ft in height, and had above it a layer, 2ft in thickness, of earth and small stones, while it rested upon a thick stratum of yellow clay which itself was laid upon the natural surface. Under this oolitic rubble, and lying upon the clay, were found the original interments. . . . Amongst the loose rubble were deposited the remains. . . . At its west end the line of rubble expanded into a regularly constructed cairn of stones. . . .'

Hanging Grimston

The two large axial pits, that described by Mortimer as a 'chamber' and the other, ten feet removed from it, could, judging by their fillings, have held posts which eventually rotted. In the first 'many streaks of burnt and decayed matter ran obliquely—and in some places almost vertically—into the pit dwelling, reaching in places nearly the bottom'. In the second there was 'a considerable quantity of burnt wood' and in its bottom 'a small dish-shaped hole, filled entirely with burnt wood'. The snail shells (*Helix nemoralis*) found all through the filling of the first hole could be considered as further evidence of decay and collapse.

Helperthorpe

Axial pits in two groups, separated by a considerable spread of wood ashes, were the subterranean features of this barrow. The pits at the proximal end were of considerable size and could have housed commensurate vertical trunks.

Kilburn, G.ccxxv

'. . . there extended towards the north a linear deposit of burnt earth and stone, 3¼ft wide, and reaching upward from the original level of the ground to the present surface of the barrow. . . . At a distance of 11ft north from the centre of the hollow already described (L-shaped and at the proximal end, perhaps an end-façade bedding trench) was a second one, of oval form, 3½ft by 2¾ft and 2ft deep, running east-by-north and west-by-south. Like the first, it was filled with burnt earth and stones, having charcoal scattered here and there amongst the filling in. . . . Two feet from the northern edge of this hollow was a third, also oval, lying north and south, 4ft long by 3ft wide, and 3ft deep. This, like the other two, was filled with burnt matter. . . . At the northern extremity of this hollow, which was 18½ft from the highest part of the barrow, the linear deposit of burnt matter ceased, the place where it terminated being situated at a distance of 20ft from the southern edge of the first hollow. All these holes . . . were placed beneath the line of the deposit. . . . The burials were found placed as well in the lowermost layer of the burnt earth and stones, as beneath it upon the natural surface of the ground, in confused intermixture with earth, clayey sand and stones.'

Kilham, G.ccxxxiv

Two of the 'several holes, sunk beneath the natural surface', his first and third, appear to have been axial. The remainder, if his compass directions are to be literally followed, seem unrelated to these.

Market Weighton, G.ccxxvi

'. . . a deposit of chalk rubble down the mesial line of the barrow, varying from 2¾ft to 5½ft in width, and reaching in height to the present surface of the mound. This deposit, on the level of the natural surface, commenced at the extreme east end, and continued for a length of 66ft towards the west, and in it were contained, at different depths, the human and some of the animal bones. . . . Amongst the chalk-rubble, which had been subjected to the very severe action of fire, was interspersed much charcoal and other burnt matter.'

Axially and beneath this chalk rubble were five elongated pits, each described as a *transverse trench*. The bones and other objects found in them could have fallen in as replacement following upon the decay of timbers.

Over Silton, G.ccxxvii

'. . . there were some stones along the middle of the barrow over that part where the burial deposit had been made.'

Rudstone, G.ccxxiv

At least two of the 'holes', described by Greenwell, appear to have been axial. There was a burned 'mesial' deposit which appears to have been 'principally of turf, with a little chalk and no flint'.

Westow, G.ccxxiii

'The mesial deposit commenced just within the eastern verge of the mound, and continued, for a distance of about 30ft, towards the west where it ceased. . . . The beginning . . . of the burial deposit . . . consisted of a trench 4½ft wide and 3ft deep; it was filled in with burnt earth, stones and charcoal, and this reached up to the present surface of the barrow. . . . Above this trench, and beyond its limits westward, extending over the whole length of the mesial deposit which contained the burials, was a pile of oolitic slabs, arranged in a sloping fashion from the middle to the outside, forming a roof-shaped ridge, 4½ft wide, and rising to the surface of the barrow. Under this, and resting upon a pavement of flag-stones 2½ft wide, which extended from a point 12ft west of the commencement of the mesial deposit to the end of the same, for a distance of 18ft the principal parts of the burials were discovered. Below the flagstones the surface-soil was reddened by the action of fire, to a depth of about 6in. Great quantities of charcoal were found all along the outside of the burnt matter and underneath the pile of stones arranged roof-fashion. . . . Without this pile, the material of the containing mound, consisting principally of earth, was also reddened by heat, the discoloured earth sometimes running for more than a foot in an irregular fashion into the surrounding and unaltered material.'

Willerby, G.ccxxii

'Along the central line of the barrow, and commencing at the east end . . . a deposit of calcined chalk and flint, 3½ft wide, and about 4ft high, resting upon the natural surface. The evidence for burning became gradually less towards the west. At a point 30ft from the east end there was a large quantity of charcoal in lumps, placed just above the natural surface and covering some burnt bones. Beyond this point, although the deposit of chalk and flint still continued there were no signs of the action of fire. . . . The mesial deposit of chalk and flint in this mound was perfectly distinct from the general material of the barrow; and the burning, even in that part where it had been the strongest, had affected the enclosing chalk rubble and earth only in the slightest degree.'

Recent excavation has disclosed the full extent of this mortuary house and the character of its collapse (Manby, 1963, fig. 4, section I–J; fig. 5).

(3) Westmorland

Crosby Garrett, G.ccxxviii

'. . . a large slab of sandstone (*menhir*), placed transversely to the line of the barrow, and apparently forming the termination of the primary burial deposits. These had all been made along the mesial line of the mound upon the natural surface . . . and under a structure, from 3½ft to 4ft wide formed in that peculiar manner which has been observed in some other barrows. . . . In the barrow . . . what may be regarded as flues had been formed, at close intervals, by an evidently designed arrangement of the stones. These rose from the level of the deposit of bones through the over-lying limestones up to the surface of the mound.'

Appendix 7

BURIALS

1. Synopsis of Primary Burial Rites in Earthen Long Barrows

PRIMARY BURIALS IN EARTHEN LONG BARROWS / SOUTHERN REGION	Articulated Skeletons	Articulated Skeletons and Disarticulated Bones	Disarticulated Bones	Unburned Articulated and Burned Disarticulated Bones	Unburned and Burned Disarticulated Bones	Burned Articulated Skeletons and Disarticulated Bones	Burned Disarticulated Bones
(1) Dorset Ridgeway and Coast Maiden Castle bank barrow	★	–	–	–	–		–
(2) Cranborne Chase Wor Barrow	–	★	–	–	–		–
(3) Hampshire Uplands Barton Stacey Nutbane	★ ★	– –	– –	– –	– –		– –
(4) Salisbury Plain East (Stonehenge) Amesbury 14 Figheldean 31 Chute 1 Fittleton 5 Fussell's Lodge	– – – – –	– – – – –	★ ★ ★ ★ ★	– – – – –	– – – – –	– – – – –	– – – – –

PRIMARY BURIALS IN EARTHEN LONG BARROWS SOUTHERN REGION	Articulated Skeletons	Articulated Skeletons and Disarticulated Bones	Disarticulated Bones	Unburned Articulated and Burned Disarticulated Bones	Unburned and Burned Disarticulated Bones	Burned Articulated Skeletons and Disarticulated Bones	Burned Disarticulated Bones
(4) Salisbury Plain East (*continued*)							
Milton Lilbourne 7	–	–	★	–	–	–	–
Netheravon 6	–	–	★	–	–	–	–
Wexcombe Tow Barrow	–	–	★	–	–	–	–
Wilsford 30	★	–	–	–	–	–	–
Winterbourne Stoke 1	★	–	–	–	–	–	–
Winterbourne Stoke 53	–	–	–	–	–	–	★
(5) Salisbury Plain West							
Boyton 1	★	–	–	–	–	–	–
Bratton 1	–	–	–	–	–	–	★
Edington 7	–	–	★	–	–	–	–
Heytesbury 1	–	–	★	–	–	–	–
Heytesbury 4	–	–	★	–	–	–	–
Knook 2	–	–	–	–	–	–	★
Knook 5	★	–	–	–	–	–	–
Maiden Bradley 8a	–	–	★	–	–	–	–
Norton Bavant 13	–	–	★	–	–	–	–
Stockton 1	★	–	–	–	–	–	–
Tilshead 1	–	–	–	–	–	–	★
Tilshead 2	★	–	–	★	–	–	–
Tilshead 5	★	–	–	–	–	–	–
Tilshead 7	–	–	★	–	–	–	–
Warminster 1	–	–	★	–	–	–	–
Warminster 6	★	–	–	–	–	–	–
Wilsford (N) 3	–	–	★	–	–	–	–
(6) North Wiltshire (Avebury) and Berkshire Downs							
Bishop's Cannings 65	–	–	★	–	–	–	–
Calne-Cherhill	★	–	–	–	–	–	–
Heddington 3	★	–	–	–	–	–	–
Wayland's Smithy 1	–	★	–	–	–	–	–
(8) The Chilterns and East Anglia							
Therfield Heath	–	–	★	–	–	–	–
Whiteleaf	–	–	★	–	–	–	–

PRIMARY BURIALS IN EARTHEN LONG BARROWS NORTHERN REGION	Articulated Skeletons	Articulated Skeletons and Disarticulated Bones	Disarticulated Bones	Unburned Articulated and Burned Disarticulated Bones	Unburned and Burned Disarticulated Bones	Burned Articulated Skeletons and Disarticulated Bones	Burned Disarticulated Bones
(1) Lincolnshire Wolds Giants' Hills, Skendleby	–	★	–	–	–	–	–
(2) Yorkshire							
Bradley Moor	–	–	–	–	★	–	–
Cropton	★	–	–	–	–	–	–
Ebberston G.ccxxi	–	–	–	–	–	–	★
Kilburn G.ccxxv	–	–	–	–	–	–	★
Kilham G.ccxxxiv	★	–	–	–	–	–	–
Market Weighton G.ccxxvi	–	–	–	–	–	–	★
Over Silton G.ccxxvii	–	–	★	–	–	–	–
Pickering 4 miles NW from	★	–	–	–	–	–	–
Rudstone G.ccxxiv	–	–	–	–	–	–	★
Westow G.ccxxiii	–	–	–	–	–	★	–
Willerby G.ccxxii	–	–	–	–	–	–	★
(3) Westmorland Crosby Garrett G.ccxxviii	–	–	–	–	–	–	★

2. Numbers of Individuals, their Sex and Age, in Earthen Long Barrow Burials

PRIMARY BURIALS IN EARTHEN LONG BARROWS / SOUTHERN REGION	Articulated Skeletons					Articulated Skeletons and Disarticulated Bones					Disarticula[ted] Bones		
	I	A	M	F	C	I	A	M	F	C	I	A	M
(1) Dorset Ridgeway and Coast Maiden Castle bank barrow	—	—	1	—	2	—	—	—	—	—	—	—	—
(2) Cranborne Chase Wor Barrow	—	—	—	—	—	—	—	6	—	—	—	—	—
(3) Hampshire Uplands Barton Stacey	—	1	—	—	—						—	—	—
Nutbane	—	—	3	—	1	—	—	—	—	—	—	—	—
(4) Salisbury Plain East (Stonehenge)													
Amesbury 14	—	—	—	—	—	—	—	—	—	—	3	—	—
Chute 1	—	—	—	—	—	—	—	—	—	—	—	—	?
Figheldean 31	—	—	—	—	—	—	—	—	—	—	1	—	—
Fittleton 5	—	—	—	—	—	—	—	—	—	—	—	—	?
Fussell's Lodge	—	—	—	—	—	—	—	—	—	—	—	—	14
Milton Lilbourne 7	—	—	—	—	—	—	—	—	—	—	3	—	—
Netheravon 6	—	—	—	—	—	—	—	—	—	—	1	—	—
Wexcombe Tow Barrow	—	—	—	—	—	⁊	—	—	—	—	?1	—	—
Wilsford 30	4	—	—	—	—	—	—	—	—	—	—	—	—
Winterbourne Stoke 1	—	—	1	—	—	—	—	—	—	—	—	—	—
Winterbourne Stoke 53	—	—	—	—	—	—	—	—	—	—	—	—	—
(5) Salisbury Plain West													
Boyton 1	—	7	—	—	1	—	—	—	—	—	—	—	—
Bratton 1	—	—	—	—	—	—	—	—	—	—	—	—	—
Edington 7	—	—	—	—	—	—	—	—	—	—	—	—	?
Heytesbury 1	—	—	—	—	—	—	—	—	—	—	?14	—	—
Heytesbury 4	—	—	—	—	—	—	—	—	—	—	—	—	?
Knook 2	—	—	—	—	—	—	—	—	—	—	—	—	—
Knook 5	3	1	—	—	—	—	—	—	—	—	—	—	—
Maiden Bradley 8a	—	—	—	—	—	—	—	—	—	—	—	—	?
Norton Bavant 13	—	—	—	—	—	—	—	—	—	—	?18	—	—
Stockton 1	—	3	—	—	—	—	—	—	—	—	—	—	—
Tilshead 1	—	—	—	—	—	—	—	—	—	—	—	—	—
Tilshead 2	3	—	—	—	—	—	—	—	—	—	—	—	—
Tilshead 5	2	—	—	—	—	—	—	—	—	—	—	—	—
Tilshead 7	—	—	—	—	—	—	—	—	—	—	—	—	3

Key: I, 'Individuals' or Skeletons (where articulated burials have been encountered)
A, Adults (no sex given); M, Males; F, Females; C, Children and Adolescents.*

...ned Articulated Burned Dis- ulated Bones				Unburned and Burned Disarticulated Bones					Burned Articulated Skeletons and Disarticulated Bones					Burned Disarticulated Bones					TOTALS
A	M	F	C	I	A	M	F	C	I	A	M	F	C	I	A	M	F	C	
—	—	—	—	—	—	—	—	—	—	—	—	—	—	—	—	—	—	—	3
—	—	—	—	—	—	—	—	—	—	—	—	—	—	—	—	—	—	—	6
—	—	—	—	—	—	—	—	—	—	—	—	—	—	—	—	—	—	—	1
—	—	—	—	—	—	—	—	—	—	—	—	—	—	—	—	—	—	—	4
—	—	—	—	—	—	—	—	—	—	—	—	—	—	—	—	—	—	—	3
—	—	—	—	—	—	—	—	—	—	—	—	—	—	—	—	—	—	—	?
—	—	—	—	—	—	—	—	—	—	—	—	—	—	—	—	—	—	—	1
—	—	—	—	—	—	—	—	—	—	—	—	—	—	—	—	—	—	—	?
—	—	—	—	—	—	—	—	—	—	—	—	—	—	—	—	—	—	—	51
—	—	—	—	—	—	—	—	—	—	—	—	—	—	—	—	—	—	—	3
—	—	—	—	—	—	—	—	—	—	—	—	—	—	—	—	—	—	—	1
—	—	—	—	—	—	—	—	—	—	—	—	—	—	—	—	—	—	—	?1
—	—	—	—	—	—	—	—	—	—	—	—	—	—	—	—	—	—	—	4
—	—	—	—	—	—	—	—	—	—	—	—	—	—	—	—	—	?	—	1
—	—	—	—	—	—	—	—	—	—	—	—	—	—	—	—	—	—	—	?
—	—	—	—	—	—	—	—	—	—	—	—	—	—	—	—	—	—	—	8
—	—	—	—	—	—	—	—	—	—	—	—	—	—	1	—	—	—	—	1
—	—	—	—	—	—	—	—	—	—	—	—	—	—	—	—	—	—	—	?
—	—	—	—	—	—	—	—	—	—	—	—	—	—	—	—	—	—	—	?14
—	—	—	—	—	—	—	—	—	—	—	—	—	—	—	—	—	—	—	?
—	—	—	—	—	—	—	—	—	—	—	—	—	—	?7	—	—	—	—	?7
—	—	—	—	—	—	—	—	—	—	—	—	—	—	—	—	—	—	—	4
—	—	—	—	—	—	—	—	—	—	—	—	—	—	—	—	—	—	—	?
—	—	—	—	—	—	—	—	—	—	—	—	—	—	—	—	—	—	—	?18
—	—	—	—	—	—	—	—	—	—	—	—	—	—	—	—	—	—	—	3
—	—	—	—	—	—	—	—	—	—	—	—	—	—	—	—	?	—	—	?
—	—	—	—	2	—	—	—	—	—	—	—	—	—	—	—	—	—	—	5
—	—	—	—	—	—	—	—	—	—	—	—	—	—	—	—	—	—	—	2
—	—	—	—	—	—	—	—	—	—	—	—	—	—	—	—	—	—	—	8

PRIMARY BURIALS IN EARTHEN LONG BARROWS	Articulated Skeletons					Articulated Skeletons and Disarticulated Bones					Disarticulated Bones			
SOUTHERN REGION	I	A	M	F	C	I	A	M	F	C	I	A	M	
Warminster 1	–	–	–	–	–	–	–	–	–	–	3	–	–	
Warminster 6	I	–	–	–	–	–	–	–	–	–	–	–	–	
Wilsford (N) 3	–	–	–	–	–	–	–	–	–	–	–	–	?	
(6) North Wiltshire (Avebury) and Berkshire Downs														
Bishop's Cannings 65	–	–	–	–	–	–	–	–	–	–	–	–	2	
Calne-Cherhill	–	–	I	2	–	–	–	–	–	–	–	–	–	
Heddington 3	I	–	–	–	–	–	–	–	–	–	–	–	–	
(8) The Chilterns and East Anglia														
Therfield Heath	I	–	–	–	–	–	–	–	–	–	–	–	–	
Whiteleaf	–	–	–	–	–	–	–	–	–	–	–	–	I	
NORTHERN REGION														
(1) Lincolnshire Wolds														
Giants' Hills, Skendleby	–	–	–	–	–	–	–	2	5	I	–	–	–	
(2) Yorkshire														
Cropton	–	2	–	–	–	–	–	–	–	–	–	–	–	
Ebberston G.ccxxi	–	–	–	–	–	–	–	–	–	–	–	–	–	
Kilburn G.ccxxv	–	–	–	–	–	–	–	–	–	–	–	–	–	
Kilham G.ccxxxiv	9	–	–	–	–	–	–	–	–	–	–	–	–	
Market Weighton G.ccxxvi	–	–	–	–	–	–	–	–	–	–	–	–	–	
Over Silton G.ccxxvii	–	–	–	–	–	–	–	–	–	–	5	–	–	
Pickering, 4 miles NW from	3	–	–	–	–	–	–	–	–	–	–	–	–	
Rudstone G.ccxxiv	–	–	–	–	–	–	–	–	–	–	–	–	–	
Westow G.ccxxiii	–	–	–	–	–	–	–	–	–	–	–	–	–	
Willerby G.ccxxii	–	–	–	–	–	–	–	–	–	–	–	–	–	
(3) Westmorland														
Crosby Garrett G.ccxxviii	–	–	–	–	–	–	–	–	–	–	–	–	–	

* This information is not always available from early accounts even though reasonably clear indications of rite may be given. Where there is variation regarding the *precise* numbers in any category the lower total is given. When there is uncertainty regarding a number it is prefixed with a question mark, and where the basic accounts give no indication, Grinsell [1957] has been followed.

...rned Articulated ...d Burned Dis-...iculated Bones				Unburned and Burned Disarticulated Bones					Burned Articulated Skeletons and Disarticulated Bones					Burned Disarticulated Bones					TOTALS
A	M	F	C	I	A	M	F	C	I	A	M	F	C	I	A	M	F	C	
—	—	—	—	—	—	—	—	—	—	—	—	—	—	—	—	—	—	—	3
—	—	—	—	—	—	—	—	—	—	—	—	—	—	—	—	—	—	—	1
—	—	—	—	—	—	—	—	—	—	—	—	—	—	—	—	—	—	—	?
—	—	—	—	—	—	—	—	—	—	—	—	—	—	—	—	—	—	—	4
—	—	—	—	—	—	—	—	—	—	—	—	—	—	—	—	—	—	—	3
—	—	—	—	—	—	—	—	—	—	—	—	—	—	—	—	—	—	—	1
—	—	—	—	—	—	—	—	—	—	—	—	—	—	—	—	—	—	—	1
—	—	—	—	—	—	—	—	—	—	—	—	—	—	—	—	—	—	—	1
—	—	—	—	—	—	—	—	—	—	—	—	—	—	—	—	—	—	—	8
—	—	—	—	—	—	—	—	—	—	—	—	—	—	—	—	—	—	—	2
—	—	—	—	—	—	—	—	—	—	—	—	—	—	14	—	—	—	—	14
—	—	—	—	—	—	—	—	—	—	—	—	—	—	—	—	?	—	—	?
—	—	—	—	—	—	—	—	—	—	—	—	—	—	—	—	—	—	—	9
—	—	—	—	—	—	—	—	—	—	—	—	—	—	26	—	—	—	—	26
—	—	—	—	—	—	—	—	—	—	—	—	—	—	—	—	—	—	—	5
—	—	—	—	—	—	—	—	—	—	—	—	—	—	—	—	—	—	—	3
—	—	—	—	—	—	—	—	—	—	—	—	—	—	—	—	?	—	—	?
—	—	—	—	—	—	—	—	—	—	1	2	2	2	—	—	—	—	—	7
—	—	—	—	—	—	—	—	—	—	—	—	—	—	—	—	?	—	—	?
—	—	—	—	—	—	—	—	—	—	—	—	—	—	6	—	—	—	—	6

3. Rites and Furnishing of Neolithic and Bronze Age Secondary Burials

SECONDARY BURIALS IN EARTHEN LONG BARROWS	FURNISHINGS													
SOUTHERN REGION	Contracted or Flexed Inhumation Burials	Cremations	Leaf Arrowheads	Scrapers	Plano-Convex Knives	Flakes	Bell Beakers	Long-Necked Beakers	Short-Necked Beakers	Food Vessels	Cinerary Urns	Miniature Vessels	Awls	Whetstones
(1) Dorset Ridgeway and Coast Bradford Peverell II	1	–	–	–	–	–	–	–	–	–	–	–	–	–
(2) Cranborne Chase Wor Barrow	1	–	★	–	–	–	–	–	–	–	–	–	–	–
Thickthorn Down	4	–	–	–	–	–	★	–	–	–	–	–	★	–
(4) Salisbury Plain East (Stonehenge) Amesbury 14	2	–	–	–	–	–	–	–	–	–	–	–	–	–
Amesbury 42	2	–	–	–	–	–	–	–	–	–	–	–	–	–
Figheldean 31	1	–	–	–	–	–	–	★	–	–	–	–	–	–
Wilsford 34	5	–	–	–	–	–	–	★	–	–	–	–	–	★
Winterbourne Stoke 1	6	–	–	★	–	–	–	–	–	★	–	–	–	–
(5) Salisbury Plain West Boyton 1	1	–	–	–	–	–	–	–	–	–	★	–	–	–
Warminster 6	–	–	–	–	–	–	–	–	–	–	–	★	–	–
Warminster 14	1	–	–	–	–	–	–	–	–	–	★	–	–	–
(8) The Chilterns and East Anglia Whiteleaf	1	–	–	–	–	–	–	–	–	–	★	–	–	–
NORTHERN REGION														
(2) Yorkshire Ebberston G.ccxxi	1	–	–	–	–	–	–	–	–	–	–	–	–	–
Gilling G.ccxxxiii	? 1	–	–	★	★	–	–	–	–	★	–	–	–	–
Kilburn G.ccxxv	1	–	–	–	–	–	–	–	–	–	–	–	–	–
Kilham G.ccxxxiv	1	–	–	–	–	–	–	–	–	★	–	–	–	–
Rudstone G.ccxxiv G.lxvi	5 or 6	–	–	★	–	–	–	★	★	–	–	–	–	–
Willerby G.ccxxii	1	–	–	–	–	–	–	–	–	–	–	–	–	–
Westow G.ccxxiii	4	–	–	–	–	–	–	–	–	–	–	–	–	–

SECONDARY BURIALS IN EARTHEN LONG BARROWS NORTHERN REGION	FURNISHINGS													
	Contracted or Flexed Inhumation Burials	Cremations	Leaf Arrowheads	Scrapers	Plano-Convex Knives	Flakes	Bell Beakers	Long-Necked Beakers	Short-Necked Beakers	Food Vessels	Cinerary Urns	Miniature Vessels	Awls	Whetstones
(4) Scotland Hill of Foulzie, Aberdeenshire	−	3	−	−	−	−	−	−	−	−	★	−	−	−

4. Details of Burials in Earthen Long Barrows

A Details of Primary Burials

SOUTHERN REGION

(1) Modern excavations

(a) Articulated Skeletons

Barton Stacey: a single skeleton, probably articulated.
Heddington 3: a single 'crouched skeleton'.
Maiden Castle Bank Barrow: the contracted skeletons of one adult, extensively mutilated, and two children.
Nutbane: the contracted skeletons of three adult males and one adolescent.

(b) Articulated Skeletons and Disarticulated Bones

Wor Barrow: the remains of six adult males. Three with their bones 'in sequence' (articulated) and three 'put in as bones' (disarticulated).

(c) Disarticulated Bones

Chute 1: '. . . circular arrangement of human skulls with long bones within the circle, the long bones showing evidence of having been tied up in bundles'.
Fussell's Lodge: the stacked remains of between 53 and 57 individuals: 14–15 adult males, 15–16 adult females, 22–24 children.
Wexcombe ,Tow Barrow: '. . . scattered fragments of skull and other human bones'.
Whiteleaf: '. . . the skeleton was scattered'.

143

(2) Early digging

(a) Articulated Skeletons

Richard Colt Hoare and William Cunnington

> Boyton 1: '... eight skeletons lying promiscuously in various directions. Seven of them were adults, the eighth a child'.
>
> Knook 5: '... an entire skeleton, probably that of an elderly man ... three others lying in the same direction'.
>
> Stockton 1: Three adult skeletons and one of a young person. A skull close by.
>
> Tilshead 2 (Western End): '... three human skeletons ... two of them side by side ... the third lying at the heads of the former'.
>
> Cunnington does not seem to have found burials at the eastern end.
>
> Warminster 6: '... a skeleton ... in a cist'.
>
> Wilsford 30: '... on reaching the floor of the barrow, four other skeletons strangely huddled together'.

William Cunnington F.G.S.

> Calne-Cherhill: Three skeletons in a large shallow grave.

John Thurnam

> Tilshead 5: '... a skeleton in the contracted position at the base of the barrow, near the east end. This and the skeleton from which skull 231 was taken no doubt formed the primary interment, and separated only from that by a space of about one foot. Like it, its doubling up, or contraction, was excessive'.
>
> Winterbourne 1: '... the skeleton of a man laid on its right side, with the knees drawn up in a closely contracted posture'.

(b) Disarticulated Bones

Richard Colt Hoare and William Cunnington

> Heytesbury 1: '... the remains of several human bodies deposited in no regular order'.
>
> Heytesbury 4: '... the remains of a great many human skeletons crossing each other in every direction, but the decayed state of the bones prevented his ascertaining the number of bodies'.
>
> Maiden Bradley 8a: '... the remains of several skeletons that had been disturbed before'.
>
> Warminster 1: '... the bones of three skeletons'.

William Cunnington

> Fittleton 5: '... a great quantity of human bones, very much broken, and interred in complete confusion'.

E. B. Nunn

> Therfield Heath: 'A skeleton was found, the bones being placed in a kind of heap or circle.'

John Thurnam

> Amesbury 14: 'The impression made by the appearance of the deposit was that the bodies had been dismembered and the skulls more or less shattered and broken before their final interment in the place where they were found.'

144

Bishop's Cannings 65: 'the scattered remains of four individuals near the east end of the barrow'.

Edington 7: 'traces of human remains in the usual situation at the east end'.

Figheldean 31: 'The primary interment consisted of a skeleton doubled up . . . within a space not more than 1½ft square. There was reason for thinking that the bones had been separated, in part before interment, the head of one tibia being in apposition with the malleolus of the other, though lying side by side'.

Milton Lilbourne 7: 'a heap of three or four skeletons was found'.

Netheravon 6: 'the broken scattered bones of one or perhaps two skeletons'.

Norton Bavant 13: 'a confused mass of skeletons spread over a space about 8ft long and 3ft broad'.

Tilshead 7: 'a pile of human bones closely packed within a space of less than 4ft in diameter, and about 18in. in depth'.

Wilsford (N) 3: 'Remains of skeletons.'

(c) Articulated Skeleton and Burned Disarticulated Bones

John Thurnam

Tilshead 2 (East End): '. . . a small skeleton well preserved in the contracted position. . . . Within a foot or two of the skeleton to the east . . . a heap of imperfectly burnt bones, in larger pieces than is usual in round barrows. This very exceptional deposit after cremation must have been made contemporaneously with that of the body to which the entire skeleton belonged. The burnt bones, which were unmixed with charcoal, were perhaps buried whilst still hot, many of the flints around them being of a red or blue colour and very brittle as if from the effect of heat'.

(d) Burned Burial of Disarticulated Bones

Richard Colt Hoare & William Cunnington

Winterbourne Stoke 53: 'several pieces of burnt bones, intermixed with great masses of mortar'.

Richard Colt Hoare, William Cunnington & John Thurnam

Bratton 1: Cunnington apparently did not reach the primary burials, Thurnam found 'a heap of imperfectly burnt, or rather charred human bones, as many as would be left by the incineration of one or two adult bodies. Careful search was made for an entire unburnt skeleton or skeletons, but without success'.

Knook 2: Cunnington, in 1802, found that a 'ridge of flints and stones was piled over the burned bones'. Thurnam, in 1866, came upon 'traces of the burnt bones and many scattered brittle flints, some of a red and others of a blackish-grey colour, as if scorched by heat. Though no pains were spared in clearing out the base of the barrow, no trace whatever was met with of any unburnt skeleton or skeletons'.

John Thurnam

Tilshead 1: 'The primary interment consisted of piles of burnt bones on the floor of the barrow at the east end. One of these to the east of the other, would have about filled a peck; the other, 6ft or 7ft nearer the middle of the barrow, was in much greater quantity. These burnt bones were some of the curiously (mixed) with burnt flints, sarsen chips, etc., into what I have called an ossiferous breccia, and many were stained of a beautifully vivid blue and green colour. These burnt bones were unequally burnt, and many merely charred were quite black. Above the bones the chalk rubble of the barrow was curiously changed into a delicate friable cream coloured substance like burned shells. I fancy this an imperfect lime, formed probably from the burned bones having been deposited whilst hot. This substance was very abundant, and would probably have filled a bushell.'

NORTHERN REGION

(1) Modern excavations

(a) Articulated Skeletons and Disarticulated Bones

Giant's Hills, Skendleby: 'The remains of four, and perhaps of five, complete bodies, and skulls belonging to three others were found closely packed within a narrow compass on a rectangular bed of chalk slabs placed directly on the old ground surface. . . . Scattered over the southern half of the mass were other bones belonging to disjointed skeletons, presumably those to be associated with the three skulls, and the largest concentration of these bones was in the south-west corner where there was a closely packed pile. Among these bones were some which could not be attributed to any of the eight bodies implied by the presence of eight skulls in all . . . the total assemblage represents remains from more than eight human beings.'

(b) Unburned and Burned Disarticulated Bones

Bradley Moor: a slab-covered depression in the floor of the large cist was filled with bones broken to fragments. With them were burnt bones.

(2) Early digging

(a) Articulated Skeletons

Thomas Bateman

Cropton: 'two skeletons, with their legs drawn up close to the trunk, and the heads to the north'.
Pickering, 4 miles NW. from: 'a skeleton . . . lying east and west . . . but strange to say wanting the skull . . . more bones . . . a grave . . . another skeleton placed with its head to the east . . . another grave . . . a skeleton, with its head to the west'.

William Greenwell

Kilham, G.ccxxxiv: At least nine skeletons, some flexed or contracted, were found along the axis of the mound on the ancient surface.

(b) Disarticulated Bones

William Greenwell

Over Silton, G.ccxxvii: 'The burials . . . along the mesial line of the barrow . . . on the natural surface . . . much decayed bone . . . the tibia of an adult

... part of a lower jaw ... a large portion of the bones of probably a man, past middle life; they were not in their proper order ... close to these ... the similarly disjointed and imperfect bones of a person about the time of puberty; and almost in contact with them were some bones ... of another person ... the bones of a young person also disjointed and fragmentary. Thus at least five bodies seem to have been buried in the barrow, but none of them had been placed there in a complete condition, all having the appearance as though they had been brought from some previous place of deposit.'

(c) Burned Burial of Articulated Skeletons and Disarticulated Bones
Westow, G.CCXXIII: 'The principal primary burials. . . . The first met with consisted of a large number of calcined bones belonging to three bodies irregularly disposed, and not presenting the appearance of having been complete when first deposited in the mound. . . . The bones which are those of two young women . . . and of an infant, extended over a space about 5ft in length and 2½ft in width . . . west of the first deposit . . . a body, laid on the right side, in the ordinary contracted position. . . . The bones were completely calcined, though still remaining in their natural order . . . the body was that of an adult, probably a man. Immediately to the west . . . a second body, that of an adult of no great strength and of uncertain sex . . . close by . . . further to the west . . . the body of a child . . burnt like the two last. The signs of burning began to be less evident about this point . . . to the west of the child . . . some burnt bones of a strongly made adult man . . . only fragmentary ones, and never having formed (though all the bones of one leg were present) a perfect body . . . the evidence of fire became gradually more scanty . . . the burning, flagging and ridge-shaped pile of stones disappeared together, the ordinary earthen material of the mound taking their place.'

(d) Burned Burials of Disarticulated Bones
Crosby Garrett, G.CCXXVII: 'the interments . . . certainly six, and possibly of seven, bodies, all of which, with the exception of two, and those themselves doubtful, had been placed in the barrow in the condition of deposits of disconnected and incomplete bones. . . . The bones were frequently encased with charcoal in a mass of calcined limestone. The bodies interred had been those of three adults and three younger persons, and possibly of a fourth. Two of the adults were strongly-made males, the third, probably a male of slighter make than the other two . . . a few feet west of the "menhir" and 7ft above the natural surface, a few burnt bones were met with; these appeared to have been burnt elsewhere and placed in the barrow afterwards. . . . Throughout that part of the mound which was to the west of the "menhir" many unburnt human bones, principally of children, were discovered at various levels. . . . The children's bones were less scattered than those of the adults, which in some cases were found as separate bones. . . . All these bones were incomplete, and no entire skeleton seemed to have been interred'.
Ebberston, G.CCXXI: '. . . the remains of at least fourteen bodies, not laid in any order, but with the component bones broken, scattered, and lying in the most

confused manner; half a jaw, for instance, upon part of a thigh bone, and a fragment of a skull amidst the bones of a foot, whilst other portions of apparently the same skull were found some distance apart . . . from the dislocated and broken state in which they occurred there can be little doubt that, before they were entombed, the flesh had been removed . . . towards the east there were found signs of burning, at first slight but gradually becoming more evident . . . until at the east end the oolitic limestone had become lime and all trace of bone had disappeared'.

Kilburn, G.ccxxv: '. . . the burials in the shape of a large quantity of burnt bones, broken and scattered. . . . At the south end of the linear deposit the calcined bones were more frequently met with amongst the burnt stones . . . at the north end they were confined to the bottom and rested on the natural surface. At one point . . . was part of an upper jaw and the whole of a lower jaw, with the left temporal bone, these being found lying close together, with a portion of a skull placed a little distance from them; two cervical vertebrae . . . near the bones just mentioned. . . . There was no appearance, indeed in any part of the linear deposit, as if a whole body had ever been placed there . . . the linear deposit . . . had evidently been subjected to a most intense heat'.

Market Weighton, G.ccxxvi: '. . . the bones of an adult and of a child and some ox bones . . . a trench. . . . In the trench . . . the bones of a young person . . . above it . . . the bones of an adult woman . . . west of this . . . the bones of an adult man . . . the bones of three adults, one of them having all the bones present and in their proper order, close to them to the west . . . the remains of four bodies . . . further to the west the bones of an adult woman . . . another transverse trench . . . and in it were the skull and lower jaw of a child . . . immediately over this . . . a human jaw and some ox bones . . . another transverse trench. . . . In it . . . the remains of two adults, one of which seemed to have been a complete body when it had been interred, apparently in a sitting posture . . . also . . . in the trench bones of red-deer, ox and goat . . . further west . . . the bones of an adult woman and a child. Another trench . . . contained some human bones. The last deposit was 60ft from the east end and consisted of those of an adult and child. In all parts of twenty-six bodies were discovered . . .'

Rudstone, G.ccxxiv: '. . . the broken and dislocated remains of several human bodies, all laid upon the natural surface. . . . At the east end where the calcination was complete, the burnt bones were mixed up with the burnt earth. . . . As the deposit was examined progressively towards the west, and the burnt matter became gradually less in quantity and at last entirely ceased, the bones still continued to be calcined, until . . . some bones quite unburnt were met with, though others were still calcined . . . still further to the west the bones were all, with a very few exceptions, untouched by the fire. . . . It would seem almost necessary to conclude that . . . when the bodies were placed on the surface . . . some bones previously calcined had been laid there with them . . . the bones were most numerous at the two ends of the deposit, very few . . . in the middle . . . just upon the edge of the large hole before described was a body imperfectly

burnt, though all the bones were to some extent calcined . . . to the west of this
was a skull perfectly burnt . . . west of this was another skull, having the finger
bones and those of the back, belonging probably to the same body, in their
proper positions. All the bones were completely calcined . . . a few more burnt
bones . . . the unburnt skull of a man of middle age . . . no lower jaw with the
head. . . . One foot further west was the unburnt skull of an aged man. . . .
With the head was a lower jaw, occupying its proper position, but which did not
belong to it . . . about a foot to the west was the lower jaw belonging to the
skull first named. In front of the face were portions of another unburnt skull,
and about to the south of it was part of a burnt skull . . . the skull of a child
about ten years old, unburnt, the lower jaw of which was placed at the back of
the head . . . no other bones . . . in connection with any of the heads . . . a few
unburnt and some imperfectly burnt bones'.

Willerby, G.ccxxii: 'The evidence of burning became gradually less towards
the west . . . the mass of burnt chalk and flints was in some places so hard that it
required the vigorous use of the pick-axe to break it up. . . . At the bottom of
the calcined matter . . . numerous fragments of human bones evidently disjointed and dislocated, and probably incomplete before they had been there
deposited . . . where the bones have been subjected to the action of fire whilst
placed under an overlying mass, there is a marked difference in their appearance
from what is presented by those which have been burnt on a pile and where the
air had free access during the process, these latter being such as are found in the
deposits of bones met with in the round barrows.'

B Secondary Burials in Earthen Long Barrows

1. Neolithic, Bronze Age and Later

SOUTHERN REGION

(1) Dorset Ridgeway and Coast

Bradford Peverell II: a possible secondary burial, contracted or flexed, from
just below the surface of the mound at the north-western end.

(2) Cranborne Chase

The Wor Barrow: contracted interment of an adult male with leaf arrowhead
in ribs, accompanied by skeleton of an adolescent in primary filling of ditch at
SE.

Thickthorn Down: the remains of four individuals in two interments, one
marked by a shallow depression, set into the top of the barrow. With each interment was a bell (type B1) beaker and with one a bronze awl. (See Appendix 11.)

(4) Salisbury Plain East (Stonehenge)

Amesbury 14: two contracted skeletons, one an adolescent, considered as
secondary burials.

Amesbury 42: skeleton '. . . lying within a foot of the present surface. . . . It was in the contracted posture, and close to it was the skeleton of an infant'.

Figheldean 31: '. . . about a foot below the surface . . . the skeleton was in a moderately contracted [? flexed] posture. . . . Near the hips a fine drinking cup of red ware [long-necked beaker] much broken but since restored'.

Wilsford 34: at least five contracted single burials set into the top of the barrow between its western end and centre. With the third burial was what has been designated a 'finger biscuit whetstone' and with the fourth was a long-necked beaker. (See Appendix 11.)

Winterbourne Stoke 1: six skeletons, contracted or flexed, and considered as those of a man, woman and four children, and furnished with a food-vessel and a scraper, found about 2ft from the surface of the mound.

(5) Salisbury Plain West

Boyton 1: '. . . a rude urn containing burned human bones at the west end'.

Warminster 6: 'near the surface was a small cup of rude British pottery', Devizes Museum Catalogue, I (1896), 202.

Warminster 14: in the top of the barrow, apparently disturbed by Saxon burials, was 'the fragment of an urn, very rude yet prettily ornamented, which probably contained an interment of burned bones'.

(8) The Chilterns and East Anglia

Whiteleaf: An inverted urn covering cremated human bones was found just under the turf in the southern lobe of the mound.

NORTHERN REGION

(2) Yorkshire

Ebberston, G.ccxxi: '. . . an unburnt body, laid 2ft below the surface of the mound. On account of . . . disturbance it could not be ascertained with certainty whether the body had been interred at full length or in a contracted position; but I think, from the narrow compass within which the bones were placed, it is scarcely possible that it had been laid at full length. There can be no doubt, however, that it was a secondary interment'.

Gilling, G.ccxxxiii: A slab cist set in the mound had in it a food-vessel, two plano-convex flint knives and a flake. Little trace of the burial remained owing to acid soil conditions.

Kilburn, G.ccxxv: '. . . a cist on the south-east side, at a distance of about 14ft from the highest part of the mound. It was placed about 2½ft above the natural surface, and was formed of four flagstones set on edge, with one large cover stone, the bottom being paved with small stones. It contained a skeleton in a contracted position, with the head laid to the north. This was, no doubt, a secondary interment, made long after the mound had been raised over the primary burials'.

Kilham, G.ccxxxiv: 'Six feet south-west by west of the centre, and on the mesial line, about a foot above the natural surface, lay the disturbed body of an aged woman, in company with the bones of which were four pieces of what had once been a very fine "food-vessel" with pierced ears.'

'At the west end of the barrow, and rising about a foot above the due level of the long barrow proper, if such this mound ever had been, was (as noticed before) what looked like a small round barrow placed upon the end of the existing long mound. Beneath it, and only just above the natural surface, was the body, probably of a girl under 16 years of age, laid on the right side, the head to W. by S., the right hand up to the face, the left hand on the hips. In front of the face was a "food-vessel".'

Rudstone, G.ccxxiv: 'A deposit of calcined bones of the ordinary kind, of the time of the round barrows . . . was met with 3ft north-by-east of the centre point, and 1ft above the natural surface. They were placed in a round heap, 14in in diameter. This was probably a secondary interment.'

Rudstone, G.lxvi: the contiguous part of the composite monument: 'At the west end, and below the centre of what had something of the appearance of a round barrow raised upon the surface of the long mound, and 2ft above the level of the natural surface, was the body of a young adult woman, laid on the right side, with the head to W., and the hands up to the face. Just in front of the right tibia was a "drinking cup" [long-necked beaker]. . . . At a level 6in. higher . . . the body of a child . . . associated with the body, was a flint knife, 1¾in. long . . . Underneath the woman . . . a beam of wood . . . a grave. . . . In it . . . the body of an adult of uncertain sex. . . . Behind the head was a 'drinking cup'; in front of the chest two round flint scrapers and a chipping; at the knees one round scraper and a chipping; and at the feet a small oval scraper. . . . Just beyond the feet of this body were the bones of a young woman which had been disturbed and relaid. They were placed in a heap, the skull being on the top of the other bones. . . . The appearance suggested that a cutting had been made into an already existing grave . . . seventy-six feet east of the grave . . . many bones belonging to a man of large stature, together with many others of a child's body, and a single piece of burnt bone. They were all laid in a heap. . . . Immediately south of them . . . was the body of a child, during the period of first dentition. . . . On the south side of the mound . . . was a single human metacarpal bone.'

(These burials can now be seen as associated with a cursus [Dymond, 1966].)

Willerby, G.ccxxii: '. . . secondary . . . met with at a place 38ft distant from the east end, on the central line of the barrow, and 2ft below its surface. It was that of an unburnt body, laid on the back, but inclining to the left side, the legs drawn up, the hands crossed upon the chest, and the head to E. It was very much broken up by rabbit digging, and the skull in consequence was only fragmentary'.

Westow, G.ccxxiii: Greenwell considered that the mound had originally been a long barrow 'of the usual proportions as to length and breadth' to which additions had been made on its south side to house burials. These were in cists of oolitic slabs.

(a) 'At a distance of 14½ft south-south-west of the present centre, an oval cist was met with, placed on the natural surface of the ground. It was formed by ten oolitic flag-stones set on edge, and had two similar stones for a cover, and was paved at the bottom with three more. It was 3ft 10in. long, 2ft 10in. wide and 1½ft deep, and had a direction east-south-east and west-north-west. In it was the body of a child, about 10 years old, laid on the right side, the head to W. by N., the hands being to the hips; the head was placed close to the south-west side of the cist. There were also some few disturbed bones of a second and adult body in the cist.'

(b) 'At the same distance south-south-east of the centre was a second cist, formed like the first, but having only eight stones for the sides, with three as covers, and the bottom, which was a foot above the surface-level, paved with a number of small flags. It had a direction south-west-by-west and north-east-by-east, and was 3ft long, 2ft wide, and 1ft deep. In it was the body of probably a woman, at least twenty years of age, laid on the left side, the head to WSW., and the hands to the hips. Just above the level of this cist, and a little to the east of it, were some disturbed human bones, and the core of an ox-horn, with other ox-bones; under them and alongside a large slab set on its edge, and on the natural surface, was much burnt earth.'

(c) 'A third cist was discovered 16½ft south-east of the centre. It was placed 3ft above the surface-level, and consisted of two side slabs, and across the corner, with three flags on the bottom; the cover stones and the other side stones had, probably, been removed when the mound was ploughed over, as the top was so close to the surface that they must have come in contact with the plough. It was 2ft 8in. by 2ft 6in., and 1ft deep; and on the bottom was the body of a woman, past the middle period of life, laid on the right side, the head to SW. by W., the hands being on the hips; some few burnt bones were likewise found in the cist.'

(4) Scotland

Hill of Foulzie, Aberdeenshire: Three cinerary urns inverted over cremated bones, one from the long sector, the others from the 'round part of the cairn' at its proximal end.

2. Roman and Saxon Secondary Burials in Earthen Long Barrows
Roman–R; Saxon–S; extended unfurnished burials are unspecified; doubtful sites are queried.

SOUTHERN REGION

(1) Dorset Ridgeway and Coast
Wimbourne St Martin 1 (Maiden Castle bank-barrow), S.

(2) Cranborne Chase
Chettle 1 ?; Handley 1 (Wor Barrow), R; Tarrant Launceston 1.

(3) Hampshire Uplands
Nil.

(4) Salisbury Plain East (Stonehenge)
Wilsford (South) 30.

(5) Salisbury Plain West
Heytesbury 1; Knook 2; Sherrington 1, S;
Tilshead 1; Tilshead 5, S; Warminster 14, S.

(6) North Wiltshire (Avebury) and Berkshire Downs
Nil.

(7) Sussex and Kent
Chilham, Julliberrie's Grave, R; Piddinghoe.

(8) The Chilterns and East Anglia
Therfield Heath, S.

NORTHERN REGION

(1) Lincolnshire Wolds
Spellow Hills ?

(2) Yorkshire
Rudstone, G.ccxxiv, S.

Appendix 8

ARTIFACTS FROM EARTHEN LONG BARROWS

1. Artifacts: pottery, flint, bone with or about primary burials.

(a) Earlier Neolithic 'Windmill Hill' and other pottery

SOUTHERN REGION

Modern Excavation: Fussell's Lodge; Maiden Castle bank barrow; Wor Barrow.
Early Digging: Edington 7; Norton Bavant 13.

NORTHERN REGION

Modern Excavation: Giants' Hills, Skendleby.
Early Digging (for full details of this pottery see *The Neolithic Pottery of Yorkshire*, by N. Newbigin [1937]): Hanging Grimston; Heslerton; Kilburn, G.ccxxv; Kilham, G.ccxxxiv; Market Weighton, G.ccxxvi; Westow, G.ccxxiii; Willerby, G.ccxxii.

(b) Flint Artifacts

SOUTHERN REGION

Modern Excavation: Fussell's Lodge.
Early Digging: Norton Bavant 13; Milton Lilbourne 7; Tilshead 2; Winterbourne Stoke 1.

NORTHERN REGION

Early Digging: Cropton; Heslerton; Kilham, G.ccxxxiv; Pickering, 4 miles NW. from.

(c) Bone Pins

NORTHERN REGION

Early Digging: Heslerton; Willerby, G.ccxxii.

2. Artifacts: pottery, flint, stone, chalk, bone and antler in and beneath mounds.

(a) Pottery

SOUTHERN REGION

Modern Excavation: Avebury 68; Bishop's Cannings 76; Nutbane; Wexcombe, Tow
Barrow (Grafton 5); Whiteleaf.
Early Digging: Bratton 1; Warminster 14.

NORTHERN REGION

Modern Excavation: Giants' Hills, Skendleby.
Early Digging: Rudstone, G.ccxxiv.

(b) Flint Artifacts

SOUTHERN REGION

Modern Excavation: Fussell's Lodge; Holdenhurst; Julliberrie's Grave; Nutbane;
Therfield Heath; Thickthorn Down; West Rudham; Whiteleaf; Wor Barrow.

NORTHERN REGION

Early Digging: Seamer Moor.

(c) Stones and Stone Artifacts

SOUTHERN REGION

Modern Excavation: Wor Barrow.
Early Digging: Bratton 1; Warminster 14.

(d) Chalk Artifacts

SOUTHERN REGION

Modern Excavation: Thickthorn Down.

(e) Bone and Antler Artifacts

SOUTHERN REGION

Modern Excavation: Whiteleaf.

NORTHERN REGION

Modern Excavation: Giants' Hills, Skendleby.
Early Digging: Market Weighton, G.ccxxvi.

3. Artifacts: pottery, flint, stone, chalk, bone, antler and metal from lower, middle and upper ditch silts.

(a) Pottery
From lower ditch silts.

SOUTHERN REGION

Modern Excavation: Badshot; Holdenhurst; Julliberrie's Grave; Lamborough (alleged); Maiden Castle bank barrow; Nutbane; Wor Barrow; Thickthorn Down.

NORTHERN REGION

Modern Excavation: Giants' Hills, Skendleby.

From middle and upper ditch silts.

SOUTHERN REGION

Modern Excavation: Badshot; Fussell's Lodge; Holdenhurst; Maiden Castle bank barrow; Nutbane; Thickthorn Down; West Rudham; Wor Barrow.

NORTHERN REGION

Modern Excavation: Giants' Hills, Skendleby.

(b) Flint Artifacts
From lower ditch silts.

SOUTHERN REGION

Modern Excavation: Badshot; Fussell's Lodge; Holdenhurst; Julliberrie's Grave; Thickthorn Down; Wor Barrow.

NORTHERN REGION

Modern Excavation: Giants' Hills, Skendleby.

From middle and upper ditch silts.

SOUTHERN REGION

Modern Excavation: Badshot; Fussell's Lodge; Holdenhurst; Therfield Heath; Thickthorn Down; Wor Barrow.

NORTHERN REGION

Modern Excavation: Giants' Hills, Skendleby.

(c) Stone and Stone Artifacts
From lower ditch silts.

SOUTHERN REGION

Modern Excavation: Windmill Hill, Horslip Barrow; Wor Barrow.

NORTHERN REGION
Modern Excavation: Giants' Hills, Skendleby.

(d) Chalk Artifacts
From lower ditch silts.

SOUTHERN REGION
Modern Excavation: Thickthorn Down.

(e) Bone and Antler Artifacts
From lower ditch silts.

SOUTHERN REGION
Modern Excavation: Thickthorn Down; Windmill Hill, Horslip Barrow.

(f) Pre-Roman Metal Objects
From upper ditch silts.

SOUTHERN REGION
Modern Excavation: Wor Barrow.

NORTHERN REGION
Modern Excavation: Giants' Hills, Skendleby.

4. Bronze Age Secondary Burials from Earthen Long Barrows: pottery and other objects furnishing burials. (See Appendix 7, 3.)

5. Romano-British pottery, coins and other objects found associated with Earthen Long Barrows.

SOUTHERN REGION
Modern Excavation: Fussell's Lodge; Julliberrie's Grave; Nutbane; Thickthorn Down; Whiteleaf; Wor Barrow.

NORTHERN REGION
Modern Excavation: Giants' Hills, Skendleby.

Appendix 9

ANIMAL SKELETAL REMAINS

1. Remains with or about primary burials.

(a) Ox heads and hooves and other portions.

Modern Excavation

Fussell's Lodge: Ox foot bones found at the top and upon the axis of the flint cairn covering the burials and an ox skull beneath it by the first bone group at the entrance to the enclosure.

Early Digging (RCH: Richard Colt Hoare; JT: John Thurnam).

Amesbury 14 [JT]: skull and feet as well as 'broken bones of the fleshy parts' appear to have been found in this long barrow.

Amesbury 42 [JT]: '. . . the skeletons of at least three individuals of *Bos longifrons* consisting of several entire carpi and tarsi, every bone, down to the sesamoids, being in situ; and parts of pelvis and of a skull of the same animal. . . . They had evidently been cut off from the carcases with the hoofs and probably the enteguments entire, and thrown on the incomplete funeral mound, whilst the flesh was probably cooked and eaten on the occasion of a feast and sacrifice'.

Fittleton 5 [JT]: '. . . remains of *Bos longifrons* . . . scattered'.

Heytesbury 1 [RCH]: At the proximal end of the mound and presumably associated with the burial complex: '. . . the head and horns of seven or more oxen'.

Knook 2 [RCH]: on top of the barrow, immediately under the turf (at the proximal end of the mound) . . . 'part of the head and horns of an ox which a butcher pronounced to have been larger than ever he saw of that species of animal'.

Norton Bavant 13 [JT]: Skull and feet are noted by Thurnam as having been found 'not far from the human remains'.

Sherrington 1 [RCH]: '. . . a neat circular cist, made in the original soil, about two feet in diameter, and sixteen inches in depth, in which were deposited the head of an ox and one small horn of a deer'.

Tilshead 5 : 'With neither skeleton was there any relic, but about a foot to the west of the last was a fine skull of *Bos longifrons*. At the base of the barrow near the west end was a second skull of the same species of *Bos* somewhat less perfect than the last. Though with six or seven of the cervical vertebrae in situ a foot or so above the first skull of *Bos l.* were several fine antlers of red deer and a metatarsal bone and phalanges of *Bos l.*'

(b) Animal remains other than those of oxen with or about primary burials.

SOUTHERN REGION

Early Digging

Amesbury 14 [JT]: The 'entire skeleton of a goose'.
Knook 2 [RCH]: 'Amongst these bones were those of birds, and on top of the barrow (at the proximal burial end), were several pieces of stags horn, and part of the head and horns of an ox. . . .'
Sherrington 1 [RCH]: '. . . a neat circular cist . . . one small horn of a deer'.
Tilshead 5 [RCH]: '. . . several fine antlers of red deer'.

NORTHERN REGION

Early Digging

Hanging Grimston: jaws representing at least twenty pigs were found at the proximal end of this barrow.

2. Bones and remains in or beneath mounds.

SOUTHERN REGION

Modern Excavation

Beckhampton Road: *Domestic:* Ox.
Fussell's Lodge: *Domestic:* Ox. *Wild:* Red deer; ? Horse.
Julliberrie's Grave, Chilham, Kent: *Domestic:* Ox, sheep, pig. *Wild:* Red deer, roe deer, bird (unidentified).
Nutbane: *Domestic:* Ox, pig, sheep or goat. *Wild:* Red deer, marten and fox were also noted but they might well be the remains of creatures that burrowed into the mound.
Thickthorn Down: *Domestic:* Ox. *Wild:* Red deer, Urus or wild ox.
Whiteleaf: *Domestic:* Ox, pig, sheep. *Wild:* Beaver, red deer, roe deer, unidentified bird.

NORTHERN REGION

Modern Excavation

Giants' Hills, Skendleby: *Domestic:* Ox, sheep. *Wild:* Red deer.

SOUTHERN REGION

Early Digging

Heytesbury 4: '... pieces of stag's horns'.
Tilshead 2: '... small pieces of stag's horns, a few animal bones, and numerous bones of birds, particularly in one place'.
Tilshead 4: '... a few pieces of stag's horns'.
Warminster 14: '... pieces of stag's horns, animal bones, boar's tusks ... the floor ... was strewed with animal bones of birds and beasts ... near the edge of the section, was found the skeleton of a horse'.

NORTHERN REGION

Early Digging

Crosby Garrett, G.CCXXVIII: *Domestic:* Ox, pig, sheep or goat. *Wild:* fulmar, grouse, horse, water-vole. These bones are noted as 'in the barrow, but all superficially placed'.
Hanging Grimston: *Wild:* pig, red deer, roe deer.
Helperthorpe: *Domestic:* Ox. *Wild:* ? wolf or dog.

3. Bones and remains from ditches.

SOUTHERN REGION

Modern Excavation

Badshot: *Domestic:* Ox, pig, dog. *Wild:* Red deer, roe deer.
Fussell's Lodge: *Domestic:* Ox, pig, sheep. *Wild:* Fallow deer, red deer, horse, dog.
Julliberrie's Grave, Chilham, Kent: *Domestic:* Ox, pig. *Wild:* Fox, red deer, roe deer.
Maiden Castle bank barrow: *Domestic:* Ox.
Nutbane: *Domestic:* Ox, pig, sheep or goat. *Wild:* Pine marten, red deer, roe deer.
Therfield Heath: *Domestic:* Ox, pig, sheep. *Wild:* Red deer.
Thickthorn Down: *Domestic:* Ox, pig, sheep. *Wild:* Fox, horse, red deer, roe deer.
Windmill Hill: *Domestic:* Ox.
Wor Barrow: *Domestic:* Ox, pig, sheep, dog. *Wild:* Badger (modern), fox, horse, red deer, roe deer.

NORTHERN REGION

Modern Excavation

Giants' Hills, Skendleby: *Domestic:* Ox, pig, sheep. *Wild:* Dog, fallow deer, horse, red deer.

Appendix 10

REGISTER. SITE, LENGTH AND ORIENTATION

(Indeterminate sites have been excluded)

Long Barrow numbers (e.g. Amesbury 42) follow L. V. Grinsell's (Appendix 2) and J. F. Dyer's (1961) lists for appropriate areas.

National Grid references: those within the county of Dorset (starting with 5, 6, 7, 8, 9) should be prefixed with SY or ST; those of Wiltshire (starting with 7, 8 and 9) ST or (starting with 0, 1, 2 and 3) SU, those of Berkshire SU, those of Bedfordshire, Buckinghamshire and Hertfordshire TL, those of Norfolk TF, those of Sussex TQ and that of Kent TR.

1. Dorset Ridgeway and Coast

(At least four barrows apparently incorporated sarsen stones, while one (Long Bredy IV) was apparently façaded and chambered.)

(a) Earthen

DORSET		Nat. Grid ref.	Map Neo. Wessex no.	Length in feet	Orientation (larger end first)
(1) Bradford Peverell	1	637923	152	120	SSE.NNW
(2)	2	669919	153	150	SE.NW
(3)	3	647923	—	87	NE.SW
(4)	4	648924	—	210	NNE.SSW
(5) Broadmayne	1	702853	—	600	ESE.WNW
(6) Cerne Abbas (U-ditch) 1		657993	138	98	S.N

DORSET (continued)		Nat. Grid ref.	Map Neo. Wessex no.	Length in feet	Orientation (larger end first)
(7) Corfe Castle (Surrounding ditch)	1	995815	185	115	E.W
(8) Frampton	1	627925	151	140	E.W
(9) Kingston Russell	1	580905	—	300	ESE.WNW
(10)	2	580904	—	250	SE.NW
(11) Long Bredy	1	571911	—	645	NE.SW
(12)	2	573909	—	110	E.W
(13) Whitcombe	1	699856	154	170	ENE.WSW
(14) Winterborne Abbas	1	604900	95	147	E.W
(15) Winterborne St Martin (Maiden Castle)	1	668885	—	1790	E.W
(16) Winterborne Steepleton	1	604883	146	180	SE.NW ?

(b) Sarsen Stones and Chamber

(17) Bere Regis	1	829972	155	190	E.W
(18) Long Bredy (Grey Mare & Colts)	4	583870	142	80	SE.NW
(19) Portesham	1	595868	144	54ft apparent	E.W ?
(20)	2	605867	145	—	SE.NW ?
(21) Winterborne Steepleton	2	614897	148	—	E.W ?
HAMPSHIRE					
Earthen					
(22) Holdenhurst		—	183	300	NNW.SSE

2. Cranborne Chase

DORSET		Nat. Grid ref.	Map Neo. Wessex no.	Length in feet	Orientation (larger end first)
(1) Chettle	1	950128	161	320	E.W
(2)	2	937135	160	190	SSE.NNW
(3) Child Okeford (Hambledon Hill)	1	845127	136	225	SSE.NNW

DORSET (continued)		Nat. Grid ref.	Map Neo. Wessex no.	Length in feet	Orientation (larger end first)
(4) Child Okeford (Hambledon Hill)	2	849120	137	84	SE.NW
(5) Gillingham	1	787272	132	130	E.W
(6) Gussage St Michael (Thickthorn Down)	1	970124	163	153	SE.NW
(7)	2	971122	163a	100	SE.NW
(8) (Gussage Down)	3	993138	164	165	SE.NW
(9)	4	994136	165	170	SE.NW
(10)	5	992131	166	210	E.W
(11)	6	981113	—	85	SSE.NNW
(12) Handley (Wor Barrow)	1	012172	170	150	SE.NW
(13) Pentridge	1	041187	171	336	SE.NW
(14)	2a	041190	172	300 } ? one barrow c.500ft.	SE.NW
(15)	2b	040191	173	175 }	
(16)	3	039195	—	95	SE.NW
(17) (Cursus)	4	025169	169	140	NE.SW
(18) Pimperne	1	917105	159	350	SE.NW
(19) Tarrant Hinton	1	964131	162	100?	ENE.WSW
(20)	2	922093	158	315	E.W
(21) Tarrant Launceston	1	929088	157	115	SE.NW
(22) Tarrant Rawston	1	915066	156	125	SE.NW
(23) Verwood (Pistle Down)	1	097105?	—	66	SE.NW
(24) Wimborne St Giles	1	014147	168	120?	E.W
WILTSHIRE					
(25) Ansty (Whitesheet Hill)	1	942242	134	135	ENE.WSW
(26) Broadchalke	2	034211	—	76	E.W
(27) Coombe Bissett	2	095224	178	165	E.W
(28) Donhead St Mary	4	916196	135	132	ENE.WSW
(29) Downton	2	161230	180	200	NNE.SSW

HAMPSHIRE		Nat. Grid ref.	Map Neo. Wessex no.	Length in feet	Orientation (larger end first)
(30) Martin (Woodyates)	1	035204	174	110	SE.NW
(31) (Knap Barrow)	2	088198	175	330	SE.NW
(32) (Grans Barrow)	3	090197	176	190	SSE.NNW
(33) Rockbourne (Duck's Nest)	1	104203	177	150	N.S
(34) (Round Clump)	2	112227	179	200	SE.NW
(35) (Giants' Grave)	3	138200	181	190	NE.SW
(36) (Rockbourne Down)	4	102222	—	185	SE.NW

3. Hampshire Uplands (Barrow names and not parish names given)

BERKSHIRE	Nat. Grid ref.	Map Neo. Wessex no.	Length in feet	Orientation (larger end first)
(1) Coombe Gibbett	365622	41	—	
HAMPSHIRE				
(1) Chilbolton Down (Chilbolton)	393368	51	172	SE.NW
(2) Danebury East (Nether Wallop)	320384	54	173	ESE.WNW
(3) Danebury North East (Nether Wallop)	320383	—	85	E.W
(4) Danebury West (Nether Wallop)	319383	55	210	SE.NW
(5) Freefolk Wood (Freefolk Manor)	498448	43	165	E.W
(6) Houghton Down (Broughton)	329358	52	180	SE.NW
(7) Lamborough (Hinton Ampner)	592283	44	220	E.W
(8) Manor Down	335381	53	180	E.W
(9) Moody's Down Northwest (Barton Stacey)	433386	50	220	SE.NW

HAMPSHIRE (continued)		Nat. Grid ref.	Map Neo. Wessex no.	Length in feet	Orientation (larger end first)
(10) Moody's Down Southeast (Barton Stacey)		434386	49	160	SE.NW
(11) Nutbane		330495	—	180	E.W
(12) Old Winchester Hill (Meonstoke)		638196	45	185	NNE.SSW
(13) Withering Corner East (Ashley)		395291 (centred on)	47	90	E.W
(14) Withering Corner West (Ashley)		395291 (centred on)	48	130	E.W
(15) Woodcott (Woodcott)		428545	42	240	NE.SW
(16) Upper Cranbourne Farm (Wonston)		489424	—	210	SE.NW
ISLE OF WIGHT					
(17) Afton Down (Freshwater)		351857	186	114	E.W
(18) Long Stone (Mottistone)		408843	187	100	E.W
SURREY					
(19) Badshot		861478	—	140	ENE.WSW

4. Salisbury Plain East (Stonehenge) (One barrow incorporated sarsen stones)
(a) Earthen

WILTSHIRE		Nat. Grid ref.	Map. Neo. Wessex no.	Length in feet	Orientation (larger end first)
(1) Amesbury	10a	119421	67	—	E.W
(2)	14	115417	64	100	SSE.NNW
(3)	42	137432	69	265	S.N
(4) Bulford	1	163430	72	133	E.W
(5) Clarenden Park (Fussell's Lodge)	4a	192324	58	170	ENE.WSW

WILTSHIRE (continued)		Nat. Grid ref.	Map Neo. Wessex no.	Length in feet	Orientation (larger end first)
(6) Collingbourne Kingston	21	256567	36	140	E.W
(7) Durrington	24	124444	79	142	SE.NW
(8) Figheldean	27	127453	80	182	E.W
(9)	31	108458	82	148	SE.NW
(10)	36	168482	77	—	SSE.NNW
(11) Fittleton	5	199516	76	140	NNE.SSW
(12) Grafton (Tow Barrow)	5	274577	37	90	NNE.SSW
(13) Idmiston	26	204348	—	80	NE.SW
(14) Milston	1	189459	78	—	NE.SW
(15)	22	203473	75	100	SE.NW
(16)	39	217462	73	160	E.W
(17)	40	217463	74	88	E.W
(18) Milton Lilbourne	7	189582	35	315	NE.SW
(19) Netheravon	6	114466	81	111	SSE.NNW
(20) Shalbourne	5	294599	39	170	S.N
(21)	5a	310592	40	162	SE.NW
(22) Wilsford (S)	13	118413	63	65	NE.SW
(23)	30	114410	62	126	E.W
(24)	34	104411	65	117	NE.SW
(25)	41	108401	61	140	SE.NW
(26) Winterbourne Stoke	1	100415	66	240	NE.SW
(27)	53	091428	—	104	E.W
(28) Woodford	2	100377	60	67	S.N

(b) With Sarsen Stones

(29) Tidcombe and Fosbury 1		292576	38	185	NNE.SSW

5. Salisbury Plain West

WILTSHIRE		Nat. Grid ref.	Map Neo. Wessex no.	Length in feet	Orientation (larger end first)
(1) Boyton	1	930403	99	210	E.W
(2) Bratton	1	900516	109	230	E.W
(3) Brixton Deverill	2	847383	129	230	SSE.NNW
(4)	7	872374	130	260	ESE.WNW
(5) East Knoyle	1a	879340	131	130	SE.NW
(6) Edington	7	939523	108	210	ENE.WSW
(7) Heytesbury	1	942467	92	150	E.W
(8)	4	924441	103	160	S.N
(9) Imber	4a	962481	91	—	SSE.NNW
(10) Knook	2	956446	94	100	NNE.SSW
(11)	5	967462	93	78	E.W
(12) Norton Bavant	13	925459	104	180	E.W
(13)	14	918459	105	84	SE.NW
(14) Sherrington	1	968391	98	97	ESE.WNW
(15)	4	951384	97	150	E.W
(16) Stockton	1	965376	96	110	NNE.SSW
(17) Sutton Veny	3	911415	100	105	SE.NW
(18) Tilshead	1	000478	89	170	SE.NW
(19)	2	023468	87	390	ENE.WSW
(20)	4	033468	86	255	E.W
(21)	5	021475	88	173	E.W
(22)	7	059494	85	210	SE.NW
(23)	10	996480	90	c.170	NNE.SSW
(24) Warminster	1	873470	106	132	SSW.NNE
(25)	6	903471	107	106	SE.NW
(26)	14	897444	101	206	SSE.NNW
(27) Wilsford (N)	3	073513	84	170	E.W

6. North Wiltshire (Avebury) and Berkshire Downs

The majority of long barrows in this group are, or appear to have been, chambered or to have incorporated sarsen stones in their structure. As the group is an entity, details of both forms are given.

(a) Earthen

WILTSHIRE		Nat. Grid ref.	Map Neo. Wessex no.	Length in feet	Orientation (larger end first)
(1) Avebury	17	087691	17	225	NE.SW
(2)	47	086705	16	135	SE.NW
(3) Bishop's Cannings	76	066677	24	160	NE.SW
(4)	92	054657	—	230	E.W
(5) Heddington	3	010659	26	100	NE.SW

(b) Chambered or incorporating Sarsen Stones

(6) Alton	14	112633	31	200	SE.NW
(7) Avebury (West Kennet)	22	104677	23	340	E.W
(8)	68	090692	18	105	ESE.WNW
(9) Bishop's Cannings	44	066648	28	106	NE.SW
(10)	65	063661	27	140	E.W
(11)	91	076658	29	132	SSE.NNW
(12) Calne-Cherhill	5	046693	25	180	E.W
(13) East Kennet	1	116668	22	344	SE.NW
(14) Liddington-Wanborough	4	225797	9	150	SE.NW
(15) Ogbourne St Andrew	19	148725	10	—	E.W ?
(16) Preshute	1	151714	11	65	SE.NW
(17)	3a	152696	12	230?	SSE.NNW
(18) West Overton	12	156656	32	105	ENE.WSW
BERKSHIRE					
(19) Ashbury Wayland's Smithy		281854	—	185	SE.NW
(20) Lambourn		323834	—	220	ENE.WSW

7. Sussex and Kent

SUSSEX		Nat. Grid ref.	Map Neo. Wessex no.	Length in feet	Orientation (larger end first)
(1) Alfriston	54	—	—	90	SSE.NNW
(2) (Long Burgh)	55	510034	—	180	NE.SW
(3) Arlington	2	541034	—	180	NE.SW
(4) Folkington-Wilmington (Hunter's Burgh)	9	550036	—	220	S.N
(5) Litlington	2	536007	—	175	SW.NE
(6) Piddinghoe (Money Burgh)	22	425037	—	120	E.W
(7) South Malling	40	431110	—	120	E.W
(8) Stoughton	12	825122	—	110	SE.NW
(9)	14	Close by	—	80	NNW.SSE
(10) West Firle	13	483058	—	115	E.W
(11) Up Marden	1	789154	—	210	E.W
KENT					
(12) Chilham Julliberrie's Grave		518716	—	180	N.S

8. The Chilterns and East Anglia

BEDFORDSHIRE		Nat. Grid Reference	Length in feet	Orientation (larger end first)
(1) Dunstable	21	012222	100	E.W
(2) Leagrave	20	057247	100	E.W
(3) Pegsdon	13	133311	100	W.E (? larger end less ploughed)
(4) Streatley	22	086268	300	E.W

BUCKINGHAMSHIRE		Nat. Grid Reference	Length in feet	Orientation (Larger end first)
(5) Monks Risborough (Whiteleaf)	9	822040	70	SSE.NNW
HERTFORDSHIRE				
(6) Royston	26	342402	110	E.W
NORFOLK				
(Prefixes given to Nat. Grid refs.) (Norfolk Archaeology (1941), XXVII, 316)				
(7) Ditchingham Broome Heath		TM/345913	160	E.W
(8) West Rudham	1	TF/810254	210	S.N
(9)	2	TF/809254	150	? N.S

NORTHERN REGION

1. Lincolnshire Wolds (Nat. Grid. refs. prefixed TF) (After Phillips, 1933b)

LINCOLNSHIRE		Nat. Grid Reference	Length in feet	Orientation (Larger end first)
(1) Candlesby		459675	100	E.W
(2) Claxby by Alford Deadmen's Grave	1	444719	160	ENE.WSW
(3)	2	445718	173	E.W
(4) Cuxwold, Ash Holt		189010	78	SSW.NNE
(5) Langton by Spilsby Spellow Hills		401722	182	SSE.NNW
(6) Normanby le Wold		133964	190	SE.NW
(7) Skendleby, Giants' Hills	1	428711	210	SE.NW
(8)	2	429708	180	SSE.NNW
(9) Swinhope Ash Hill	1	208961	128	NE.SW
(10) Hoe Hill	2	489529	180	E.W

LINCOLNSHIRE (continued)	Nat. Grid Reference	Length in feet	Orientation (Larger end first)
(11) Tathwell	294822	105	SE.NW
(12) Walmsgate (Beacon Plantation)	371776	257	SE.NW

2. Yorkshire (after Elgee, 1930) (Prefixes given to National Grid references.)

THE WOLDS GROUP	Nat. Grid Reference	Length in feet	Orientation (Larger end first)
(1) Flotmanby	TA/065787	250	N.S
(2) Hanging Grimston	SE/810608	78	E.W
(3) Helperthorpe	SE/963679	96	E.W
(4) East Heslerton	SE/938753	410	ENE.WSW
(5) Kilham	TA/056674	170	ENE.WSW
(6) Market Weighton	SE/906410	110	E.W
(7) Rudstone 1	Sites not to	210	ESE.WNW
(8) 2	be found	255	NE.SW
(9) Westow	SE/769652	75	SE.NW
(10) Willerby Wold	TA/029760	132	E.W
SCARBOROUGH GROUP			
(11) East Ayton	TA/000864	85	N.S
(12) Peasholm	TA/031897	66	ENE.WSW
SCAMRIDGE GROUP			
(13) Ebberston	SE/892861	165	E.W
(14) Scamridge 1 Rob Howe	SE/903860	120	E.W
(15) 2	SE/893861	75	E.W

CROPTON GROUP	Nat. Grid Reference	Length in feet	Orientation (Larger end first)
(16) Cropton 1 ⎫ (17) 2 ⎭	Sites not to be found	72 —	N.S E.W
HAMBLETON GROUP			
(18) Over Silton, Kepwick	SE/492904	100	SE.NW
(19) Kilburn Wass Moor	Site not to be found	60	N.S
(20) Gilling, Yearsley	SE/601741	140	SE.NW

Demonstrable Long Cairns: Highland Zone. England.

ESKDALE	Nat. Grid Reference	Length in feet	Orientation (Larger end first)
(21) Grosmont Sleights Moor	? NZ/827024	90	S.N
WESTMORLAND			
(22) Crosby Garett Raiset Pike	NY/684072	180	SE.NW
(23) Crosby Ravensworth Cumberland	—	87	E.W
CUMBERLAND			
Ennerdale, Stockdale Moor (Samson's Bratful)	NY/098080	90	E.W
NORTHUMBERLAND			
Redesdale, Bellshiel Law	NT/813014	367	E.W
Kielder, Devil's Lapful	NY/642928	200	NNE.SSW

YORKSHIRE	Nat. Grid Reference	Length in feet	Orientation (Larger end first)
Bradley Moor (W.R.)	SE/009476	230	SE.NW
Great Ayton Moor (N.R.)	NZ/594115	? 300	E.W
Hinderwell (N.R.)	NZ/804170	—	NE.SW

For Long Cairns in Scotland see Henshall (1963), 40: the Balnagowan group and references there cited.

Appendix 11

POSSIBLE 'OVER-GRAVE', SMALL & OVAL LONG BARROWS, ENDITCHED MULTIPLES OF ROUND BARROWS

(Barrow numbers where quoted follow L. V. Grinsell for appropriate regions and counties)

(a) Possible 'Over-grave' Long Barrows.

SOUTHERN REGION

(2) Cranborne Chase
Thickthorn Down

(4) Salisbury Plain East (Stonehenge)
Wilsford 34

NORTHERN REGION

(2) Yorkshire
Rudstone, G.LXVI. (Now seen to be part of a cursus [Dymond, 1966].)

(b) Small and Oval Long Barrows (Colt Hoare's XII, Long Barrow no. 2: see also Cunnington [1914, 411] for other details.)

SOUTHERN REGION

(2) Cranborne Chase
Wimbourne St Giles (Oakley Down) nos. 10, 22. [Colt Hoare, 1810, 241–2, pl. XXXIII, 4; Crawford, 1928, 174–83; Grinsell, 1959, pl. II, B.]

(4) Salisbury Plain East (Stonehenge)
Durrington 61 [Colt Hoare, 1810, 169]; Figheldean 1 [Hawley, 1910, 624]; Winterbourne Stoke 35 [Thurnam, 1864, 429].

(5) Salisbury Plain West
East Knoyle 1 [Grinsell, 1957, 173].

(6) North Wiltshire and Berkshire Downs
Wilcot 3 [Huish, Thurnam, 1864, 428]; Roundway 5 [Cunnington, W., 1860, 162–3; Thurnam, 1864, 428].

(c) Enditched Multiples of Round Barrows

By this definition are meant such monuments as the triple bell-barrow on Amesbury Down [Crawford, 1928, 202–7, pl. xxxv]. However, when damaged, an encircling ditch is difficult to detect, thus some (e.g. Amesbury 59–60) may well be sequential monuments. Barrows are listed by counties (cf. L. V. Grinsell: appropriate works).

CORNWALL
Bowl and Bell Forms
Triple Barrow
Advent, near Camelford [Crawford, 1928, 14].

DORSET
Twin Barrows
Winterborne Abbas (Poor Lot); Tyneham 4a (Povington Heath).
Triple Barrow
Winterborne St Martin 40 (three mounds are enclosed by a single ditch, one mound appears as an addition).
Oval Twin, Disc Form
Gussage St Michael 17a (Gussage Down); Wimborne St Giles (Oakley Down).

HAMPSHIRE
Bowl and Bell Forms
Twin Barrows
Roundwood 25 S.W.

SUSSEX
Stoughton 2 (Bow Hill)

WILTSHIRE
Amesbury 44; Amesbury 59, 60 (one barrow added to ditch enclosed twin mounds); Collingbourne Ducis 4; Enford 5, 6; Wilsford 15, 16.
Triple Barrows
Amesbury 91 (Amesbury Down); Durrington 63–65.
Oval Twin, Disc Form
Amesbury 10; Bishop's Cannings 95; Milton Lilbourne 1.

Appendix 12

ROUND BARROWS WITH MULTIPLE CAUSEWAYED DITCHES

(Monuments are listed by counties and specific references are given)

Barrows	*Contents where known*
DORSET	
Nine Barrows, Corfe Castle 12 [Grinsell, 1959, 102.]	
HAMPSHIRE	
Stockbridge Down [Stone, 1940.]	Contracted inhumation with bell beaker, cremations in grave infill. Satellite inurned cremation with jet beads.
ISLE OF WIGHT	
Brook Down 3 [Grinsell and Sherwin, 1940.]	
WILTSHIRE	
Amesbury 51 [*P.P.S.*, XXVII, 345 (note).]	Earlier under- and ground-burials with necked beaker(s) dug out by Colt Hoare. Over-burial with necked beaker and satellite in ditch with bell beaker found in 1960.
Shrewton, Rollestone Field 24 [*P.P.S.*, XXV, 274 (note).]	Necked beaker burials.
Wilsford (S) 51 [*P.P.S.*, XXV, 275 (note).]	Necked beaker recovered. Colt Hoare's description suggests superimposed burials.
Winterbourne Stoke, Fargo Plantation [Stone, 1938.]	Necked beaker and food vessel.

Appendix 13

ROUND BARROWS WITH CONTENTS OF NEOLITHIC AFFINITY

Barrow numbers after L. V. Grinsell for appropriate areas.

Earlier Neolithic

(2) Cranborne Chase
Tarrant Launceston 4; Winterborne Herringston 1.

(5) Salisbury Plain West
Mere 13d.

(6) North Wiltshire and Berkshire Downs
Alton 13; Westbury 7 [Upton Down, Colt Hoare, 1810, 54].

(7) Sussex and Kent
Patching [Blackpatch, Pull, 1932, 69–72].

(8) The Chilterns and East Anglia
Mildenhall [Fox, 1923, 12]; Newmarket Heath [Fox, 1923, 12]; Triplow [Fox, 1923, 12].

Late Neolithic

(2) Cranborne Chase
Handley 26.

(5) Salisbury Plain West
Warminster 10.

(8) The Chilterns and East Anglia (numbers follow Dyer, 1961)
Dunstable 2; Dunstable 5; Royston Heath 4 [Fox, 1923, 32]; Streatley 30 [Barton

Hill 1, Childe & Smith, 1954, 228]. Oxford Region: Linch Hill Corner [Grimes, 1960, 154–64].

Earlier and Late Neolithic Material with Bronze Age Associations

(4) Salisbury Plain East (Stonehenge)
Collingbourne Ducis 10.

(6) North Wiltshire and Berkshire Downs
Lambourn [Greenwell, 1890, 60, G.CCLXXXIX]; Ogbourn St Andrew 7.

NORTHERN REGION

(2) Yorkshire (with outliers in Cumberland, Derbyshire and Northumberland). The extensive operations of Bateman, Greenwell and Mortimer have made possible classified lists for this region. G and roman numerals refer to Greenwell [1877], M and arabic numerals to Mortimer [1905]. Neolithic pottery lists are based on Newbigin [1937].

Earlier Neolithic

(a) Multiple disarticulated burials
Calais Wold, M.275; Duggleby 1, G.VII; Duggleby II, G.VIII; Towthorpe, M.18.

(b) Early Neolithic pottery with burials of one or two bodies
Cowlam, G.LII; Cowlam, G.LIII; Duggleby Wold, G.III; Huggate Wold, M.230; Towthorpe, M.7; Weaverthorpe, G.XLVII.

(c) Leaf-shaped arrowheads with burials of one or more bodies
Aldro, M.88; Ganton, G.xxx; Riggs Group, M.19.

(d) Stone axes with burials of one or more bodies
Calais Wold, M.86; Huggate Wold, M.229.

Late Neolithic

Burials of the Duggleby Group
Aldro, M.C75; Aldro, M.94; Crosby Garrett, G.CLXXIV; Howe Hill, Duggleby, M.273; Liff's Low [Bateman, 1848, 41–3; Fowler, 1956, 99]; Seamer Moor [Londesborough, 1848; Smith, R. A., 1927, 90]; Waterhouses [Bateman, 1861, 131]; Wharram Percy, M.65.

Earlier and Late Neolithic Rites and Material with Bronze Age and later Association

(1) Multiple disarticulated burials
Cowlam, G.LVII; Garton Slack, M.C51; Painsthorpe, M.99; Towthorpe, M.72.

(2) Burned burials with 'trenches' (burned and collapsed mortuary houses)
Copt Hill, Houghton-le-Spring [Trechmann, 1914, 123–30]; Cowlam, Willie

Howe Plantation, M.277; Garton Slack, M.C34; Garton Slack, M.80; Garton Slack, M.81; Helperthorpe, G.XLIX; Heslerton, G.VI; Huggate Wold, M.224; Huggate Wold, M.254.

SCOTLAND

Early Neolithic Pottery

(a) East Finnercy [Callender, 1928–9, 62–3].

(b) Pitnacree [Coles & Simpson, 1965, 41–3].

Mortuary House

Pitnacree [Coles & Simpson, 1965, 39, fig. 3].

(3) Multiple articulated burials

A number of normally large barrows of Beaker and Food-vessel affinity, examined by Mortimer and Greenwell, had beneath them multiple articulated burials in graves and upon ancient surfaces, as well as sometimes cremations, in such circumstances as would suggest simultaneous burial.

Mortimer

I   The Towthorpe Group: 6; 72; 276.
III   The Aldro Group: 116; 52; 54.
IV   The Acklam Wold Group: 204; 205.
V   The Hanging Grimston Group: 12; 55.
VI   The Painsthorpe Wold Group: 4.
VII The Garrowby Wold Group: C69.
XI   The Garton Slack Group: 37; C40; C52; C62; C63; C67; C71; 79.
XIII The Huggate Wold Group: 226; 228.
XV   The Blanch Group: 237.

Greenwell

Barrows: Weaverthorpe, XLIII: Rudstone, LXII: LXVII: Folkton, LXX: Goodmanham, LXXXIX: Ferry Fryston, CLXI.

(4) Single disarticulated burials: Mortimer [1905, xxxiii, xxxvi] and Greenwell [1877, 17] noted what they described as 'dismembered bodies' or 're-interred bodies'. They were encountered beneath barrows of Beaker and Food-vessel affinity, and were side by side with articulated skeletons and in some instances may have been buried simultaneously.

Mortimer: 50; 52; 53; 54; 55; 72; 81; 107; 265.
Greenwell: XXVI, LXVII, CXVI.

(5) Early Neolithic pottery from barrows of Beaker, Food-vessel and later affinity. Based on Neolithic A Pottery list for Yorkshire by N. Newbigin [1937, 203–215]. Numbers are her bracketed map numbers.

Newbigin: 3; 5; 6; 7; 8; 13; 15; 16; 17; 18; 19; 20; 21; 27; 31; 33; 35; 37; 42; 45.

179

(6) Leaf-shaped arrowheads from barrows of Beaker, Food-vessel and later affinity.
Barrow numbers after Mortimer [1905] and Greenwell [1877].

Mortimer: 10; 12; 13; 32; C38; 41; 56; 99; 111; 116; 281.

Greenwell: CLIX.

(7) Polished flint and stone axes and axe pieces from barrows of Beaker, Food-vessel
and later affinity. Barrow numbers after Mortimer [1905] and Greenwell [1877].

Mortimer: 10; 32; C38; C59; C63; 79; 86; 100; 229; 249.

Greenwell: I, XXXI, CX.

(8) Antler combs from Round Barrows.
Barrow numbers after Mortimer [1905].

C37; 242.

Appendix 14

HENGES CLOSE BY CAUSEWAYED CAMPS

BIBLIOGRAPHY

The following abbreviations have been used:

A.A.	*American Anthropologist*
A.J.A.	*American Journal of Archaeology*
A.N.L.	*Archaeological News Letter*
Ant. J.	*Antiquaries Journal*
Arch. Ael.	*Archaeologia Aeliana*
Arch. Camb.	*Archaeologia Cambrensis*
Arch. Cant.	*Archaeologia Cantiana*
Arch. J.	*Archaeological Journal*
B.A.	*Bedfordshire Archaeologist*
B.S.P.F.	*Bulletin Société Préhistorique Française*
Bull. Inst. Arch.	*Bulletin of the Institute of Archaeology, University of London*
D.A.J.	*Journal of the Derbyshire Archaeological and Natural History Society*
Dorset A.S.	*Dorset Archaeological & Natural History Society Proceedings*
J.B.A.A.	*Journal of the British Archaeological Association*
J.M.V.	*Jahreschrift für Mitteldeutsche Vorgeschichte, Halle*
J.S.T.	*Jahreschrift für die Vorgeschichte der sächsisch-thüringischen Länder*
M.A.S.	*Memoirs, Anthropological Society*
P.D.A.E.S.	*Proceedings of the Devon Archaeological Exploration Society*
P.D.N.H.A.S.	*Proceedings of the Dorset Natural History and Archaeological Society*
P.H.F.C.	*Papers and Proceedings of the Hampshire Field Club and Archaeological Society*
P.I.W.N.H.A.S.	*Proceedings of the Isle of Wight Natural History and Archaeological Society*
P.P.S.	*Proceedings of the Prehistoric Society*
P.P.S.E.A.	*Proceedings of the Prehistoric Society of East Anglia*
P.R.I.A.	*Proceedings of the Royal Irish Academy*
P.S.A.L.	*Proceedings of the Society of Antiquaries of London*
P.S.A.S.	*Proceedings of the Society of Antiquaries of Scotland*
S.A.C.	*Sussex Archaeological Collections*
S.N.Q.	*Sussex Notes and Queries*

T.G.A.S.	*Transactions of the Glasgow Archaeological Society*
T.N.A.S.	*Transactions Norfolk Archaeological Society*
U.J.A.	*Ulster Journal of Archaeology (New Series)*
U.L.I.A.R.	*University of London, Institute of Archaeology, Annual Report and Bulletin*
W.A.M.	*Wiltshire Archaeological Magazine*
Y.A.J.	*Yorkshire Archaeological Journal*

ABERCROMBY, J. (1912) *The Bronze Age Pottery of Great Britain and Ireland*. Oxford, 1912.

ACLAND, J. E. (1916) List of Dorset Barrows opened by Mr E. Cunnington or described by him. *Dorset A.S.*, XXXVII (1916), 40–7.

AITKEN, M. J. (1961) *Physics and Archaeology*. London, 1961.

ALEXANDER, J. (1961) The Excavation of the Chestnuts Megalithic Tomb at Addington, Kent. *Archaeologia Cantiana*, LXXVI (1961), 1–57.

ARKELL, W. J. (1947) *The Geology of Oxford*. Oxford, 1947.

ASHBEE, P. (1957a) The Great Barrow at Bishop's Waltham, Hampshire. *P.P.S.*, XXIII (1957), 137–66.
　(1957b) Stake and Post Circles in British Round Barrows. *Arch. J.*, CXIV (1957), 1–9.
　(1958) The Fussell's Lodge Long Barrow. *Antiquity*, XXXII (1958), 106–11.
　(1960) *The Bronze Age Round Barrow in Britain*. London, 1960.
　(1963) *Nature, Science and Experiment in Field Archaeology*. Jewell (Ed.), 1963, 1–17.
　(1964) The Radiocarbon Dating of the Fussell's Lodge Long Barrow. *Antiquity*, XXXVIII (1964), 139–40.
　(1966) The Fussell's Lodge Long Barrow, *Archaeologia*, C (1966), 1–80.

ASHBEE, P. *and* CORNWALL, I. W. (1961) An Experiment in Field Archaeology. *Antiquity*, XXXV (1961), 129–34.

ASHBEE, P. *and* SMITH, I. F. (1960) The Windmill Hill Long Barrow. *Antiquity*, XXXIV (1960), 297–9.
　(1966) The Date of the Windmill Hill Long Barrow. *Antiquity*, XL (1966), 299.

ATKINSON, R. J. C. (1951) The Excavations at Dorchester, Oxfordshire, 1946–51. *A.N.L.* IV (1951), 56–9.
　(1953) The Neolithic Long Mound at Maiden Castle. *P.D.N.H.A.S.*, LXXIV (1953), 36–8.
　(1955) The Dorset Cursus. *Antiquity*, XXIX (1955), 4–9.
　(1956) *Stonehenge*. London, 1956.
　(1957) Worms and Weathering. *Antiquity*, XXXI (1957), 219–33.
　(1961) Neolithic Engineering. *Antiquity*, XXXV (1961), 292–9.
　(1962) Fishermen and Farmers. *The Prehistoric Peoples of Scotland* (ed. S. Piggott). London, 1962, 1–38.

(1964a) Wayland's Smithy, Berkshire; a report on further excavations. *Paper to the Royal Archaeological Institute*, 11th March 1964.

(1964b) The Prehistorian's Task. *Paper to the Prehistoric Society*, 12th April 1964 (Conference on Culture and Culture Change).

(1965) Wayland's Smithy. *Antiquity*, XXXIX (1965), 126–33.

ATKINSON, R. J. C., PIGGOTT, C. M. *and* SANDARS, N. K. (1951) *Excavations at Dorchester, Oxon*. Ashmolean Museum, Oxford, 1951.

AUSTEN, J. H. (1857) On the Tumuli, etc., of the Chalk Range. *Papers read before the Purbeck Society*. Wareham (1856–67), 110–15.

BANKS, J. (1900) Journal of an Excursion to Eastbury and Bristol, etc., in May and June, 1767. *Dorset A.S.*, XXI (1900) 143–9.

BASSE DE MÉNORVAL, E. (1953) 'Allée sépulcrale néolithique de Bonnières-sur-Seine', *Bulletin de la Société archaeologique et scientifique de la région de Bonnières-sur-Seine* (1953), 17.

BATEMAN, T. (1848) *Vestiges of the Antiquities of Derbyshire*. London, 1848.

(1861) *Ten Years' Diggings in Celtic and Saxon Grave Hills*. London, 1861.

BECK, H. C. *and* STONE, J. F. S. (1936) Faience Beads of the British Bronze Age. *Archaeologia*, LXXXV (1936), 203–52.

BEHN-BLANCKE, G. (1953–4) Die schnurkeramische Totenhütte Thüringens. *Alt-Thüringen*, I (1953–4), 68–83.

BEHRENS, H. (1953) Einsiedlungs- und Begräbnisplatz der Trichterbecherkultur bei Weissenfels an der Saale. *J.M.V.*, Bd. 37 (1953), 67–108.

(1957) Ein jungsteinzeitlicher Grabhügel von mehrschichtigen Aufbau in der Dölauer Heide bei Halle (Saale). *J.M.V.*, Bd. 41–42 (1957–8), 213–42.

BIBBY, G. (1957) *The Testimony of the Spade*. London, 1957.

BOSANQUET, R. C. (1928) Pillow-Mounds. *Antiquity*, II (1928), 205.

BRAMWELL, F. G. S. (1938) Barrow formerly existing in Preston Drove, Brighton. *S.N.Q.*, VII (1938–9), 73–6.

BRANDT, K. *and* BECK, H. (1954) Ein Grosshaus mit Rössenerkeramik in Bochum-Hiltrop. *Germania*, XXXII (1954), 260–9.

BROTHWELL, D. R. (1961) Cannibalism in Early Britain. *Antiquity*, XXXV (1961), 304–7.

(1963) *Digging Up Bones*. London, 1963.

BROTHWELL, D. R. *and* BLAKE, M. L. (1966) The Human Remains from the Fussell's Lodge Long Barrow. *Archaeologia*, C (1966), 48–63.

BUNTING, G. H, VERITY, D. K. *and* CORNWALL, I. W. (1959) Report on the Human Remains from Nutbane, *P.P.S.*, XXV (1959), 46–7.

BURCHELL, J. P. T. *and* PIGGOTT, S. (1939) Decorated Prehistoric Pottery from the Bed of the Ebbsfleet, Northfleet, Kent. *Ant. J.*, XIX (1939), 405–20.

BUTTERFIELD, A. (1939) Structural details of a Long Barrow on Black Hill, Bradley Moor, West Yorkshire. *Y.A.J.*, XXXIV (1939), 223–7.

BUTTLER, W. (1938) *Der Donauländische und der Westische Kulturkreis der Jungeren Steinzeit*. Berlin und Leipzig, 1938.

BUTTLER, W. and HABEREY, W. (1936) Die bandkeramische Ansiedlung von Köln-Lindental. *Römische-Germanische Forschungen*, XI, 1936.

CALLENDER, J. G. (1928–9) Scottish Neolithic Pottery. *P.S.A.S.*, LXIII (1928–9), 29–98.

CAMPBELL, M., SCOTT, J. G. and PIGGOTT, S. (1960–1) The Badden Cist Slab. *P.S.A.S.*, XCIV (1960–1), 46–61.

CAMPS, F. E. (1953) *Medical and Scientific Investigations in the Christie Case*. London, 1953.

CARNEY, J. (1961) *The Problem of St Patrick*. Dublin, 1961.

CARRÉ, H., DOUSSON, J. and POULAIN, P. (1958) Habitat néolithique dans les alluvions Yonne-et-Cure de la plaine de Sainte-Pallaye. *B.S.P.F.*, LV (1958), 133–4.

CASE, H. (1952) The Excavation of Two Round Barrows at Poole, Dorset. *P.P.S.*, XVIII (1952), 148–59.
 (1956) The Neolithic Causewayed Camp at Abingdon, Berks. *Ant. J.*, XXXVI (1956), 11–30.
 (1959) The Sherds of Beaker Ware from Nutbane. *P.P.S.*, XXV (1959), 42–5.
 (1961) Irish Neolithic Pottery: Distribution and Sequence. *P.P.S.*, XXVII (1961), 174–233.
 (1962) Long Barrows and Causewayed Camps. *Antiquity*, XXXVI (1962), 212–16.
 (1963) Foreign Connections in the Irish Neolithic. *U.J.A.*, XXVI (1963), 3–17.

CAVE, A. J. E. (1936) Human Remains from the Long Barrow at Skendleby, Lincs. *Archaeologia*, LXXXV (1936), 90–5.
 (1938) Report on The Neolithic Skeletons (from the Lanhill Long Barrow). *P.P.S.*, IV (1938), 131–50.

CHILDE, V. G. (1925) *The Dawn of European Civilisation*. London, 1925.
 (1929) *The Danube in Prehistory*. Oxford, 1929.
 (1931a) *Skara Brae*. London, 1931.
 (1931b) The Continental Affinities of British Neolithic Pottery. *Arch. J.*, LXXXVIII (1931), 37–66.
 (1932) Chronology of Prehistoric Europe: a Review. *Antiquity*, VI (1932), 206–12.
 (1933) Scottish Megalithic Tombs and their Affinities. *T.G.A.S.*, VIII, pt III (1933), 120–37.
 (1939) The Orient and Europe. *A.J.A.*, XLIV (1939), 10–26.
 (1940) *Prehistoric Communities of the British Isles*. London, 1940.
 (1944) *Progress and Archaeology*. London, 1944.
 (1947) *The Dawn of European Civilisation*. London, 1947 (4th ed.).
 (1948) Cross-dating in the European Bronze Age. *Festschrift für Otto Tschumi*, Frauenfeld (1948), 70–6.

(1949a) The Origin of Neolithic Culture in Northern Europe. *Antiquity*, XXIII (1949), 129–39.

(1949b) Neolithic House-types in Neolithic Europe. *P.P.S.*, XV (1949), 77–86.

(1950) Cave Men's Buildings. *Antiquity*, XXIV (1950), 4–11.

(1951) *Social Evolution*. London, 1951.

(1956) *Piecing Together the Past*. London, 1956.

(1957) *The Dawn of European Civilisation*. London, 1957 (6th ed.).

(1959) Valediction. *Bull. Inst. Arch.*, I (1959), 1–8.

CHILDE, V. G. *and* SMITH, I. F. (1954) The Excavation of a Neolithic Barrow on White-leaf Hill, Bucks. *P.P.S.*, XX (1954), 212–30.

CHMIELEWSKI, W. (1952) *Zagadnienie Grobowców Kujawskich w Świetle Ostatnich Badań.* Łódź, 1952.

CLARK, J. G. D. (1932) *The Mesolithic Age in Britain*. Cambridge, 1932.

(1937) Earthen Long Barrows. *P.P.S.*, III (1937), 173–5.

(1940) *Prehistoric England*. London, 1940.

(1945) Farmers and Forests in Neolithic Europe. *Antiquity*, XIX (1945), 57–71.

(1947) *Archaeology and Society*. London, 1947.

(1952) *Prehistoric Europe: The Economic Basis*. London, 1952.

(1954) *Excavations at Star Carr*. Cambridge, 1954.

(1966) The Invasion Hypothesis in British Archaeology. *Antiquity*, XL (1966), 172–189.

CLARK, J. G. D. *and* GODWIN, H. (1962) The Neolithic in the Cambridgeshire Fens. *Antiquity*, XXXVI (1962), 10–23.

CLARK, J. G. D., GODWIN, H. *and* CLIFFORD, M. H. (1935) Report on Recent Excavations at Peacock's Farm, Shippea Hill, Cambridgeshire. Analysis of the Peats (H. & M. E. G. & M. H. C.). *Ant. J.*, XV (1935), 284–319.

CLIFFORD, E. M. (1950) The Cotswold Megalithic Culture: The Grave Goods and their Background. *Early Cultures of North-West Europe* (Chadwick Memorial Studies), 23–50. Cambridge, 1950.

COGHLAN, H. H. *and* CASE, H. (1957) Early Metallurgy of Copper in Ireland and Britain. *P.P.S.*, XXIII (1957), 91–123.

COLES, J. M. *and* SIMPSON, D. D. A. (1965) The Excavation of a Neolithic Round Barrow at Pitnacree, Perthshire, Scotland. *P.P.S.*, XXXI (1965), 34–57.

COLLINGWOOD, R. G. (1946). *The Idea of History*. Oxford, 1946.

COLLINS, A. E. P. *and* WATERMAN, D. M. (1955) *Millin Bay, A Late Neolithic Cairn in Co. Down*. Belfast (H.M.S.O.), 1955.

COLT HOARE, R. (1810) *The History of Ancient Wiltshire*. London, 1810.

(1819) *The Ancient History of North Wiltshire*. London, 1819.

CONNAH, H. G. (1965) Excavations at Knap Hill, Alton Priors, 1961. *W.A.M.*, LX (1965), 1–23

CORCORAN, J. X. W. P. (1960) The Carlingford Culture. *P.P.S.*, XXVI (1960), 98–148.

CORNWALL, I. W. (1953) Soil Science and Archaeology. *P.P.S.*, XIX (1953), 129–47.
  (1956) *Bones for the Archaeologist*. London, 1956.
  (1958) *Soils for the Archaeologist*. London, 1958.

CRAW, J. H. (1925) The Mutiny Stones, Berwickshire. *P.S.A.S.*, LIX (1925), 198–204.

CRAWFORD, O. G. S. (1924) The Long Barrows and Megaliths in the area covered by Sheet 12 of the ¼ inch Map (Kent, Surrey and Sussex). *Ordnance Survey Professional Papers, New Series, no. 8* (1924).
  (1925) *The Long Barrows of the Cotswolds*. Gloucester, 1925.
  (1928) *See* Crawford, O. G. S. & Keiller, A. (1928).
  (1930) Lowland Long Barrows. *Antiquity*, IV (1930), 357–8.
  (1932) *Map of Neolithic Wessex*. Ordnance Survey, 1932.
  (1936) Varia. *Antiquity*, X (1936), 479.
  (1938) Bank-Barrows. *Antiquity*, XII (1938) 228–32.
  (1953) *Archaeology in the Field*. London, 1953.
  (1955) *Said and Done*. London, 1955.

CRAWFORD, O. G. S. *and* KEILLER, A. (1928) *Wessex from the Air*. Oxford, 1928.

CUNNINGTON, B. H. (1909) Notes on Barrows on King's Play Down, Heddington. *W.A.M.*, XXXVI (1909), 311–17.

  (1920) 'Blue hard stone, ye same as at Stonehenge', found in Boles (Bowles) Barrow (Heytesbury, I). *W.A.M.*, XLI (1920), 172–4.
  (1924) The 'Blue Stone' from Boles Barrow. *W.A.M.*, XLII (1924), 431–7.

CUNNINGTON, M. E. (1912) Knap Hill Camp. *W.A.M.*, XXXVII (1912), 42–65.
  (1914) List of the Long Barrows of Wiltshire. *W.A.M.*, XXXVIII (1914), 379–414.
  (1929) *Woodhenge*. Devizes, 1929.
  (1931) The 'Sanctuary' on Overton Hill near Avebury. *W.A.M.*, XLV (1931), 300–335.
  (1935) Blue Stone from Boles Barrow. *W.A.M.*, XLVII (1935), 267.
  (1938) *An Introduction to the Archaeology of Wiltshire*. Devizes, 1938.

CUNNINGTON, W. (1860) Roundway Hill, Account of Ancient British and Anglo-Saxon Barrows. *W.A.M.*, VI (1860), 159–67.
  (1895) Opening of Barrows, etc., near Haxon. *W.A.M.*, XXVIII (1894–96), 172–3.

CURWEN, E. C. (1929) *Prehistoric Sussex*. London, 1929.
  (1930) Neolithic Camps. *Antiquity*, IV (1930), 22–54.
  (1934) Excavations in Whitehawk Neolithic Camp, Brighton, 1932–3. *Ant. J.*, XIV (1934), 99–133.
  (1954) *The Archaeology of Sussex*. London, 1954.

DANIEL, G. E. (1950) *The Prehistoric Chamber Tombs of England and Wales*. Cambridge, 1950.
  (1961) The Date of the Megalithic Tombs of Western Europe. *L'Europe à la fin de*

l'âge de la pierre (Actes du Symposium consacré aux problèmes du Néolithique européen). Praha, 1961, 575–83.

(1963) 'The Personality of Wales' in *Culture and Environment*. Essays in Honour of Sir Cyril Fox (ed. I. Ll. Foster & L. Alcock). London, 1963.

(1965) Editorial. *Antiquity*, XXXIX (1965), 81–6.

(1967) Northmen and Southmen. *Antiquity*, XLI (1967), 313–17.

DARBISHIRE, R. D. (1874) Notes on Discoveries in Ehenside Tarn, Cumberland. *Archaeologia*, XLIV (1874), 273–92.

DILLON, M. (1946) *The Cycles of the Kings*. London, 1946.

DIMBLEBY, G. W. (1954) The Ecological Study of Buried Soils. Techniques in Archaeology. *British Association for the Advancement of Science*, 1954.

(1962) *The Development of British Heathlands and their Soils*. Oxford Forestry Memoirs, 23, 1962.

DREW, C. D. *and* PIGGOTT, S. (1936) The Excavation of Long Barrow 163a on Thickthorn Down, Dorset. *P.P.S.*, II (1936), 77–96.

DUNNING, G. C. (1946) A new Long Barrow in Hampshire. *Ant. J.*, XXVI (1946), 185–6.

DYER, J. F. (1955) A Secondary Neolithic Camp at Waulud's Bank, Leagrave, Bedfordshire. *B.A.*, I (1955), 9–16.

(1961) Barrows of the Chilterns. *Arch. J.*, CXVI (1961), 1–24.

DYMOND, D. P. (1966) Ritual Monuments at Rudston, E. Yorkshire, England. *P.P.S.*, XXXII (1966), 86–95.

EBERT, H. (1955) Neue Grabfunde auf dem 'Grossen Berg' bei Aspenstedt, Kr. Halberstadt. *J.M.V.*, XXXIX (1955), 70–80.

EDLIN, H. L. (1958) *The Living Forest*. London, 1958.

ELGEE, F. (1930) *Early Man in North-east Yorkshire*. Gloucester, 1930.

ELGEE, F. *and* ELGEE, H. W. (1933) *The Archaeology of Yorkshire*. London, 1933.

ELGEE, H. W., *and* ELGEE, F. (1949) An Early Bronze Age Burial in a Boat-shaped Wooden Coffin from North-east Yorkshire. *P.P.S.*, XV (1949), 87–106.

EVANS, E. E. (1938) Doey's Cairn, Dunloy, Co. Antrim. *U.J.A.*, I (1938), 59–78.

EVANS, J. (1864) *The Coins of the Ancient Britons*. London, 1864.

(1881) *The Ancient Bronze Implements* . . . London, 1881.

(1897) *The Ancient Stone Implements* . . . *of Great Britain*. (2nd ed.), London, 1897.

EVANS, J. D. (1958) Two Phases of Prehistoric Settlement in the Western Mediterranean. *U.L.I.A.R.*, 13 (1958) 49–70.

EVANS, J. H. (1948) Smythe's Megalith. *Arch. Cant.*, LXI (1948), 135–40.

(1950) Kentish Megalith Types. *Arch. Cant.*, LXIII (1950), 63–81.

FARRAR, R. A. H. (1952) Archaeological Fieldwork in Dorset in 1951. *Dorset A.S.*, LXXIII (1952), 85–115.

BIBLIOGRAPHY

BIBLIOGRAPHY

(1956) Archaeological Fieldwork in Dorset in 1953 and 1954. *Dorset A.S.*, LXXVI (1956), 74–99.

FEUSTEL, R., *and* ULLRICH, H. (1965) Tötenhütten der Neolithischen Walternienberg Gruppe. *Alt. Thüringen*, VII (1965), 105–202.

FOWLER, M. J. (1956) The Transition from Late Neolithic to Early Bronze Age in the Peak District of Derbyshire and Staffordshire. *D.A.J.*, LXXV (1956), 66–122.

FOX, A., *and* STONE, J. F. S. (1951). A Necklace from a Barrow in North Molton Parish, North Devon. *Ant. J.*, XXXI (1951), 25–31.

FOX, C. (1923) *The Archaeology of the Cambridge Region*. Cambridge, 1923.
(1952) *The Personality of Britain*. Cardiff, 1952.

GANDERT, O. F. (1953) Neolithische Gräber mit Rinderbeigaben und Rinderbestattungen in Mitteleuropa. *Actes de la IIIe Session*, Congrès International de Sciences Préhistoriques et Protohistoriques, Zürich, 1950 (Zürich, 1953), 201.

GERHARDT, K. (1951) Künstliche Veränderungen am Hinterhauptsloch vorgeschichtlicher Schädel. *Germania*, XXIX (1951), 182–4.

GIFFORD, J. (1957) The Physique of Wiltshire. *Victoria County History of Wiltshire*, I, pt. I, 1–20. London, 1957.

GJESSING, G. (1944) Circumpolar Stone Age. *Acta Artica*, Fasc. II.

GLASBERGEN, W. (1954) Barrow Excavations in the Eight Beatitudes. *Palaeohistoria*, II (1954), 1–134.
(1955) Barrow Excavations in the Eight Beatitudes. *Palaeohistoria*, III (1955), 1–204.

GLØB, P. V. (1949) Barkaer, Danmarks ældste landsby. *Fra Nationalmuseets Arbejdsmark* (1949), 5–16.

GODWIN, H. (1956) *The History of the British Flora*. Cambridge, 1956.

GOMME, G. L. (1886) Ed. *The Gentleman's Magazine Library. Archaeology: part 1*. London, 1886.

GREENFIELD, E. (1963) The Romano-British Shrines at Brigstock. *Ant. J.*, XLIII (1963), 228–63.

GREENWELL, W. (1877) *British Barrows*. Oxford, 1877.
(1890) Recent Researches in Barrows. *Archaeologia*, LII (1890), 1–72.

GRIMES, W. F. (1948) Pentre-Ifan burial chamber, Pembrokeshire. *Arch. Camb.*, C (1948). 3–23.
(1951) A review of Daniel (1950). *P.P.S.*, XVII (1951), 235–8.
(1960) *Excavations on Defence Sites, 1939–1945. I: Mainly Neolithic-Bronze Age*. London, 1960.

GRINSELL, L. V. (1934) Sussex Barrows. *S.A.C.*, LXXV (1934), 217–75.
(1936) *The Ancient Burial-Mounds of England*. London, 1936.
(1938) Hampshire Barrows. *P.H.F.C.*, XIV, pt. I (1938), 9–40.

(1939) Hampshire Barrows. *P.H.F.C.*, XIV, pt. 2 (1939), 195–229.
(1941) The Bronze Age Round Barrows of Wessex. *P.P.S.*, VII (1941), 73–113.
(1953) *The Ancient Burial-Mounds of England*. London, 1953. (2nd ed.).
(1957) Archaeological Gazetteer. *Victoria County History of Wiltshire*, I, pt. I, London, 1957.
(1958) *The Archaeology of Wessex*. London, 1958.
(1959) *Dorset Barrows*. Dorchester, 1959.

GRINSELL, L. V., *and* SHERWIN, C. A. (1940) Isle of Wight Barrows. *P.I.W.N.H.A.S.*, III (1940), 179–222.

GRÖSSLER, H. (1907) Das Fürstengrab im grossen Galgenhügel am Paulsschachte bei Helmsdorf (im Mansfelder Seekreise). *J.S.T.*, VI (1907). 1–87.

HANSEN, H. O. (1962) Ungdommelige Oldtidshuse. *Kuml*, 1961 (1962), 28–45.

HARTING, J. E. (1880) *British Animals extinct within Historic Times, with some account of British Wild White Cattle*. London, 1880.

HARTNETT, P. J. (1957) Excavation of a Passage Grave at Fourknocks, Co. Meath. *P.R.I.A.*, LVIII (1957), 197–277.

HAWKES, C. F. C. (1940) *The Prehistoric Foundations of Europe to the Mycenaean Age*. London, 1940.
(1948) From Bronze Age to Iron Age: Middle Europe, Italy, the North and West. *P.P.S.*, XIV (1948), 196–218.
(1954) Archaeological Theory and Method: Some suggestions from the Old World. *A.A.*, LVI (1954), 155–68.
(1959) The A B C of the British Iron Age. *Antiquity*, XXXIII (1959), 170–82.

HAWKES, J. (1934) Aspects of the Neolithic and Chalcolithic Periods in Western Europe. *Antiquity*, VIII (1934), 24–42.

HAWLEY, W. (1910) Notes on Barrows in South Wilts. *W.A.M.*, XXXVI (1909–10), 615–28.
(1928) Report on the Excavations at Stonehenge during 1925 and 1926. *Ant. J.*, VIII (1928), 149–76.

HENSHALL, A. S. (1963) *The Chambered Tombs of Scotland*, I. Edinburgh, 1963.

HIGGS, E. S., *and* WHITE, J. P. (1963) Autumn Killing. *Antiquity*, XXXVII (1963), 282–9.

HODGSON, J. C. (1918) Memoir of The Rev. William Greenwell. *Arch. Ael.*, XV (1918), 3rd series, 1–21.

HÖFER, P. (1906) Der Leubinger Grabhügel. *J.S.T.*, V (Der Leubinger Hügel) (1906), 1–59.

HOGG, A. H. A. (1940) A Long Barrow at West Rudham. *T.N.A.S.*, XXVII, (1940), 315–31.

HUBBARD, A. J., *and* HUBBARD, G. (1905) *Neolithic Dew-Ponds and Cattle-Ways*. London, 1905.

JACKSON, J. W. (1936a) The Animal Remains from Giants' Hills. *Archaeologia*, LXXXV (1936), 95–8.

(1936b) Report on the Animal Remains (from Long Barrow 163a on Thickthorn Down, Dorset). *P.P.S.*, II (1936), 93–4.

(1937) Report on Animal Remains from Julliberrie's Grave. *Ant. J.*, XVII (1937), 133–5.

(1939a) Report on Animal Remains (from Julliberrie's Grave). *Ant. J.*, XIX (1939), 278–9.

(1939b) Bone (from the Badshot Long Barrow). A Survey of the Prehistory of the Farnham District. *Surrey Archaeological Society*, 1939, 146–8.

(1943) Animal Bones, I, Neolithic (from Maiden Castle, Dorset). *Wheeler*, 1943, 360–7.

JAŹDŹEWSKI, K. (1938) Cmentarzyska Kultury Ceramiki Wstęgowej: Związane Ź Nimi Slady Osadnictwa Brześciu Kujawskim. *Wiadomosci Archaeologiczne*, XV (1938), 1–105.

JESSUP, R. F. (1937) Excavations at Julliberrie's Grave, Chilham, Kent. *Ant. J.*, XVII (1937), 122–37.

(1939) Further Excavations at Julliberrie's Grave, Chilham. *Ant. J.*, XIX (1939), 260–81.

JEWELL, P. A. (1958) Natural History and Experiment in Archaeology. *The Advancement of Science*, XV (1958), 165–72.

(1962) Changes in size and type of cattle from Prehistoric to Mediaeval times in Britain. *Zeitschrift für Tierzüchtung und Züchtungsbiologie*, Band 77, Heft 2, (1962), 159–67.

(1963) Cattle from British Archaeological Sites. *Occasional Paper no. 18 of the Royal Anthropological Institute*, 1963.

JEWELL, P. A. (1963) Ed. *The Experimental Earthwork on Overton Down, Wiltshire*, 1960. London, 1963.

JOHNSON, W. (1912) *Byways in British Archaeology*. Cambridge, 1912.

JONES, G. (1961) Settlement Patterns in Anglo-Saxon England. *Antiquity*, XXXV (1961), 221–32.

JØRGENSEN, S. (1953) Skovrydning med Flintøkse. *Fra Nationalmuseets Arbejdsmark* (1953), 36–43.

KAELAS, L. (1956) Dolmen und Ganggräber in Schweden. *Offa*, XV (1956), 5–24.

KEILLER, A. (1939) Avebury, Summary of Excavations, 1937 and 1938. *Antiquity*, XIII (1939), 223–33.

KEILLER, A., *and* PIGGOTT, S. (1938) Excavation of an Untouched Chamber in the Lanhill Long Barrow. *P.P.S.*, IV (1938), 122–50.

(1939) Badshot Long Barrow (in *A Survey of the Prehistory of the Farnham District*, *Surrey Archaeological Society*, 1939, 133–49).

KEITH, A. (1916) The Human Remains (St Nicholas Chambered Tumulus), *Arch. Camb.*, Ser. 6, XVI (1916), 268–93.
(1925) *The Antiquity of Man*. London, 1925.

KENDRICK, T. D. (1925) *The Axe Age*. London, 1925.

KENDRICK, T. D., *and* HAWKES, C. F. C. (1932) *Archaeology in England and Wales, 1914–1931*. London, 1932.

KERSTEN, K. (1936) Das Tötenhaus von Grünhof-Tesperhude, Kreis Herzogtum Lauenberg. *Offa*, I (1936), 56–87.

KLINDT-JENSEN, O. (1957) *Denmark before the Vikings*. London, 1957.

KLIMA, B. (1956) Coal in the Ice Age. *Antiquity*, XXX (1956), 98–101.

LEEDS, E. T. (1921) An Archaeological Survey of Oxfordshire (by the late Percy Manning, Esq., M.A., F.S.A. and E.T.L.) *Archaeologia*, LXXI (1921), 227–65.
(1927) A Neolithic Site at Abingdon, Berks. *Ant. J.*, VII (1927), 438–64.
(1928) A Neolithic Site at Abingdon, Berks. *Ant. J.*, VIII (1928), 461–77.

LEROI-GOURHAN, A., BAILLOUD, G., *and* BREZILLON, M. (1962) L'Hypogée II Des Mournouards. *Gallia Préhistoire*, V (1962), 23–133.

LETHBRIDGE, T. C. (1950) *Herdsmen & Hermits*. Cambridge, 1950.

LIBBY, W. F. (1955) *Radiocarbon Dating*. Chicago, 1955.

LONDESBOROUGH, LORD (1848) Discoveries in Barrows near Scarborough. *J.B.A.A.*, IV (1848), 101–7.

LONG, W. (1876) Stonehenge and its Barrows. *W.A.M.*, XVI (1876), 1–244.

LONGWORTH, I. H. (1961) The Origins and Development of the Primary Series in the Collared Urn Tradition in England and Wales. *P.P.S.*, XXVII (1961), 263–306.

MACALISTER, R. A. S. (1921) *A Text-Book of European Archaeology*. Cambridge, 1921.

MACKIE, E. W. (1963–4) New excavations on the Monamore Neolithic chambered cairn, Lamash, Isle of Arran. *P.S.A.S.*, XCVII (1963–4), 1–34.

MALMER, M. P. (1962) *Jungneolithische Studien*. Lund, 1962.

MANBY, T. G. (1963) The Excavation of the Willerby Wold Long Barrow. *P.P.S.*, XXIX (1963), 173–205.
(1965) The Excavation of Green Low Chambered Tomb. *D.A.J.*, LXXXV (1965), 1–24.
(1967) Radiocarbon Dates for the Willerby Wold Long Barrow. *Antiquity*, XLI (1967), 306–7.

MARIËN, M. E. (1952) *Oud-Belgie*, Antwerp, 1952.

MATHESON, C. (1932) *Changes in the Fauna of Wales within Historic Times*. Cardiff, 1932.

MENGHIN, O. (1925) *Urgeschichte der Bildenden Kunst in Europa*. Wien, 1925.

MODDERMAN, P. J. R. (1958–9) Die bandkeramische Siedlung von Sittard. *Palaeohistoria*, VI–VII (1958–9), 33–120.

    (1964) The Neolithic Burial Vault at Stein. *Analecta Praehistorica Leidensia*, I (1964).

MORANT, G. M., *and* GOODMAN, C. (1943). Human Bones (from Maiden Castle). *Wheeler*, (1943), 337–60.

MORGAN, F. de M. (1959) The Excavation of a Long Barrow at Nutbane, Hants. *P.P.S.*, XXV (1959), 15–51.

MORTIMER, J. R. (1905) *Forty Years' Researches into British and Saxon Burial Mounds of East Yorkshire.* London, 1905.

MOVIUS, H. L. (1942) *The Irish Stone Age.* Cambridge, 1942.

NAVARRO, J. M. DE (1950) The British Isles and the Beginning of the Northern Early Bronze Age. *Early Cultures of North-West Europe* (Chadwick Memorial Studies, 1950), 77–105.

NEWBIGIN, N. (1936) Excavations of a long and round cairn on Bellshiel Law, Redesdale. *Arch. Ael.*, (4th ser.), XIII (1936), 293–309.

    (1937) The Neolithic Pottery of Yorkshire. *P.P.S.*, III (1937), 189–216.

NICHOLS, J. (1822) *Illustrations of the Literary History of the Eighteenth Century*, IV. London, 1822.

NIETSCH, S. (1939) Wald und Siedlung im Vorgeschichtliche Mitteleuropa. *Mannus-Bucherei*, no. 64 (1939).

O'KELLY, M. J. (1966) New Discoveries at the Newgrange Passage-Grave in Ireland. *Sborník*, XX (1966), 95–9.

O'NEIL, H., *and* GRINSELL, L. V. (1961) Gloucestershire Barrows. *Transactions of the Bristol and Gloucestershire Archaeological Society for* 1960, LXXIX (1961).

ONIANS, R. B. (1951) *The Origins of European Thought.* Cambridge, 1951.

Ó RÍORDÁIN, S. P. (1937) The Halberd in Bronze Age Europe. *Archaeologia*, LXXXVI (1937), 195–321.

Ó RÍORDÁIN, S. P., *and* DE VALERA, R. (1952) Excavation of a Megalithic Tomb at Ballyedmonduff, Co. Dublin. *P.R.I.A.*, LV (1952), 61–81.

PASSMORE, A. D. (1922) Notes on Field-Work in N. Wilts, 1921–1922. *W.A.M.*, XLII (1922–4), 49–51.

    (1942) Chute, Barrow 1, *W.A.M.*, L. (1942–4), 100–1.

PEATE, I. (1961) Review of 'The English Farmhouse and Cottage' by M. W. Barley. *Antiquity*, XXXV (1961), 249–51.

PENGUIN CLASSICS (1954) *Herodotus, the Histories,* translated by Aubrey de Selincourt. The Penguin Classics, ed. E. V. Rieu, Harmondsworth, 1954.

PEQUART, M., *and* S. J. (1954) *Höedic, deuxième Station-Nécropole du Mésolithique côtier armoricain.* Anvers, 1954.

PEQUART, M., S. J., BOULE, M., *and* VALLOIS, H. V. (1937) *Téviec, Station-Nécropole Mésolithique du Morbihan*. Archives de l'Institut de Paléontologie Humaine, XVIII, Paris, 1937.

PHILLIPS, C. W. (1933a) *Map of the Trent Basin showing the distribution of Long Barrows*. Ordnance Survey, 1933.

(1933b) The Long Barrows of Lincolnshire. *Arch. J.*, LXXXIX (1933), 174–202.

(1934) Some New Lincolnshire Long Barrows. *P.P.S.E.A.*, VII (1934), 423.

(1935) A Re-examination of the Therfield Heath Long Barrow, Royston. *P.P.S.*, I (1935), 101–7.

(1936) The Excavation of the Giants' Hills Long Barrow, Skendleby, Lincolnshire. *Archaeologia*, LXXXV (1936), 37–106.

PIGGOTT, C. M. (1938) A Middle Bronze Age Barrow and Deverel-Rimbury Urnfield, at Latch Farm, Christchurch, Hampshire. *P.P.S.*, IV (1938), 169–87.

(1943) Excavation of Fifteen Barrows in the New Forest, 1941–2. *P.P.S.*, IX (1943), 1–27.

PIGGOTT, S. (1929) Neolithic Pottery and other remains from Pangbourne, Berks, and Caversham, Oxon. *P.P.S.E.A.*, VI (1929), 30–9.

(1930) Butser Hill. *Antiquity*, IV (1930), 187–200.

(1931) The Neolithic Pottery of the British Isles. *Arch. J.*, LXXXVIII (1931), 67–158.

(1934) The Mutual Relations of the British Neolithic Ceramics. *P.P.S.E.A.*, VIII (1934), 373–81.

(1935) A Note on the Relative Chronology of the English Long Barrows. *P.P.S.*, I (1935), 115–26.

(1936) Handley Hill, Dorset—a Neolithic Bowl and the Date of the Entrenchment. *P.P.S.*, II (1936), 229–30.

(1937a) The Excavation of a Long Barrow in Holdenhurst Parish, near Christchurch. *P.P.S.*, III (1937), 1–14.

(1937b) The Long Barrow in Brittany. *Antiquity*, XI (1937), 441–55.

(1938) The Early Bronze Age in Wessex. *P.P.S.*, IV (1938), 52–106.

(1940a) A Trepanned Skull of the Beaker Period from Dorset and the Practice of Trepanning in Prehistoric Europe. *P.P.S.*, VI (1940), 112–32.

(1940b) Timber Circles: A Re-examination. *Arch. J.*, XCVI (1940), 193–222.

(1941) The Sources of Geoffrey of Monmouth, II. The Stonehenge Story. *Antiquity*, XV (1941), 305–19.

(1947–8) The Excavations at Cairnpapple Hill, West Lothian, *P.S.A.S.*, LXXXII (1947–8), 68–123.

(1950) *William Stukeley*, Oxford, 1950.

(1951) 'Stonehenge Reviewed' in *Aspects of Archaeology*. Essays presented to O. G. S. Crawford (ed. W. F. Grimes). London, 1951.

(1954) *The Neolithic Cultures of the British Isles*. Cambridge, 1954.

(1955) Windmill Hill—East or West? *P.P.S.*, XXI (1955), 96–101.

(1956) Excavations in Passage-Graves and Ring-Cairns of the Clava Group, 1952–3. *P.S.A.S.*, LXXXVIII (1956), 173–207.

(1959) *Approach to Archaeology*. London, 1959.

(1961a) The British Neolithic Cultures in their Continental Setting. *L'Europe à la fin de l'âge de la pierre* (Actes du Symposium consacré aux problèmes du Néolithique européen). Praha, 1961, 557–74.

(1961b) *The Dawn of Civilisation* (ed.). London, 1961.

(1962a) *The West Kennet Long Barrow Excavations*, 1955–6. London, 1962.

(1962b) From Salisbury Plain to Siberia. *W.A.M.*, LVIII (1962), 93–7.

(1962c) Heads and Hoofs. *Antiquity*, XXXVI (1962), 110–18.

(1962d) Archaeological Considerations (Fourth Report of the Sub-Committee . . . on the Petrological Identification of Stone Axes). *P.P.S.*, XXVII (1962), 209–66.

(1963) 'Abercromby and After: the Beaker Cultures of Britain Re-examined' in *Culture and Environment*, Essays in Honour of Sir Cyril Fox (ed. I. Ll. Foster *and* L. Alcock). London, 1963.

(1967) 'Unchambered' Long Barrows in Neolithic Britain. *Palaeohistoria*, XII (1966), 381–93.

PIGGOTT, S., *and* C. M. (1939) Stone and Earth Circles in Dorset. *Antiquity*, XIII (1939), 138–58.

PIGGOTT, S., *and* POWELL, T. G. E. (1949) Excavation of three Neolithic Chambered Tombs. *P.S.A.S.*, LXXXIII (1948–49), 103–61.

PITT-RIVERS, A. (né Lane Fox) (1876) Excavations in Cissbury Camp, Sussex. *The Journal of the Anthropological Institute of Great Britain and Ireland*, V (1876), 357–90.

(1898) *Excavations in Cranborne Chase*, IV (1898).

PITTIONI, R. (1955) Contributions to a Study of 'The Problem of Pile Dwellings'. *P.P.S.*, XXI (1955), 102–7.

POWELL, A. (1948) *John Aubrey and his Friends*. London, 1948.

(1949) *Brief Lives . . . by John Aubrey* (ed.). London, 1949.

POWELL, T. G. E. (1958). *The Celts*. London, 1958.

(1963) The Chambered Cairn at Dyffryn Ardudwy. *Antiquity*, XXXVII (1963), 19–24.

POWELL, T. G. E., *and* DANIEL, G. E. (1956). *Barclodiad y Gawres*. Liverpool, 1956.

PREHISTORIC SOCIETY (1962). Prehistoric Society, Summer Conference, 1962. *Dorchester –Dorset, Guide.*

PRESTON, J. P., *and* HAWKES, C. F. C. (1933) Three Late Bronze Age Barrows on the Cloven Way. *Ant. J.*, XIII (1933), 414–54.

PULL, J. H. (1932) *The Flint Miners of Blackpatch*. London, 1932.

QUIDAM (1855) Tumulus at Langbury Hill. *Notes and Queries*, XII (1855), 364.

R C H M, (1960) *A Matter of Time*. London, H.M.S.O., 1960.

RADFORD, C. A. R., *and* ROGERS, E. H. (1947) The Excavation of Two Barrows at East Putford. *P.D.A.E.S.*, III (1947), 156–63.

RADIG, W. (1930) *Der Wohnbau im jungsteinzeitlichen Deutschland*. Leipzig, 1930.

RAISTRICK, A. (1931) Prehistoric Burials at Waddington and at Bradley, West York-shire. *Y.A.J.*, XXX (1930–1), 248–55.

RAJEWSKI, Z. (1958) New Discoveries in Western Poland. *Archaeology*, XI (1958).

REINERTH, H. (1928) Die schnurkeramischen Totenhäuser von Sarmenstorf. *Mannus* VI, *Ergänzungsband* (1928) (Kossina Festgabe), 202–20.

RETZER, J. L., SWOPE, H. M., REMINGTON, J. D., *and* RUTHERFORD, W. H. (1956) *Beaver Management*. State of Colorado, Dept. of Game and Fish, Technical Bulletin no. 2. March, 1956.

RICHARDSON, N. M. (1897) The Proceedings, Dorset Natural History and Antiquarian Field Club. *Dorset A.S.*, XVIII (1897), xxi–lv.

RITCHIE, J. (1920) *The Influence of Man on Animal Life in Scotland.* Cambridge, 1920.

RIVET, A. L. F. (1962) *Map of Southern Britain in the Iron Age.* Ordnance Survey, Ches-sington, Surrey, 1962.

ROCHE, J. (1960) *Le Gisement Mesolithique de Moita do Sebastão (Muge-Portugal),* Lisboa, 1960.

RODDEN, R. J. (1962) Excavations at the Early Neolithic Site at Nea Nikomedeia, Greek Macedonia (1961 season). *P.P.S.*, XXVIII (1962), 267–88.

SANDELL, R. E. (1961) Sir Richard Colt Hoare. *W.A.M.*, LVIII (1961), 1–6.

SAVORY, H. N. (1948) Two Middle Bronze Age Palisade Barrows at Letterston, Pem-brokeshire. *Arch. Camb.*, C (1948), 67–87.

SCHMIDT, R. R. (1930 u. 1936) *Jungsteinzeitsiedlungen im Federseemoor.* Augsberg-Stuttgart, 1930 u. 1936.

SCHUCHHARDT, C. (1919) *Alteuropa.* Berlin und Leipzig, 1919.

SCOTT, J. G. (1958) The Excavation of the Chambered Cairn at Brackley, Kintyre, Argyll. *P.S.A.S.*, LXXXIX (1958), 22–54.
    (1962) Clyde, Carlingford and Connaught Cairns—a Review. *Antiquity*, XXXVI (1962), 97–101.

SCOTT, W. L. (1936) Whiteleaf Barrow, Monk's Risborough, Bucks. *P.P.S.*, II (1936), 213.
    (1937) Whiteleaf Barrow, Monk's Risborough, Bucks. *P.P.S.*, III (1937), 441.

SHIPP, W., *and* HODSON, J. W. (1868) Ed. *History of Dorset by J. Hutchins.* III. West-minster, 1868.

SJOESTEDT, M-L. (1949) *Gods and Heroes of the Celts.* London, 1949.

SMITH, A. C. (1884) *British and Roman Antiquities of North Wiltshire.* Marlborough College Natural History Society, 1884.

SMITH, I. F. (1959) Excavations at Windmill Hill, Avebury, Wilts. 1957–8. *W.A.M.*, LVII (1959), 149–62.

(1960) Radio-carbon Dates from Windmill Hill. *Antiquity*, XXXIV (1960), 212–13.

(1965) *Windmill Hill and Avebury: Excavations by Alexander Keiller, 1925–1939*, Oxford, 1965.

(1966) Windmill Hill and its Implications. *Palaeohistoria*, XII (1966), 469–81.

SMITH, I. F., *and* EVANS, J. G. (1968) Excavation of Two Long Barrows in North Wiltshire. *Antiquity*, XLII (1968), 138–42.

SMITH, M. A. (1955) The Limitations of Inference in Archaeology. *A.N.L.*, VI (1955), 3–7.

SMITH, R. A. (1910) The Development of Neolithic Pottery. *Archaeologia*, LXII (1910), 340–52.

(1926) *A Guide to the Antiquities of The Stone Age*. British Museum, 1926.

(1927) Flint Arrow-heads in Britain. *Archaeologia*, LXXVI (1927), 81–106.

SMITH, W. G. (1915) Maiden Bower, Bedfordshire. *P.S.A.L.*. XXVII (1914–15), 143–61.

SOUDSKÝ, B. (1955) Výzkum Neolitického sídliště v Postoloprtech V.R. 1952. *Archaeologické Rozhledy*, VII (1955), 5–11.

(1962) The Neolithic Site of Bylany. *Antiquity*, XXXVI (1962), 190–200.

SPIESSBACH, E. (1934) Eine Grabanlage der Kugelamphorenkultur. Gotha, Flur Ostheim, Kiesgrube Wagner. *Mannus*, XXIV (1932), 238–44.

SPROCKHOFF, E. (1938) *Die Nordische Megalithkultur*. Berlin und Leipzig, 1938.

(1952) Zwei Megalithgräber aus Schleswig und Holstein. *Offa*, X (1952), 15–28.

(1954) Kammerlose Hünenbetten im Sachsenwald. *Offa*, XIII (1954), 1–16.

(1966) Atlas der Megalithgräber Deutschlands, Teil 1: Schleswig-Holstein (Text u. Atlas-Band), Bonn, 1966.

STONE, E. H. (1924) *The Stones of Stonehenge*. London, 1924.

STONE, J. F. S. (1938) An Early Bronze Age Grave in Fargo Plantation near Stonehenge. *W.A.M.*, XLVIII (1938), 357–70.

(1940) A Round Barrow on Stockbridge Down, Hampshire. *Ant. J.*, XX (1940), 39–51.

(1943–8) A Fixed Point in the Chronology of the European Bronze Age. *Jahrbuch für Prähistorische und Ethnographische Kunst*, XVII (1943–8), 43–6.

(1948) The Stonehenge Cursus and its Affinities. *Arch. J.*, CIV (1948), 7–19.

(1958) *Wessex before the Celts*. London, 1958.

STONE, J. F. S., *and* THOMAS, L. C. (1956) The use and distribution of Faience in the Ancient East and Prehistoric Europe. *P.P.S.*, XXII (1956), 37–84.

STUKELEY, W. (1740) *Stonehenge: a Temple Restored to the British Druids*. London, 1740.

(1743) *Abury: a Temple of the British Druids*. London, 1743.

STÜRUP, B. (1965) En Ny Jordgrav fra Tidlig-Neolitisk tid. *Kuml* (1965), 13–22.

THOMAS, H. (1964) The Neolithic Causewayed Camp at Robin Hood's Ball, Shrewton. *W.A.M.*, LIX (1964), 1–27

THOMPSON, H. V., *and* WORDEN, A. N. (1956) *The Rabbit*, London, 1956.

THOMPSON, M. W. (1957) A Group of Mounds on Seasalter Level, near Whitstable. *Archaeologia Cantiana*, LXX (1957), 44–67.

THOMPSON, M. W., ASHBEE, P., *and* DIMBLEBY, G. W. (1957) Excavation of a Barrow near the Hardy Monument, Black Down, Portesham, Dorset. *P.P.S.*, XXIII (1957), 124–36.

THURNAM, J. (1860) Examination of Barrows on the Downs of North Wiltshire in 1853–7. *W.A.M.*, VI (1860), 317–36.

(1864) '... exhibited four flint implements of very careful workmanship found in a barrow near Stonehenge ...' *P.S.A.L.*, II (2nd series), 427–31.

(1865a) On the Two Principal Forms of Ancient British and Gaulish Skulls. *M.A.S.*, i (1865), 120–68: 459–519.

(1865b) On the Leaf-Shaped Type of Flint Arrow-head, and its connection with Long Barrows. *P.S.A.L.*, III (2nd series), 168–72.

(1867) Further Researches and Observations on the two Principal Forms of Ancient British Skulls. *M.A.S.*, iii (1867–8–9), 41–80.

(1868) On Ancient British Barrows, especially those of Wiltshire and the adjoining Counties. Part 1, Long Barrows. *Archaeologia*, XLII (1868), 161–244.

(1869) On Leaf and Lozenge-shaped Flint Javelin Heads from an Oval Barrow near Stonehenge. *W.A.M.*, XI (1869), 40–9.

(1870) On Ancient British Barrows. Part II, Round Barrows. *Archaeologia*, XLIII (1870), 285–552.

(1872) On Long Barrows and Round Barrows. *W.A.M.*, XIII (1872), 339–42.

TOMS, H. S. (1922) Long Barrows in Sussex. *S.A.C.*, LXIII (1922), 157–65.

TRECHMANN, C. T. (1914) Prehistoric Burials in the County of Durham. *Arch. Ael.*, XI (1914), 3rd series, 119–76.

DE VALERA, R. (1960) The Court Cairns of Ireland. *P.R.I.A.*, LX (1960), 9–140.

(1961) The 'Carlingford Culture', the Long Barrow and the Neolithic of Great Britain and Ireland. *P.P.S.*, XXVII (1961), 234–52.

DE VALERA, R., *and* Ó NUALLÁIN, S. (1961) *Survey of the Megalithic Tombs of Ireland, I, County Clare.* Dublin, 1961.

VATCHER, F. DE M. (1959) The Radio-Carbon Dating of the Nutbane Long Barrow. *Antiquity*, XXXIII (1959), 289.

(1961a) The Excavation of the Long Mortuary Enclosure on Normanton Down, Wiltshire. *P.P.S.*, XXVII (1961), 160–73.

(1961b) Seamer Moor, Yorkshire. *P.P.S.*, XXVII (1961), 345.

(1965) East Heslerton Long Barrow, Yorkshire: The Eastern Half. *Antiquity*, XXXIX (1965), 49–52.

WACE, A. J. B. (1932) Chamber Tombs at Mycenae. *Archaeologia*, LXXXII (1932), 1–242.

WAINWRIGHT, F. T. (1962) *Archaeology and Place-names and History.* London, 1962.

WARNE, C. (1866) *The Celtic Tumuli of Dorset.* London, 1866.

WARREN, S. H. *et al.* (1936) Archaeology of the Submerged Land-Surface of the Essex Coast. *P.P.S.*, II (1936), 178–210.

WATERBOLK, H. T. (1958–9) Die bandkeramischen Siedlung von Geleen. *Palaeohistoria*, VI–VII (1958–9), 121–61.

WATSON, D. M. S. (1931) The Animal Bones from Skara Brae. *Childe*, 1931, 198–204.

WATTS, W. A. (1960) C-14 Dating and the Neolithic in Ireland. *Antiquity*, XXXIV (1960), 111–16.

WELLS, C. (1960) A Study of Cremation. *Antiquity*, XXXIV (1960), 29–37.

WELLS, L. H. (1962) Report on the Inhumation Burials from the West Kennet Barrow. *Piggott* (1962a), 79–89.

WHEELER, R. E. M. (1943) *Maiden Castle, Dorset.* Society of Antiquaries, London. Reports of Research Committee, XII (1943).
    (1952) Earthwork since Hadrian Allcroft. *Arch. J.*, CVI (1952), (Supplement), 62–82.

WIEGAND, F. (1953–4) 'Ein Grabhaus am Egelsee bei Arnstadt', *Alt-Thüringen*, I (1953–4), 213–22.

WILLIAMS-FREEMAN, J. P. (1915) *An Introduction to Field Archaeology as illustrated by Hampshire.* London, 1915.

WILLIAMSON, W. C. (1872) *Description of the Tumulus opened at Gristhorpe near Scarborough.* (3rd ed.) Scarborough, 1872.

WILLIS, E. H. (1963) Radio-Carbon Dating. *Science in Archaeology* (ed. Brothwell & Higgs), London, 1963, 35–46.

ZEUNER, F. E. (1963) *A History of Domesticated Animals.* London, 1963.

INDEX

Barrow numbers are separated from page numbers by colons

Pickering, Vale of, 9
Piddinghoe 22 (Money Burgh), 119, 153, 169
Piggott, Stuart, 8, 13, 75, 76, 81, 83, 85, 94, 101
pig's jaws, 76, 159
pillow mounds, 18
Pimperne 1 : 163
pine marten, 160
pioneer digging, 117–19
pitched (mortuary houses), 52, 53, 57, 83, 88, 92, 93, 96, 103, 107, 109, 126–33
Pitnacree, 92, 104, 179
pits, 50, 53
Pitt-Rivers, Lt-Gen., 24, 25, 63, 69, 74, 111
platform cremation(s), 57, 66
Poland, 87
Pole's Wood South long barrow, 81
Pomerania, 94
Poor Lot (Winterborne Abbas), 175
portal dolmen, 92
Portesham 1 : 162
Portesham 2 : 162
Portsdown, 117
post-glacial deposits, 86
post-holes, 50, 63
post-marked Early Neolithic single graves, 83
Postolprty, Czechoslovakia, 99, 100, 108
posts, 53, 80, 83, 86, 90
pottery, broken, 83, 84
    Early Neolithic, 6, 71, 72, 154, 155, 178, 179
    from Yorkshire, 72
    Later Neolithic, 6, 71, 72, 156
    Whiteleaf long barrow, 73
Povington Heath (Tyneham 4a), 175
prehistory, 3
Preshute 1; 3a: 168
primary burials, 135–6, 138–41, 154, 158
    absence of, 68
primitive tools, 78
Purbeck Hills, 8

quarry ditches, 13

radio-carbon dating, 85–7, 99
Raiset Pike (Crosby Garrett G.CCXXVIII), 119, 172
Randwick, 81
Ratcliffe-on-Soar, 13
rectangular, 15
red deer, 77, 159, 160
Redesdale (Bellshiel Law), 172
Regency, 1
Reinerth, H., 97
Ritchie, J., 75
rites, 58
    (of burial), 135–53
Rob Howe (Scamridge 1), 171
Robin Hood's Ball, 9, 105, 181
Rockbourne 1 (Duck's Nest), 164
Rockbourne 2 (Round Clump), 164
Rockbourne 3 (Giant's Grave), 164
Rockbourne 4 (Rockbourne Down), 164
Rockbourne Down (Rockbourne 4), 164
Rodmartin cairn, 78
roe deer, 77, 159, 160
Roman, 68, 74, 105, 152
Romano-British, 69, 74, 157
roof-fashion, 53
round barrows, 50, 59, 103, 104
Round Clump (Rockbourne 2), 164
Roundway 5 : 174
Roundwood 25 : 175
Royston (Therfield Heath), 6, 170
Royston Heath 4 : 177
'rude pottery', 71
Rudstone G.LXVI, 68, 119, 151, 174
Rudstone G.CCXXIV, 46, 66, 67, 70, 119, 123, 132, 137, 140, 148, 151, 153, 155, 171

Sachsenwald, 291, 292, 299 : 91, 95, 96, 108
Salisbury Plain, 5, 7, 61, 75

Salisbury Plain East, 8, 9, 16–17, 26, 29, 69, 113, 115, 117, 126, 135, 138, 149, 153, 165, 174, 178
Salisbury Plain West, 8, 9, 16–17, 26, 29, 45, 69, 113, 115, 118, 127, 136, 138, 150, 153, 167, 174, 177
Samson's Bratful (Ennerdale, Stockdale Moor), 172
Sanctuary, 80, 105
Sarmenstorf, 103
sarsen stone(s), 46, 50–1, 52, 162, 165, 166
Saxo-Thuringian royal barrows, 97
Saxon, 68, 69, 70, 152
Saxons, 4–5
Saxony, Germany, 67
Scamridge (Ebberston), 119
Scamridge 1 (Rob Howe), 2: 171
Scamridge Group, 171
Scarborough Group, 171
Schleswig-Holstein, 91
Schuchthardt, C., 94
Scotland, 8, 13, 27, 92, 114, 116, 143, 173, 179
Scott, Sir Lindsay, 6
scramasax, 70
scraper(s), 72, 142, 143
Seamer Moor, 46, 74, 76, 86, 116, 119, 155, 178
Second World War, 6
secondary burials, 58, 68–70, 142–3, 149–53, 157
Secondary Neolithic, 101
segmented chambers, 90
Seine-Oise-Marne, 61
semblance of articulation, 64
separation, long bones and skulls, 83
Severn Estuary, 8
Severn-Cotswold, 90, 92, 93
sex, 61, 138–41
Shalbourne 5; 5a: 166
sherds, Beaker, 77
sherds (of pottery), 71, 103
    stratified, 72
sherds, Romano-British, 74